PROMISCUOUS GRACE

A series edited by Kathryn Lofton and John Lardas Modern

Earthquakes and Gardens: Saint Hilarion's Cyprus
Virginia Burrus

Awkward Rituals: Sensations of Governance in Protestant America
Dana Logan

Sincerely Held: American Secularism and Its Believers
Charles McCrary

Unbridled: Studying Religion in Performance
William Robert

Profaning Paul
Cavan W. Concannon

Making a Mantra: Tantric Ritual and Renunciation on the Jain Path to Liberation
Ellen Gough

Neuromatic; or, A Particular History of Religion and the Brain
John Lardas Modern

Kindred Spirits: Friendship and Resistance at the Edges of Modern Catholicism
Brenna Moore

The Privilege of Being Banal: Art, Secularism, and Catholicism in Paris
Elayne Oliphant

Ripples of the Universe: Spirituality in Sedona, Arizona
Susannah Crockford

PROMISCUOUS GRACE

Imagining Beauty and
Holiness with Saint Mary of Egypt

SONIA VELÁZQUEZ

The University of Chicago Press
Chicago and London

The University of Chicago Press, Chicago 60637
The University of Chicago Press, Ltd., London
© 2023 by The University of Chicago
All rights reserved. No part of this book may be used or reproduced in any
manner whatsoever without written permission, except in the case of brief
quotations in critical articles and reviews. For more information, contact the
University of Chicago Press, 1427 E. 60th St., Chicago, IL 60637.
Published 2023
Printed in the United States of America

32 31 30 29 28 27 26 25 24 23   1 2 3 4 5

ISBN-13: 978-0-226-82608-0 (cloth)
ISBN-13: 978-0-226-82610-3 (paper)
ISBN-13: 978-0-226-82609-7 (e-book)
DOI: https://doi.org/10.7208/chicago/9780226826097.001.0001

Library of Congress Cataloging-in-Publication Data

Names: Velázquez, Sonia (Theologian), author.
Title: Promiscuous grace : imagining beauty and holiness with Saint Mary of
    Egypt / Sonia Velázquez.
Other titles: Class 200, new studies in religion.
Description: Chicago : The University of Chicago Press, 2023. | Series: Class 200:
    new studies in religion | Includes bibliographical references and index.
Identifiers: LCCN 2022038225 | ISBN 9780226826080 (cloth) | ISBN 9780226826103
    (paperback) | ISBN 9780226826097 (ebook)
Subjects: LCSH: Mary, of Egypt, Saint. | Christian saints in art. | Christian saints in
    literature. | Beauty, Personal—Religious aspects—Christianity. | Holiness.
Classification: LCC BR1720.M33 V45 2023 | DDC 226—dc23/eng/20221024
LC record available at https://lccn.loc.gov/2022038225

♾ This paper meets the requirements of ANSI/NISO Z39.48-1992
(Permanence of Paper).

CONTENTS

List of Figures   vii
On Translations and Spelling   ix

In a Chapel: An Invitation to Imagine   1

1 Image Theory according to Saint Mary of Egypt   23
2 The Seductions of Hagiography   50
3 The Shoes of the Sinner and the Skin of the Saint   73
4 Neither Venus nor Venerable Old Men   92
5 Appearances Are Everything   128

Epilogue: In the Artist's Studio   159

Acknowledgments 167   *Notes* 171   *Bibliography* 209   *Index* 225

FIGURES

1 Hill, *My Wife and My Mother-in-Law* 5
2 Ribera, *Saint Mary of Egypt*, Museo Civico Gaetano Filangieri, Naples, Italy 17
3 Ribera, *Saint Mary of Egypt in Ecstasy*, Colección Juan Antonio Pérez Simón, Mexico City, Mexico 18
4 Matham, *Kitchen Scene with Kitchen Maid*, Metropolitan Museum of Art, New York 40
5 Velázquez, *Kitchen Maid with the Supper at Emmaus*, National Gallery, Dublin, Ireland 41
6 Sánchez Cotán, *Still Life with Quince, Cabbage, Melon and Cucumber*, San Diego Museum of Art, San Diego 48
7 *Frau Welt*, Cathedral of Worms, Germany 79
8 Ribera, *Saint Mary of Egypt*, Musée Fabre, Montpellier, France 95
9 Ribera, *Saint John the Baptist in the Desert*, Museo Nacional del Prado, Madrid, Spain 101
10 Ribera, *Saint Bartholomew*, Museo Nacional del Prado, Madrid, Spain 102
11 Ribera, *Penitent Magdalene*, Museo Nacional del Prado, Madrid, Spain 103
12 Ribera, *Saint Mary of Egypt*, Museo Nacional del Prado, Madrid, Spain 104
13 Ribera, *The Assumption of Mary Magdalene*, Real Academia de Bellas Artes de San Fernando, Madrid, Spain 112
14 Velázquez, *The Nun Jerónima de la Fuente*, Museo Nacional del Prado, Madrid, Spain 121
15 Ribera, *Saint Mary of Egypt in Ecstasy* (detail), Colección Juan Antonio Pérez Simón, Mexico City, Mexico 125

ON TRANSLATIONS AND SPELLING

Throughout this book, all translations are mine, unless the name of a translator is indicated. I modernize spelling, punctuation, and capitalization when quoting directly from primary sources not available in modern editions.

IN A CHAPEL

An Invitation to Imagine

IN THE CITY OF PARIS, on the corner of rue de la Jussienne—a linguistic deformation of *égyptienne*—and rue Montmartre, a plaque invites the passerby to envision a medieval chapel that had once occupied that space. Imagine, then, standing inside the chapel where the light directs your gaze upward to the stained-glass windows depicting the beautiful female saint that gives the chapel its name, Saint Mary of Egypt. According to the plaque, the image portrayed the saint facing a boatman across the deck of a ship with her skirt suggestively rolled up to just above the knees. Underneath the image, one could read the following explicatory text: "*How the saint offered her body to the boatman in exchange for her passage.*"[1] The seductive image conjured by this inscription may take today's passersby aback, not least because it would have been inside a holy chapel. They are not alone: the plaque indicates that having been judged "indecent," the offending image was removed in 1660.[2]

The beauty of the nude human body, including female bodies, is certainly not foreign to Christian iconography. In imitation of Christ, male and female martyrs are often depicted unclothed, their limbs perhaps bloodied but still luminous in their sanctity. The Virgin Mary nursing a barely draped infant, too, is a common sight. So is the lovely, sometimes scantily clad, penitent Mary Magdalene. But the woman on the window panel described above does not fit any of these categories. Her body shows no signs of torture. She reveals her legs and frames what she conceals with her gathered skirt instead of letting a nurturing breast peek out from her blouse. Her demeanor, as described in textual sources, is confident, even brazen, certainly not contrite or meditative. Beauty here does not simply signify holiness, as is the case for the Virgin Mary. But neither is it a quality that must be sacrificed for holiness to surface as the great art historian Émile Mâle wrote of Mary Magdalene's beauty, "consuming itself like incense burned before God in solitude far from the eyes of men."[3] Ever since the eighth century, the rationale behind the presence of images in churches has been that they serve as aids in the instruction of the faithful. In this context, what does the image in the Jussienne chapel perform?

There is no easy way to account for this image. The contention of this book is that the body of its heroine, Saint Mary of Egypt, together with the corpus of visual and textual manifestations of her legend, have new lessons to teach us about the long-contested relationship between feminine beauty and holiness; the role played by human-made images in a religious context; and the significance of gender to both. This project was originally conceived to show art historians and literary scholars that religion matters. But there came a point where I realized that not all religionists would recognize how the literature and art of Saint Mary of Egypt speaks to their concerns. The project is, in short, an intervention in the study of religion and materiality. What it contributes to the study of the materiality of religion and the religiosity of matter is attention to beauty and, in particular, to the judgments about the beauty of women's bodies.

MARY OF EGYPT BETWEEN THE VIRGIN MARY AND MARY MAGDALENE

Theologians, poets, artists, and laypeople alike have been fascinated by Mary of Egypt's legend ever since it was first recorded in the seventh century in a version ascribed to Sophronius, patriarch of Jerusalem.[4] Recent scholarship has contested this attribution, and some have gone so far as to propose that the text should be classified as "imaginary hagiography," although both Eastern and Western Christian traditions venerate the saint.[5] What Voltaire famously wrote about God—"If he did not exist, it would be necessary to invent him"—applies to the Egyptian saint.[6] Her prominence is religious and symbolic rather than historical, and all the more important for that reason. It is easy to see why: Mary of Egypt encompasses sin and sanctity, the excesses of both concupiscence and asceticism, and, uniquely, the charms of nubile youth and the wrinkles of old age. Her story takes us from her early years in fourth-century Egypt when at the age of twelve she defied her parents to pursue her burning desire for sex by moving to Alexandria. There, she found welcome in the town's brothel, although she—pursuing pleasure, not profit—gave herself freely and indiscriminately to men for seventeen years. One day, after spying on the harbor a crew of pilgrims on their way to Jerusalem for the feast of the Adoration of the Holy Cross, she seduced the boatman (as depicted in the Jussienne chapel). On the ship, she once again turned her "lust into a free gift" offered to old and young men alike.[7] Her conversion took place in the Holy Land when she had a tearful epiphany upon encountering an image of the Virgin Mary on the porch of the Church of the Holy Sepulchre. She spent her last decades in the Jordan desert— her body ravaged by age and the austerity of her penitent life; her holiness attested by a monk, Zozimas, who found her by chance and learned from her the true meaning of ascetic virtue. When she died, Zozimas miraculously received help from a lion to bury her body.[8]

The Egyptian's life is marked by her interaction with the Virgin Mary, and the narrative arc of her written vita parallels the Magdalene's move from sinfulness to sainthood. Yet, to imagine with Mary of Egypt—the key process of this book—is to depart from a long-standing schematic understanding of how beauty and holiness are figured in a Christian context. The Virgin Mary and Mary Magdalene have traditionally stood as examples of ideal and worldly beauty, respectively.[9] When the angel Gabriel greets Mary as "full of grace" (Luke 1:28), the favors she receives are reflected in her spiritual and physical perfection. Ephraim the Syrian (AD 306–73) sings of that ideal, perfect beauty when he places it alongside that of Christ: "You alone and your Mother / are more beautiful than any others; / for there is no blemish in you, / nor any stains upon your Mother. / Who of my children / can compare in beauty to these?"[10] He is not alone in praising the Virgin's beauty as a mark of holiness and redemption. In fact, the long tradition among church fathers, relating Mary's radiant beauty to her lack of spiritual blemish (original sin) from the moment she was conceived in her mother's womb, sustains the Catholic dogma of her immaculate conception, decreed in 1854.[11] But this beauty, like the Virgin herself, is singular and exceptional. "Not like earthly beauty, dangerous to look upon," hers is a shining star guiding human souls through the darkness to God, as Cardinal Newman put it in the conclusion to his sermon on the glories of Mary.[12] The path toward the divine that the Virgin's beauty represents belongs to this world, insofar as stars are part of the cosmos—a cosmos that is itself figured as reflecting the grace and beauty of God. Importantly, however, this beautiful path also remains literally out of touch; it is a *heavenly* guide, a guide traced on ether leading the way to a spiritual beyond.

In contrast to the Virgin's ideal beauty stands Mary Magdalene, the repentant prostitute of medieval lore.[13] In the last decade of the sixth century, Pope Gregory the Great sketches her earthly beauty and the threat it poses to the soul in an influential sermon that also cemented her reputation as a penitent sinner of the flesh.[14] Gregory's homily offers the woman "who had loved much" (Luke 7:47), first, as an example of how feminine beauty leads astray by insisting on the pleasures of the earthly, and, second, as an instance of how this beauty can be corrected through sacrifice and penance.[15] When Gregory concludes that after seeking Christ, Mary Magdalene "found as many things to sacrifice as she had had ways of offering pleasure," he makes her a foundational figure of vanity.[16] She comes to represent both senses of the word: first, the sinful pride in one's appearance, and then the realization that appearances are worthless. Hence her iconographic attributes: a jar of ointment (the perfume she had once used sinfully to embellish herself before conversion, and which afterward she lavished on Christ's feet) and a skull upon which to meditate on the transience of the world's pleasures and beauty.

Against both the Virgin Mary's exclusionary model of idealized beauty and the Magdalene's sacrificial model of vanity punished, Mary of Egypt offers the generous and paradoxical logic of both/and. The Egyptian's beauty is not an ideal to follow toward transcendence, as is the case of the Virgin. Yet in all its worldly and carnal manifestation, Mary of Egypt's beauty remains a gift from God. The stained-glass window in the Jussienne chapel underscores this tension when the descriptive caption specifies that the seductive body belongs to "the saint." Unlike the lessons of the Magdalene, where spiritual enlightenment depends on the revelation that the world's wonders hide the fundamental rot and emptiness of death, Mary of Egypt invites us to imagine a more generous world and a humbler vision of revelation. The Magdalene's beauty asks us to peel back the seductive but ultimately false appeal of the flesh in order to see the truth of the bare bones underneath. Worldly beauty is replaced by its spiritual, truer counterpart. This cognitive move, as feminist philosopher and theologian Grace Jantzen notes, aligns beauty with the body and its ultimate demise. Beauty in such accounts is valuable only insofar as it teaches that true worth lies in a disembodied, spiritual beyond.[17] By contrast, beauty according to Mary of Egypt is closer to the experience of the ambiguous image known as *My Wife and My Mother-in-Law* (figure 1). The lines of this drawing depict at once the profiles of a beak-nosed old woman wearing a head rag and a dark-haired woman dressed in an elegant fur wrap and a choker.[18] The same image offers two different representations and insights, but one does not necessarily correct

FIGURE 1. W. E. Hill, *My Wife and My Mother-in-Law*. Optical illusion in *Puck* 78, no. 2018 (November 6, 1915), 11. Source: Library of Congress Prints and Photographs Division.

or invalidate the other. Instead, the scope of what it is possible to see gets enhanced. The world of the beholder becomes richer when the image is both a young woman and a hag. Unlike the revelation that all earthly beauty must die, and therefore appearances are not to be trusted, the process of reimagining here is a joyful realization that we must attend to what we see and that there is more than initially meets the eye. That is, as I will argue, one of the main lessons of Saint Mary of Egypt.

RELIGION, MATERIALITY, AND THE ABSENCE OF BEAUTY

Scholars of religion have long urged us to attend to what we see, and to the embodied experience of seeing, by focusing on materiality and the role of the senses. Insisting on the importance of matter—long denigrated as idolatrous, fetishistic, or simply less significant than spiritual ideals, beliefs, or faith—this scholarship challenges the dematerialized concept of religion typically associated with Protestant Christianity. The study of religion and materiality teaches us to consider sacred spaces, relics, images, shrines, vestments, other devotional objects, and indeed bodies as they move in the world, as sites of creative and meaningful religious experience. As David Morgan explains, materiality includes objects, spaces, and performances as well as participants' sensory perceptions. Materiality, he writes, is ultimately "an integrated process, interweaving the different senses and incorporating memory and emotion into the relationships human beings have with the physical world."[19] Transformative work has been inspired by Morgan's insight that things matter in the study of religion exactly because they are embedded and act within social networks alongside other things, ideas, and bodies. Rather than simply approach material forms as expressions of religion, this work asks how religion might "happen materially."[20] From Morgan's studies of how visual culture shapes the religious experience even of presumably aniconic Protestants, to Colleen McDannell's exploration of American religious popular culture and Charles Hirschkind's research on the popularity of recorded sermons in Cairo, we learn how the mundane experiences of wearing certain items of clothing, owning a mass-produced image of Jesus, or listening to a cassette tape, are themselves religious experiences.[21]

And yet, the study of religion and materiality has little patience for aesthetic judgments. As a category, aesthetics is usually associated with its eighteenth-century legacy. At that time, aesthetics connoted the experience of a disinterested observer contemplating an object (natural or artistically produced) judged pleasing and beautiful. This connotation, as scholars today point out, gets in the way of understanding how mass-produced objects such as garden statues of saints can be religiously significant. As Morgan and McDannell show, the aesthetic scorn for these kitschy objects carries with it also a moral condemnation that has prevented both scholars and church authorities from taking them seriously.[22] Drawing on Aristotle's *De Anima* as well as on contemporary anthropological practice, Birgit Meyer and Jojada Verrips propose an alternative definition of aesthetics, one that would refer to "our total sensoric experience of the world and to our sensuous understanding of it."[23] For Meyer, this implies a reconceptualization of religion as "sensational forms that make the transcendental sense-able."[24] The sensational forms Meyer considers include quotidian objects such as books, videotapes, or buildings, each locating the experience of what she calls the transcendental alongside the sublime. Beauty, however, is rarely addressed in anthropological, theological, or religious studies conversations about materiality. Conceived as normative and constrictive—even elitist and reactionary—beauty is seldom deemed worthy of study.[25] Hence the question that animates this project: What place might beauty, and in particular the beauty of women's bodies, have in such conversations about religion and materiality?

Other aspects of the signifying power of women's bodies have been studied especially well by those who focus on women mystics. Carolyn Walker Bynum's notable study of women and food in the Middle Ages is just one instance of works challenging the dualistic opposition of body to spirit and expanding our notions of what bodies can be and do.[26] In her work on modern theorists' obsession with medieval mystics, Amy Hollywood shows, for example, how bodies resist, while abetting, the theorization of nonnormative life. For Hollywood, the crucial question concerns our fascination with "emotional, bodily, and excessive forms" of mysticism associated with women, mysticism being "one of the few places within the West in which women have been able to give free rein to their desire to be everything."[27] More precisely, Hollywood studies the generativity of dying bodies "and the way that the body and its mortality are associated with women" and how "men's (and women's) anxieties about disease, pain, and death are projected onto women's bodies."[28] With Mary of Egypt, by contrast, we think with a didactic saint rather than a mystic, and we focus not on the relationship between the sensible and the ecstatic, but instead on the coexistence of beauty and ugliness.

THE INCARNATIONAL BEAUTY OF BODIES, TEXTS, AND IMAGES

Feminist theologians have prepared the ground for this project by recuperating beauty for ethical thought. Partly by appealing to the doctrine of the incarnation, upholding Christ's dual nature as god and as human, they have pushed back against fundamentally negative accounts of beauty and holiness. From this perspective, scholars have paid attention to the concrete and material realities of women who, as creators of beauty and not merely its silent objects, counter the mystifying aspects of beauty.[29] The symbolic and conceptual value of embodied beauty has only recently begun to be explored, however. Taking as a point of departure the incarnation as an example of the relationship between the divine and its creation, Krista Hughes calls for the deconstruction and reconstruction of Christian stories and symbols in order to find a form of beauty that is "integrated" rather than idealized.[30] Hughes pursues a model of beauty that incorporates justly, without ignoring, sugarcoating, or glorifying "all elements of one's corporeal existence," including suffering.[31] These pages offer Mary of Egypt as a powerful example of such an integrated beauty.

Understood this way, beauty resides in the concreteness of particulars rather than in abstractions. This study of the different manifestations of the Egyptian's legend thereby attends as much to what the story has to teach us about beauty and holiness as to how that doctrine is inseparable from the specific words sung on a medieval public square or pigment painted on canvas. It is a central premise of the book that the incarnation structures medieval and early modern understandings of artistic creation and interpretation.[32] Therefore, the reasons for my insistence on materiality are at once methodological, theological, and theoretical. It follows, then, that the chapters of the book hew closely to the material specifics of poetry (metaphor, wordplay, rhyme), painting (perspective, color, light), and performance (using bodies to bring to life word and image). If the Word became flesh, then words in all their wayward, fleshy ways are inextricably bound to the ideas they incarnate. Such an incarnational emphasis implies that "all thinking, and therefore all knowing, takes place *in* language and not merely *through* language."[33] There is no discarding of the letter in pursuit of the spirit.

This insight is most apparent in those texts where the uniqueness of expression makes form and content inseparable, such as the poetry of John Donne or the prose of Saint Teresa of Ávila. But our written sources for

Mary of Egypt are primarily hagiographic, and the importance of form is less obvious for a genre rarely noted for its beauty and often maligned for its repetitiveness. Each of the various versions of the hagiographic legend of Mary the Egyptian may "say the same thing," insofar as it is telling the story of the same saint. Nevertheless, the meaning of each version is inflected by *how* that narrative is told. Moreover, that the incarnational doctrine that the *word* became flesh should have an impact on the composition and interpretation of linguistic texts makes sense. But, as I outline in the first chapter, another lesson of Mary of Egypt is that that painting, too, is haunted by an incarnational poetics and the bodiliness of the paintings' poetics complicates the theory that images communicate transparently.

THINKING WITH SAINT MARY OF EGYPT

Thinking with Mary of Egypt is a promiscuous venture, and not only because of her sexiness. Promiscuity implies a willingness to attend to what is impure, what can be confusing, or what can have more than one use.[34] For this project, moving forward (*pro-*) implies mixing and assembling (*miscere*) material across boundaries of period, geography, medium, and genre. I draw the corpus studied in this book largely from a Western Christian tradition—more precisely, from an Iberian context. Each artifact is set in its own context: the anonymous thirteenth-century poem *Vida de Santa María Egipciaca* (*Life of Saint Mary the Egyptian*) (focus of chapters 2 and 3); the four known canvases depicting Mary of Egypt painted by Jusepe de Ribera (chapters 1 and 4); and the seventeenth-century play *La gitana de Menfis* (The gypsy girl from Memphis) by Juan Pérez de Montalbán (1602–38), popular Spanish playwright, inquisitorial notary, and protégé of the great poet Lope de Vega (chapter 5). Remaining true to the spirit of hagiography that transcends geographic, chronological, and generic boundaries, each chapter's focal point is linked to a constellation of translations, revisions, and strategic deployments in documents such as church councils or treatises of painting that move us forward and backward in time. Each chapter pays attention to the grammar and syntax of hagiography, in order to show how the story of Mary of Egypt mediated thinking about the beauty of bodies, words, and images and the relationship of all three—the corporeal, the verbal, and the visual—to holiness.

Rather than tracking the historic development of Mary of Egypt's cult, my ultimate goal is to offer a prismatic conceptual exercise in thinking with this particular saint. The phrase "good to think with" has become a commonplace in academia, shorthand for what Marjorie Garber calls the "validating power" of humanistic inquiry.[35] Yet, when it comes to thinking with saints, it is still worth recalling the origin of this locution in the work of Claude Lévi-Strauss. Writing about how totemic creatures are chosen, Lévi-Strauss concludes that their direct utility—that they are "good to eat"—is less of a factor than the fact that they are "good to think with."[36] To think with a totemic animal is to see how it can render abstractions such as kinship sensible and tangible. For my purposes, thinking with Mary of Egypt means that considering the particulars of the Egyptian's legend can yield a new understanding of the complex relationship of sensible beauty and holiness.

THE VISIBILITY OF HOLINESS

Let us return to the image of Mary the Egyptian in the Jussienne chapel. It is certainly normal to find the name of a saint spelled out near its corresponding image on a stained-glass window. That is the case, for example, in the depiction of Mary the Egyptian in the cathedral of Chartres, where "Egipciaca" can be read framing the saint's haloed head.[37] However, on the stained-glass window of the chapel on rue de la Jussienne, the inscription below the image of the Egyptian does not deem it necessary to spell out the woman's name. It emphasizes her sanctity instead. Those viewers already familiar with Mary of Egypt and the story of her conversion from licentious twelve-year-old to venerable anchorite would have recognized the scene as the moment when the sinner left Alexandria for Jerusalem in search of new erotic adventures. This episode, depicted in medieval churches from Burgos to Bourges, is often followed by panels that show Mary in sexual pursuit of pilgrims on their way to the Church of the Holy Sepulchre, the site of her eventual conversion.[38] Knowledgeable viewers, then, would presumably *not* need to read the proleptic reminder of the Egyptian's future holiness. In fact, the epithet "the saint" may even prove puzzling since it is more common to refer to Mary of Egypt as "the sinner."[39] But the surprise of finding a saint where one expects a sinner is, in fact, fundamental to the power of Mary's legend. The Egyptian's story—and in many cases also the visual representations of her very body—make visible a resistance to the linear chronology of youthful sinner turned venerable saint. She sets askew the axis of holiness:

she is "the saint" even in the very midst of her seduction of the pilgrims, just as she is "the sinner" in the incipit of the canonized tale of her life. This is another lesson of the Egyptian's story.

To the very few medieval and early modern faithful ignorant of the legend's details, the label of holiness, coupled with the suggestion of a sexual transaction, would have proven more bewildering than the image alone. The word "saint" reassures the reader that the displayed body is holy, that the Egyptian's displayed legs belong to God. But, as with the medium of stained-glass itself, the caption's colorful lucidity changes the light as it shines through. After all, the text describes the saint's act of offering her body to the boatman as a form of promiscuity, of sexual license, rather than an act of consecration. In the case of the stained-glass window, holiness may be a label applied to the Egyptian. Yet, this label does not clarify or confirm the viewer's conclusions about her legend. The naming of sanctity marks the beginning, rather than the conclusion, of inquiry. Or to put it another way, in the very act of proclaiming Mary's body as holy, the inscription under the image also complicates what holiness itself may mean.

To imagine Saint Mary of Egypt—and to think with her—is to inquire into the visibility of holiness. As I shall argue, interpretations of the Egyptian's story, in word, image, or performance, call on us to ask: Which stories, acts, or bodies come to be recognized as holy? When and how does holiness become manifest to the eye? Does belief follow perception? That is to ask, as Jean-Luc Marion does in *Believing in Order to See: On the Rationality of Revelation and the Irrationality of Some Believers*, is "seeing believing"? Or, must one "believe in order to see"?[40] This line of questioning offers us a dynamic way of conceptualizing holiness. Typically, a concept is "a general notion [. . .], a mental representation of the essential or typical properties of something."[41] A noun, such as "kindness," for example, stands in for a series of predetermined qualities—generosity, nobility, friendly disposition, and so on—used to judge whether an object or an action is in fact kind. In contrast, as Marion points out, to reduce holiness to such a checklist risks to become an idolatrous containment. And yet, this does not mean that holiness escapes our cognition. I maintain that holiness as much as beauty are concepts that hark back to the etymological connection between pregnancy and thought. To conceive, in this sense, is to actively create, through a relationship, something whose outcome cannot be known in advance.

If I shy away from offering specific definitions of my key terms, it is not because *holiness* and *beauty* are empty signifiers that incite the desire to fill them, as Roland Barthes famously suggests in his influential *S/Z*. When the

French semiotician writes that "beauty (unlike ugliness) cannot really be explained: in each part of the body it stands out, repeats itself, but it does not describe itself. Like a god (and as empty), it can only say: *I am what I am*,"[42] he imagines beauty and the divine as tyrannical entities that can only be known through a repetition that ultimately yields awed silence. Writing about feminine beauty, Barthes further notes that the only predicates available to speak about it pass through tautology ("*a perfectly oval face*") or a chain of comparisons ("*lovely as a Raphael Madonna, like a dream in stone, etc.*"). The chain eventually breaks down as he asks: "*lovely as Venus? But Venus lovely as what?*"[43] Barthes's account of beauty and the divine is seductive in its invisibility, freeing us from the need to locate it within bodies. Yet it is a very narrow way to imagine beauty and holiness.

By contrast, the value of beauty and holiness as concepts in this project comes precisely from the unexpected nature of the encounters they occasion. For example, the label signaling holiness ("the saint") under the image of Mary the Egyptian seducing the boatman calls for the viewer to imagine what holiness *might be*. It is an invitation to imagine that promiscuity can be holy, that holiness may encompass profanation as much as consecration. Similarly, for the purposes of this project, beauty will name an encounter produced between particulars: a seductive woman and a boatman, an ascetic woman and a holy man in the desert, an image and its beholder, and so on. Beauty, in each of these cases, is primarily a call that requires a response. The answer to the call of beauty in the legend of Mary of Egypt takes many forms. Within the story, men respond to her beauty seeking sex; Mary responds to the beauty of the image of the Virgin by converting. But the call of beauty extends outward to the audience, too. For a legend to be worthy of its name—a thing to be read, *legenda*—it is not enough to read and contemplate the story. Its words must move readers to act: to propagate the story, to change their life, and yes, even to reject the call. Beauty names the desire for a relationship, for something to be created together, unlike awe, which reduces the spectator to silence and private contemplation.

ICONOCLASM AND MEMORY AS RESPONSES TO THE CALL OF BEAUTY

If the label of "saint" functions as a call to inquiry, rather than as a verdict or conclusion for the public to accept, the responses elicited by this call are unpredictable. The call may fall—and has fallen—on deaf ears. Yet, these instances in which Mary of Egypt's sainthood is questioned become themselves part of the conceptual story. The caption at the Jussienne chapel reveals how even a rejected call speaks to responsiveness, how even acts of iconoclasm are a way of thinking with Mary of Egypt. The saintly label on the stained-glass window offered an invitation to imagine holiness present in an unexpected site, but it was unable to save the image from opprobrium and, ultimately, destruction. As confessional differences regarding the usefulness of images in a religious context changed the attitudes toward subjects deemed "inconvenient or scabrous," even Catholic leaders pushed for the removal of many stained-glass panels from churches.[44] As we saw earlier, the windowpane in the Jussienne chapel depicting Mary of Egypt on the ship was among those purged. In 1660 the priest of the nearby church of Saint Germain l'Auxerrois had the panel removed.[45] Thus, the scandal of the Egyptian's legend—the sight of a beautiful, openly seductive saint—is not simply a case of presentism, of our contemporary difficulty to imagine a form of beauty, or religiosity, different from a modern, prudish understanding.

The striking representation of Mary of Egypt caught in the act of seducing the boatman may have been physically destroyed, but it did not disappear from memory. Not only does a plaque still remind the passerby of its complex history, but references to the chapel's representation of the saint playing peekaboo with her clothes to tempt the boatman also crop up in novels by the likes of Alexandre Dumas and Anatole France in the nineteenth century. More significantly, as I show in the epilogue, the Egyptian performs a vital role in the development of the "catechism of aesthetics" that has made Honoré de Balzac's short story Le chef-d'œuvre inconnu (The Unknown Masterpiece) a favorite of philosophers and artists alike.[46]

When art historian Louis Réau writes about the ecclesiastic iconoclasm committed against medieval stained-glass windows, the only concrete example he offers is that of the destruction of the windowpane at the Jussienne chapel.[47] This honor is not arbitrary. In fact, a central claim of this book is that a radically understudied feature of the legend of Mary of Egypt is its connection to medieval and early modern debates about the merits of images (chapter 1). On the one hand, Mary's statuesque beauty, as portrayed in medieval poems, sometimes resembles the description of idols (chapter 3). On the other hand, in all versions of the legend, her conversion takes place under the aegis of an image of the Virgin Mary. Hers, in other words, is a story that not only brings together the seductive power of feminine beauty *and* its participation in surprising holiness; it also offers forceful examples of how images—textual and visual—possess the capacity to effect changes in the world, whether it be spiritual conversion or the destruction of a windowpane.

QUEER BEAUTY AND HOLINESS

The story of the stained-glass window in the Jussienne chapel and the afterlife of its provocative image of Saint Mary of Egypt is but one example of how the textured details of this legend allow us to reimagine beauty, holiness, and their interaction. This malleability is true not only at the beginning of her story, when Mary exemplifies traditional European canons of female beauty that nonetheless stand outside the typical religious tropes of feminine representations of holiness. The last part of the legend, too, challenges a number of familiar associations: of holiness with maternal or virginal bodies, of linear temporality ("before and after") with conversion stories, of sacred depths versus sinful surfaces (chapter 3).

In the Jussienne chapel, the iconographic focus is on the early life of Mary of Egypt. Most medieval and early modern visual representations of the saint, however, prioritize the post-conversion part of the legend. This bias makes sense from a doctrinal perspective. After all, the story's emphasis on repentance, forgiveness, penitence, and the eucharist align with ecclesiastic teachings and guidelines as spelled out in church councils from the Fourth Lateran Council in the thirteenth century to the Council of Trent convened three hundred years later.[48] Aesthetic considerations, however, also weigh strongly in the preference for penitent Mary as a subject (chapter 4). First and foremost, her story allows artists to grapple with how to represent a visibly aged female body in ways that honor her spiritual conversion without erasing her past. Imagining Mary of Egypt after her conversion demands that artists negotiate competing conventions for representing the female body. On the one hand, artists typically have hidden the wizened surface of the female body to portray decorously attired matriarchs, and on the other, they have depicted the old female body as a grotesque sign of physical decadence and possibly moral vice.[49]

The visual emphasis on the toll that age and the rigors of asceticism have taken on the Egyptian's body differentiates her from Mary Magdalene. With very few exceptions, the Magdalene holds on to her youthful beauty even when she is depicted in penitence in the French wilderness. When, for example, Orazio Gentileschi (1563–1639) paints a recumbent Magdalene on rocky soil, her long, reddish-blond locks cascade around the skull upon which she has been meditating. The iconographic tradition of the Egyptian, in contrast, typically shows her hair long but almost indistinguishable from fur; in fact, Mary of Egypt's hair often replaces her worn-out clothes and protects her otherwise naked, exposed, and importantly, now withered body.[50] The animality of the long hair sharpens in the depiction of the saint's death, where a hairy Mary lies on the ground awaiting burial by the monk Zozimas, aided by a furry lion. In such scenes, the texture of Mary's hair becomes a tactile echo of the lion's fur. Although Mary of Egypt is not the only hirsute saint, it is only in her case that hair denotes and emphasizes the saint's creaturely nature precisely at the moment when the spirit is supposed to have triumphed.

It is easy to interpret Mary the Egyptian's radical conversion from sinfulness to sainthood as an inversion of the logic of holy beauty: if as a sinner she represented a beautiful shell hiding a rotten soul, then as desert penitent the shriveled husk of her body would conceal a beautiful spirit. And yet, a simple reversal does not account for the ways in which her later semi-nakedness, this time marked by time and asceticism, still retained its seductive powers—as Virginia Burrus and Cary Howie have shown.[51] Missing from the neat formula of inversion and the accounts that complicate it is a feature of our heroine's body that fascinates painters and writers: the potential beauty of her aged body. Visual representations of the saint's ascetic experience—on canvas but also ekphrastically on the page—announce queer forms of both beauty and holiness. This queerness is most salient in the four poignant portraits of the saint painted by seventeenth-century Valencian artist Jusepe de Ribera (1591–1652). Ribera, best known today as a "master of gore" for his depiction of mythological and hagiographic scenes of suffering and punishment, emerges in my argument as the prophet of a paradoxically grotesque beauty.[52] In different ways, each of his four canvases visibly disrupts the expectations that the "before" of a spiritual conversion is radically different from its "after." Moreover, in doing so, Ribera's images of the Egyptian expand the palette of expressions of beauty and holiness beyond the predictable depictions of the Virgin Mary, virgin martyrs, and saintly matrons.

Visually and spiritually, the martyrdom of beautiful female virgins teaches that the faithful must discard the physical surface in favor of spiritual depth, and that transcendence takes precedence over transience. This tutorial translates into the expectation that a sacrificial treatment of the beautiful body paves the path to the virgin's sanctity. Similarly, the association of Mary Magdalene with vanity, the expectation that conventional feminine beauty is a stumbling block to holiness, also informs the representation of non-martyred, elderly female saints such as Saint Anna, widow and prophetess, or Saint Anne, the Virgin's mother. In this tradition of holy matrons, for an old female body to be *seen* as holy, it must lose the corporeal trappings of sensuality to become a vessel of visible "masculine authority."[53]

In Ribera's paintings, the queerness of the legend of Saint Mary of Egypt extends beyond the more obvious aspects of the legend. Queerness is apparent, of course, in the saint's distinctive sexuality. The details of the Egyptian's vita refuse to coalesce into either one of two stable and mutually exclusive economies—that of reproductive sex and that of virginity. Her legend even resists presenting Mary of Egypt as having a stable object of desire, for she begins seeking out every man with abandon only to then devote herself absolutely to one exceptional woman, the Virgin Mary.[54] Her story shares that particular nuance of queerness with other stories of holy harlots, but the "productive incoherence" of queerness, as identified by literary theorist and queer studies scholar Eve Kosofsky Sedgwick, uniquely animates other key aspects of the Egyptian's legend: identity, space, time, and crucially, how one conceives her holiness.[55] In *Tendencies*, Sedgwick describes the essays in her collection as themselves "queer." She glosses the adjective by referring to the etymology of the word, which recalls a transversal, twisted, and twisting movement across categories.[56] This energy, she writes, is "directed at rendering those culturally central, apparently monolithic constructions newly accessible to analysis and interrogation."[57] I can think of no better, succinct description of what imagining with Mary of Egypt entails. Although Ribera's four different figurations of Saint Mary of Egypt are notable for their unflinching realism, their affective power depends on their destabilizing nature. Without the clutch of a title, we do not know for certain what are we looking at. Is the woman on the Filangeri canvas (figure 2) a canonized, fourth-century saint or a dubious contemporary? Is the dark figure hovering diagonally across the magnificent Pérez Simón painting (figure 3) a venerable old man, a frightening hag, a levitating saint, or, as the prostrate monk Zozimas fears, a malignant desert apparition meant to test him?

As we shall see, Ribera's figurations of the Egyptian often posit her body as a site where the depiction of old age is not simply the undoing of youthful charm. Nor is transience negated in order to make room for transcendence, or the physical surface discarded to make way for spiritual depth. Instead,

FIGURE 2. Jusepe de Ribera, *Saint Mary of Egypt* (1651). Oil on canvas. Museo Civico Gaetano Filangieri, Naples, Italy. Courtesy of Directmedia Publishing. Source: Wikimedia Commons.

the wrinkles Ribera paints on Mary's skin incarnate a complex topology where youth meets age, strength touches vulnerability, and the conventional characterization of aged female flesh as disgraceful becomes the very ground for imagining a type of beauty and holiness capable of holding all these contradictions as a manifestation of what I call promiscuous grace.

FIGURE 3. Jusepe de Ribera, *Saint Mary of Egypt in Ecstasy* (ca. 1640). Oil on canvas. Colección Juan Antonio Pérez Simón, Mexico City, Mexico. Photograph from Alfonso E. Pérez Sánchez and Nicola Spinosa, *Jusepe de Ribera el Españoleto* (Barcelona: Lunwerg Editores, 2003), 159.

PROMISCUOUS GRACE

Grace is central to the project because it foregrounds that this study of religion and materiality is also an intervention in aesthetics. Like David Marno, I am interested in attending to the importance of form to religious experience, paying attention to how poetic form "raises its own questions about [its] historical and conceptual contexts."[58] Where Marno investigates the poetics of faith, however, I am interested in how the sensible and the spiritual converge. And while he assesses grace as simultaneously formalist and theological, I am interested in grace as that which bridges the putative divide between holiness and sensuality. Grace, generally understood in a Christian context as unmerited favor, a mercy freely given by God without attention to the virtue of the recipient, would seem to be promiscuous by definition.[59] This is, after all, how Paul describes grace in the epistle to the Ephesians. The connection between Mary of Egypt's sexual promiscuity and God's infinite mercy is present already in the seventh-century version of the legend, where her sexual abandon is described as the offering of a "free gift."[60] And yet, to insist on the promiscuity of grace does more than indulge in redundancy. It serves, rather, to highlight two important aspects of grace for this project: its connection with the realm of the senses and its relational structure.

First and foremost, the emphasis on promiscuity as a licentious lack of limits breaks the concept of grace free from its almost exclusive relegation to a religious sphere, where it is the subject of confessional debates between Catholicism and Protestantism. To imagine the promiscuity of grace with Mary of Egypt implies recuperating for grace its full meaning as both the gratuitous gift of mercy and salvation (holiness) and the allure of the senses (beauty). Promiscuous grace denotes a gift that is both spiritual and sensual, without simply making one the expression of the other, as is the case with the Virgin Mary's grace. This is why the Egyptian's grace is difficult to attribute exclusively to either a saintly or a sinful moment. As the caption in the Jussienne chapel indicated, at the height of her beauty (and at her most seductive moment) Mary is literally labeled as a "saint"; as a canonized legendary saint, she is inseparable from her epithet as "the sinner."

The second aspect of grace that comes into focus with promiscuity is its relational structure. As with beauty and holiness, grace, too is a calling. Grace is the quality or collection of qualities in an object that call for attention and attentiveness. Humanist Sebastián de Covarrubias eloquently observes in the first European monolingual dictionary, *Tesoro de la lengua castellana o española* (1611), that grace encompasses both "appearance and spirit" (buen talle y espíritu) so the qualities that "call out" may manifest as matters of form, such as harmony or symmetry, or comportment, such as thoughtfulness and kindness.[61] Grace, notes the lexicographer, is also the favor bestowed by a subject onto an object, one whose grace (in the sense of a quality that attracts attention) has been recognized. In a further turn, it is also the acknowledgment of the favor by the recipient (in Spanish *gracias*, thanks). Grace as a gift that requires recognition harks back to charisma, to the Greek *kharis* (gift), which may denote charm and seduction but also what is indivisible from a person, her aura as perceived by others. Applied to discourse, grace becomes a feature of rhetoric identified both with "the energy of the speaker's conviction, the rhythm of his speech, the clarity of his discourse," and more generally with a "deep certainty that an indispensable sensible joy makes possible the sharing of thought, and without it any oration would remain abstract and indifferent to its reception."[62] This way, grace becomes central to the creation of a shared sensibility.

The argument of the book takes place in three movements. The first two chapters make the case for the importance of form—the specificity and materiality of words and images—to the formational and didactic function of hagiography. Importantly, the visual and textual manifestations of the legend of Saint Mary of Egypt call for an awareness of mediation, that is to say, that the communication of beauty and holiness is not transparent or immediate. The next two chapters exemplify the generous logic of both/and that is central to paradox, holding two contradictory doxa as true side by side. In both the medieval Spanish verse vita and in Ribera's portraits, I argue for the simultaneity of beauty and holiness with what seems to be their opposite. These materials, I propose, model how to recognize a sinner who is also saint and to accept a past that does not get erased but remains. They teach how to see beauty in the grotesque. The final chapter turns to what happens when word and image come together in theatrical spectacle to bring to life the legend of Saint Mary of Egypt in the seventeenth century. The central object of study is Juan Pérez de Montalbán's *La gitana de Menfis* (ca. 1621–25). Here, Montalbán's Mary of Egypt, who is at home with appearances yet distanced from dissembling, comes to embody the encounter between what Jean-Luc Marion describes as the "ontological invisibility of sainthood" and the theatrical imperative to display. Finally, in the conclusion, I move from Spain to France, from the medieval and early modern to the nineteenth century, and from works that straddle the didactic and the aesthetic to a fictional novella. In other words, I move from the chapel of this introduction to another space that tickles the imagination, the artist's studio. Honoré de Balzac's *Le chef-d'œuvre inconnu* (1830s), long recognized as a founding fable of modernist art, contrasts two portraits. Scholars have spilled the most ink analyzing the importance of the last portrait, *La belle noiseuse*, a harbinger of abstract art and a paean to idealizing form over matter. They have written little, however, about the first portrait, the one that brings the three protagonists together—a canvas of none other than Saint Mary of Egypt. This final reflection shows how even at the birth of modernism, in the midst of a secular text, a fourth-century saint still has much to teach us.

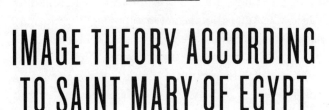

IMAGE THEORY ACCORDING TO SAINT MARY OF EGYPT

Then that other disciple, who reached the tomb first, also went in, and he saw and believed.

JOHN 20:8

The saint. What sort of saint? No one has ever seen a saint. For the saint remains invisible, not by chance, but in principle and by right.

JEAN-LUC MARION[1]

IF MARY OF EGYPT LIVED, it was sometime in the late fourth century at a time when the Christian church had not yet plunged into heated debates about the role images should play in a religious context. Still a relatively new religion in the eastern Mediterranean, Christianity welcomed the production of icons and other artifacts such as architecture, tapestries, and liturgical robes. The public visibility of these objects, after all, signaled the religion's growing civic and political power in addition to communicating any specific doctrinal content or speaking of local, noninstitutional religious practices.[2] Among these signs of splendor was the Church of the Holy Sepulchre in Jerusalem. There, a miraculous force denied Mary the Egyptian entrance while pilgrims rushed in to venerate the recently found relics of the Holy Cross. According to the legend, Mary's conversion took place thanks to her interaction with an icon of the Virgin Mary, but the very grounds where this transformation took place have a story to tell, too. Eusebius of Caesarea's fourth-century *Life of Constantine* details how the Holy Sepulchre had itself undergone two cultic alterations by the time Mary of Egypt paused at its gates. First, the historian notes, pagans had brought soil from elsewhere to cover over Christ's tomb. Then, on this newly paved ground, they built a shrine dedicated to Venus, goddess of love, hoping that the transformation would obscure the site's connection to Christ. A century later, Constantine ordered the utter destruction of pagan temples. Such was the zeal of this endeavor that he had the stones of the temple to Venus ground down to dust and the soil where they had stood dug out and removed as well. Workers in pursuit of the emperor's attempt to cleanse the past discovered the Holy Sepulchre, and Constantine subsequently turned the site into a magnificent pilgrimage destination.[3]

The Egyptian's conversion at the threshold of this twice-transformed site plots her singular spiritual transformation onto a larger map of political and religious changes. More subtly, I suggest that the juxtaposition of human and monumental conversions in the legend of Saint Mary of Egypt gestures toward two insights that guide my exploration of its visual aspects. First, the site reveals that the powerful human aspiration to build a glorious legacy often leads to an equally forceful need to break with the past, to the wish to erase it by crushing its stones into dust, as it were. Second, as Eusebius's story of multiple transformations indicates, the materiality of the past complicates the rectilinear desire that conversion be forward-looking, leaving the past behind. As Arthur D. Nock's influential account of conversion insists, conversion "implies turning from something to something else: you put earlier loyalties *behind* you."[4] This second insight—that the past does not always remain behind and out of sight—is central to the conversion story of Mary of Egypt. From this recognition of a more complicated temporality of conversion, it also follows that there is no immediacy when it comes to recognizing holiness. The experience of holiness is not instantaneous or obvious. In other words, the superimposition of conversions in the legend of Saint Mary of Egypt asks the reader to suspend the certainty that we may know, a priori, what holiness is and where it is to be found.

While arguably every conversion story may be understood as a relearning to see, the legend of Saint Mary of Egypt is unique among the legends of the holy harlots, for it insists on the visual mediations of this reeducation. In other such tales, the female sinner changes her ways thanks to the stirring words of male authority figures (Christ to Magdalene, Nonnus to Pelagia), or on account of a priest's clever reasoning (Paphnutius to Thais). By contrast, Mary of Egypt's conversion is mediated first by a spatial interdiction (the invisible force preventing her from entering the church), then a visual encounter with an icon of the Virgin Mary (which triggers self-reflection), and finally, the affective veneration of the Holy Cross. No surprise, then, that her story should appear at key moments in the history of Christian debates about images. When church authorities met at the Second Council of Nicaea (787) to counter the arguments of iconoclasts, a recitation of Mary the Egyptian's conversion is mobilized in the defense of images. And when the legitimacy of the use of images was again the center of theological controversy in the wake of the Reformation, her example appears in treatises on painting in Spain and Italy that affirmed the validity of religious images.

As I will show in this chapter, such a defense typically has hinged on the presumed immediacy of images. In the eyes of both religious authorities and artists, the appeal of images as a pedagogical tool, as the proverbial "book of the illiterate," rests upon the assumption that visual matter communicates immediately: viewers apprehend the message *all at once* and directly, as if images were no medium at all.[5] Under this logic, images say what they mean and mean what they say, and to stand before them is to *get* them: to see is to believe, *vidit et credit*. Indeed, the contexts of the use of the exemplum of Saint Mary of Egypt's conversion initially seem to corroborate the understanding of images as transparent vehicles of doctrine. But exempla, like images, are rarely only illustrative, and the exemplum of Mary the Egyptian proves productively unruly. It is invoked in contexts that underscore the power of images to affect the viewer immediately. However, a careful reading attending to the story's dependence on memory, delay, and hesitancy complicates an initial understanding of images as an immediate force. In fact, as I argue below, the story of Mary the Egyptian's conversion gestures toward how even canonical accounts of the proper role of religious images *also* affirm the importance of mediation—of how the visibility of holiness is a process that passes through a thick temporality not unlike that of spiritual conversion.

From such a perspective, then, the story of Mary's conversion constitutes what W. J. T. Mitchell calls a "discursive hyper-icon": an image like Plato's cave or the tabula rasa, which offers a condensation of particular ways of knowing. As Mitchell describes them, "in their strongest forms they [hyper-icons] don't merely serve as illustrations to theory; they picture theory."[6] In a religious context, dense images—such as the constellation of visual and textual manifestations of the conversion of Mary of Egypt—do more than illustrate doctrine; they are also theory. Theory, that is, in its etymological sense implies a site for contemplation, for thinking about what images are and what work they do. Yet, it must be stressed that this theory is not a disembodied exercise of thought.[7] It is inseparable from the material that gives rise to thinking. As S. Brent Plate puts it when writing about material religion, the point is to recognize that "ideas, beliefs, and doctrines begin in material reality" rather than seeing "theoretical ideas and doctrines all worked out, and then they find their 'expression' in the material world."[8] It is in this sense that there is a theory of images according to Saint Mary of Egypt. The title of this chapter, then, does not attribute the agency of a theorist to a saint who may not have lived. It does suggest, however, that a theory of how images work, of what they tell us about the visibility of holiness and beauty, may be drawn from the assemblage of visual and textual experiences encompassed in the mystery of her conversion.[9]

THE DREAM OF IMMEDIACY

The now commonsensical truth of the advertising statement that "a picture is worth a thousand words"—much like the popularized idea that images are the so-called Bible of the illiterate—cashes in the promise that a visual representation provides an unmediated, immediate access to the represented object. Underlying both of these common expressions is faith in a third axiom: that "seeing is believing." In a recent book on the material study of religion, David Morgan notably remarks about images that "they are able to operate on viewers with an immediacy that makes them beguiling. People are often inclined to believe what they see, as if an image were an encapsulation of reality."[10] Confidence in the communicative economy of images and their fidelity to reality depends partly on the almost intuitive association of visual representation with a spatial dimension. At its minimum, painting is matter, usually pigment, applied to a solid surface. This alone would suggest that space is the enabling dimension of painting's intelligibility, as opposed to the temporal nature of linguistic representation. Further, western European art has been marked by the dominance, from the fifteenth century onward, of perspectival representation to create an illusion of depth and solidity, a three-dimensionality that would render painting more lifelike on its two-dimensional surface.[11] However, this insistence on mimesis, the creative imitation of a recognizable world, obscures the temporal dimension of visual representation. Despite the supposed immediacy of the visual, images, like stories, take their time; they unfold slowly to the viewer rather than give themselves over immediately to whoever stands before them. Attention to the details of visual and narrative versions of the legend of Mary of Egypt will allow us to take measure of this thick temporal dimension of images.

Before turning to the complex relationship of images to time, however, I must first elaborate how the model of immediacy came to define the norm and set the foundation for the perceived efficacy of the visual over the linguistic. Imagistic immediacy speaks to the viewer's desire to understand visual representations as adhering to a favorable time of simultaneity, when perception and interpretation, thing and likeness, seem to coincide. In their influential work on remediation, Jay David Bolter and Richard Grusin describe the logic of immediacy as "the attempt to put the viewer in the same space as the objects viewed."[12] Whether dealing with perspectival painting or virtual reality software, viewers gauge the effectiveness of a medium of representation by how well it convinces them that their perception occurs with little or no mediation, that the medium represents a direct experience. Similarly, when it comes to religion, there is a tendency for the medium to disappear for the believer as it makes the connection between the divine and the immanent. Mass-produced sacred texts, like the Bible or the Koran, or devotional images are not appreciated as objects with particular material properties, but they are instead made "to vest the religious mediations in which they take part with some sense of immediacy."[13]

When it comes to humanistic Renaissance discourses on painting, immediacy also has a temporal dimension, especially as the efficacy of painting is measured against that of linguistic representation. Leonardo da Vinci articulates many of the ideas about word and image that would become commonplace among European humanist painters. Comparing the relative merits of the arts, Leonardo emphasizes the arbitrariness of linguistic signs that do not have a proper relationship to their referent. In this, he follows the insights of medieval thinkers such as Hugh of Saint Victor (1096–1141), who argued that words were the result of human invention while things were the work of God.[14] Leonardo extrapolates from this insight, asserting that there is a closer commonality between the work of God in creation and the work of the painter because both deal with images (similitudes) that pass directly to perception. In contrast, descriptive language depends on the activation of a previously established image in the mind in order to make sense. Leonardo writes, "poetry uses letters to put things into the imagination, and painting renders things really outside the eye so that the eye receives the similitudes [images] as if they were natural; and poetry renders what is natural without that similitude."[15] Only the painter whose art reflects directly the work of God can offer an unchanging, universal image or likeness of a person. Whereas a man will respond to different linguistic versions of his name—Giovanni, John, Juan—only painting can guarantee the universality of human form. Once imprinted on a surface, the human figure, rendered by the good painter according to the rules of science, will remain not only recognizable across linguistic and cultural borders but also across time. Painting, ruled as it is by mathematical principles such as proportion and perspective—which, according to Leonardo, are intelligible to any viewer—represents a more universal form of communication than the linguistic, which depends on imperfect translations to cross boundaries. In Claire Farago's words, the painter defended his medium "because it alone embodies harmony in an enduring, simultaneous mode."[16]

Furthermore, Leonardo stakes the impact of images on a perceived immediacy of the visual, on the presumption of a simultaneity of perception and comprehension:

> By these [comparisons] I only wish for a good painter to figure the fury of a battle, and for the poet to write something about it, and for both [of these battles] to be put before the public. You will see which will stop most viewers, which they will consider [more], which will be given most praise, and which will satisfy more. Certainly the painting, a great deal more useful and beautiful, will please most. Place the name of God in writing in a place and, if you set up his figure opposite this, you will see which is the more revered. [. . .] Take a poet who describes the beauties of a lady to her lover, and take a painter who figures her, you will see where nature will lead the enamoured judge.[17]

Leonardo's examples take direct aim at the highest manifestations of linguistic invention in the humanist canon. The battle scene recalls epic poetry, the name of God conjures theology, and the beauties of a lady bring to mind Petrarchan lyric. In all of them, Leonardo's claim for the superiority of painting depends on a phenomenology of the image that trades on the instantaneous pleasure that the "there-ness" of the visual is thought to provide. He further pegs the imbalanced exchange of a single image against copious words to the currency of time. According to his logic, the thousand words to describe a battle take a correspondingly long time, first to enunciate and then to assemble in the mind. In contrast, an image of combat affords the viewer the impression of taking in all at once the totality of the depicted object. The painted battle scene strikes the viewer and makes her stop and take it all in, seemingly at once. In contrast, the reader must piece together a verbal representation over time, thus lessening its arresting effect on the audience.

Elsewhere, Leonardo makes this point even more explicitly. He notes that it would be "very tedious" (tediosissima) for the audience to be presented linguistically with all the details that are otherwise gracefully presented in a painting. Indeed, as Leonardo points out mockingly, even the poet will experience pain related to his medium's association with time. After all, the poet who would compete with the painter in depicting a bloody battle would suffer from thirst, hunger, and sleeplessness in trying to say what the painter otherwise depicts "immediately" and painlessly: "the painter will surpass you because your pen will be consumed before you have fully described what the painter presents to you immediately using his science. And your tongue will be impeded by thirst, your body by sleep and hunger, before you demonstrate with words what a painter demonstrates to you in an instant."[18] Painting, in this classical paradigm, dreams of an instantaneous movement from model to copy. It hopes for an act of interpretation so immediate that it coincides with perception.

In the aftermath of the Council of Trent, treatises describing painting, its nature, and its usefulness in a religious context also presumed this sense of imagistic immediacy but this time coupled with the task of the orator to teach, to delight, and to sway or move the audience by presenting before their eyes intelligible, decorous images. This is exactly how Sevillian scholar and painter Francisco Pacheco (1564–1664) describes the importance of painting in his *Arte de la pintura, su antigüedad y grandeza* (1649). A combination of technical handbook, compendium of iconographic advice for painting religious motifs post-Trent, and humanist treatise, this text condensed a century and a half of (mostly Italian) arguments speaking to the nobility of painting as an intellectual endeavor and of its rightful place in a religious context. Following a humanist emphasis on the imitation of life for didactic purposes, Pacheco defines the purpose of painting in terms of the achievement of likeness, relegating color and ornament to an ancillary role.[19] A Christian painter, however, has yet another duty: to frame the very act of painting by virtue. Virtue is posited, first, at the conception of a canvas, painted by someone fully aware that the purpose of the human-made image is to serve divine glory rather than to achieve earthly fame. Second, virtue is also the end goal of painting since, if all goes as planned, the resulting image will lead the viewer into virtue. Here again, the integrity of the chain leading from the painter's virtue to the viewer's depends on the posited immediacy of visual medium:

> To move the soul of the viewer is not only the proper task of painting but also its most important [. . .]. For, if the orator can sway the emotions of strangers through the power of speech and deserves eternal praise for it, who can doubt that Christian painting, accompanied as it is by beauty and a spiritual conception, is able to achieve this effect all the more efficiently and nobly before the typically unlearned crowd? That the end of painting is all the more sublime and glorious the lyric poet [Horace in *Ars Poetica*] already noted in this *sententia Segnius irritant animum demissa per aures, / quam quae sunt oculis subiecta fidelibus*, which I translated this way: "Matters perceived / by the ears move but slowly. / Offered, though, / to trustworthy eyes, the quiet soul feels / a more powerful effect / and it is thus moved."[20]

In content and organization, this chapter in Pacheco's treatise follows closely Cardinal Gabriele Paleotti's *Discourse on Sacred and Profane Images* (1582), but Pacheco inserts his own translation of the classical Roman poet Horace's declaration of the superiority of "trustworthy eyes" over ears in the *Ars Poetica*. Horace's remarks are explicitly about theater and the different effects on the audience that "showing" an action upon the stage has versus "narrating" it.[21] Torn from this context, however, painters appropriated the quotation to proclaim more generally the primacy of sight, and consequently of painting, as a vehicle of trustworthiness or fidelity (*fidelidad*) over a less precise and impactful linguistic delivery of the same message.[22] Pacheco takes this polemical move one step further by translating *segnius* with an adverb of time: "lentamente" (slowly). The importance of this word becomes clearer when compared to the translation choices made by some of Pacheco's contemporaries. When translating this passage from Horace, Tomás Tamayo de Vargas emphasized the lack of force in aural impression, turning *segnius* into "feebly" (con floxedad). Alternatively, Francisco de Cascales, qualified the effect of hearing an account simply as "less moving" (menos mueve).[23] Pacheco, for his part, leaves no doubt: the power of visual impact is measured in time, where the slow motion of listening ("mueven lentamente") loses out to the immediacy and efficacy of painting.

IN PRAISE OF MEDIATION, OR IMAGE THEORY
ACCORDING TO MARY OF EGYPT

As Pacheco's words show, the Counter-Reformation's reiteration that religious images have earned their place in devotional practice because of their didactic and emotive force did not so much change as it intensified the Leonardian model of immediacy, the desire for a congruence of representation with its interpretation to be apprehended by the eye all at once. The Twenty-Fifth Session of the Council of Trent enjoined bishops to uphold the proper place of "paintings or other representations" in order to remind viewers of particular articles of faith and of divine favor more generally. According to the council, a visual object "set before the eyes of the faithful [. . .] may [result in] order[ing] their own lives and manners in imitation of the saints; and [they] may be excited to adore and love God, and to cultivate piety" (235).[24] The cultural influence of Trent in artistic activity is out of proportion with the barely six paragraphs dedicated to the topic of "The Invocation, Veneration, and Relics, of Saints, and on Sacred Images." The surprising concision of Trent is explained in part by the fact that the major conceptual battle against iconoclasm occurred eight centuries earlier, as recorded in the Fourth Session of the 787 Seventh Ecumenical Council (also known as the Second Council of Nicaea). Pacheco turns to this eighth-century text, via Paleotti, in order to demonstrate the efficacy of religious painting. After having established the "antiquity" of painting and sculpture (used by "gentiles" to honor their deities and respected by them enough to equate them with writing) and after having discussed the natural attraction of humans to images (via Pliny), Pacheco discusses three examples from the Seventh Ecumenical Council that demonstrate the power of images. The first two examples follow the logic of immediacy, as I examined it in the previous section. The last one—the story of the conversion of Mary of Egypt—narrated in greater detail than the others, does something different. The example of the Egyptian's conversion story substitutes a chain of mediations for the immediacy of painting.

The first of Pacheco's (and Paleotti's) examples corresponds to a quotation from the sermon "On the Divinity of the Son and the Holy Spirit" by Saint Gregory of Nyssa (ca. 330–95), which also appeared toward the beginning of the Seventh Council's Fourth Session. Reacting to a painting of Abraham's sacrifice of Isaac, the saint avows: "Often have I seen in pictures the representation of his trial, and never could I view the spectacle without tears, so powerfully did the work of art present the history to my eyes."[25] Pacheco, working from Paleotti's Latin, imbues the quotation with a polemic touch by contrasting the power of painting to move the holy man to tears repeatedly with the inability of the painting's caption to do the same: "I saw many times the visual representation of the inscription and could not walk past without shedding tears, for painting sets the story so vividly before the eyes."[26] Pacheco and Paleotti are careful not to claim for painting a stronger power than what is proper to scripture, but they do suggest that inscription as material language, unlike divinely inspired history *and* painting, cannot claim "to cause tears of edification" and much less "compunction" to "the uninstructed and ignorant."[27]

The second example Pacheco describes is a famous ekphrasis, that is to say the vivid description of a work of art. Here, the object of ekphrasis is a picture detailing the martyrdom of Saint Euphemia, as told by Saint Asterius, bishop of Amasea. In the Seventh Council, the bishop's narrative is told with obvious delight, and it is quoted in its entirety, including the bishop's frame, which posits a mild competition between language and visual arts. Seeking to engage his audience, Asterius prefaces his tour de force description thus: "Give me, if you please, your attention, as now there is some spare time for this narration, and I will describe the picture to you; for we sons of the Muses have resources in no way inferior to those of the painter."[28] This rhetorical bravado is missing from the painters' account of the ekphrasis. In *Arte de la pintura*, Pacheco reduces the entire episode to just two sentences that highlight, on the one hand, the image's decorum (*propiedad*) and lifelike depiction of the cruelty of the martyrdom and, on the other, the emotional effect that such a vivid depiction had on the bishop, concretized in the tears he shed.[29]

These two examples—Gregory of Nyssa's admiring the painting of Abraham's sacrifice and the description of the powerful representation of Saint Euphemia's martyrdom—help Pacheco emphasize two aspects of the efficacy of painting: its capacity to imitate life and to affect the viewer immediately upon encountering the visual object. In contrast, Pacheco's example of Saint Mary of Egypt's conversion subtly shifts emphasis. Instead of immediacy, the story highlights memory and prolepsis; instead of lifelike depictions observed by receptive viewers, the scene offers featureless images shooting violent glances back at the viewer:

> One reads about St. Mary of Egypt who, one day, upon seeing a crowd of people enter the temple and realizing that she alone was held back by

some unknown force, and remembering her libertine ways, she raised her eyes to an image of the Holy Cross and to another of the glorious Virgin; and it seemed to her that sharp darts issuing from the images were piercing her heart, and she pronounced these heartfelt words, "Dread overcame me and my soul was seized and I started to tremble and to get upset." And then that conversion and her unusual penitence came to pass.[30]

Attention to the language in this passage proves instructive. From the very beginning, Mary's conversion features and foregrounds mediation in material and temporal modes. When Pacheco quotes the description by Saint Asterius of his encounter with the canvas of Euphemia's martyrdom, he echoes the bishop's use of the historical present. This choice heightens the effect of immediacy, of presenting the image and its effects vividly before the eyes of the audience who, he posits, share both the bishop's temporal perspective and Pacheco's. In contrast, the narrative of the Egyptian's encounter with the image of the Virgin holds the listener at a distance. It is largely narrated in the past tense: she was held back; she raised her eyes; her heart was pierced. Even when Pacheco quotes Mary's words, there is no illusion of immediacy. Her description of how she had not been allowed to enter the church and her encounter with the image of the Virgin Mary both abound in the preterit: her senses and intellect were "seized," "overwhelmed," or "upset." The one surprising exception to the predominant use of the past tense is the participle that expresses Mary's first act of self-awareness: "*remembering* her libertine ways, she raised her eyes." Much like memory itself, this not-quite-verb poses a glitch in time; it interrupts and modifies the sequence of actions narrated clearly in the past while remaining itself grammatically and chronologically nonfinite. As if this strange temporality were not enough, the ostensible punch line of the story, what would lend it its exemplary value—that Mary converted as an immediate result of her encounter with the images—is shunted into the vagueness of the adverbial phrase "then it came to pass" (siguióse luego).

The different temporality of the example of Mary of Egypt stands out even more sharply compared to the story that follows it in Pacheco's text. That narrative, too, is a story of prostitution and of the important role an image played in effecting a change of heart, but it returns readers to the classical model of immediacy. After offering the example of Mary of Egypt, Pacheco inserts a poem, written by his friend, Don Juan de Arguijo, which retells a story attributed to Gregory of Nazianzus about a nameless prosti-

34 CHAPTER ONE

tute. Rushing to meet a client, she encounters an image of the pious philosopher Polemon and, suddenly shamed, desists from her sinfulness. The poem emphasizes the immediacy of the prostitute's "conversion." No sooner does she see the portrait of the virtuous philosopher than she registers her guilt: "She had *barely crossed* the threshold of the first gate *when her eyes set upon* the image of the great Polemon, and *at that very moment* [. . .] she registered her guilt."[31]

Against the insistent, immediate present of Pacheco's catalog of the power of painting to elicit an immediate emotional and spiritual response, something about Mary of Egypt troubles painting's effect of immediacy. While she too responds to the image of the Virgin Mary, the Egyptian's delay, in Pacheco's narration, creates a gap that challenges religious images' function as "silent preaching." Turning eight centuries back to Nicaea reveals a fuller picture of the peculiarity of image theory according to Mary that threads through Pacheco's text.

At the Seventh Ecumenical Council, approximately three hundred bishops met in Nicaea in 787 to address the question of the proper place of images in a religious context. The first three sessions set forth the recent history of the controversy together with Pope Adrian I's position against the iconoclasts. The Fourth Session established arguments in favor of the use of images, "whether on canvas, on wood, or in mosaics" as long as they are "for our instruction, emulation, and pattern."[32] This argument made use of extensive quotations from biblical sources, the writings of church fathers, hagiography, and other sources. In this context, the conversion of Saint Mary of Egypt is read aloud from her vita as part of a series of stories that testify not only to the power of images to teach and to persuade but also to the ways in which God may work miracles through them. One of the church authorities who participated in the council, Peter the Reader, read aloud from a version of Saint Mary of Egypt's life that belongs to the Eastern branch of the legend (as it is now known). In this version, Mary tells her life story to the pious monk Zozimas, after she has spent several years living in penitence in the desert. The focus of the quotation read at the council is on Mary's conversion:

> At length I retired and stood in a niche of the porch of the church, and there I came after some time to perceive the reason why I was not permitted to behold the life-giving wood. [. . .] While weeping I perceived above the place where I was standing an image of the immaculate Mother of God; and having fixed my eyes steadfastly upon her I said, "O Virgin

Mistress [. . .] I know, I know, indeed that it is neither right nor proper that I, utterly defiled and abandoned as I am, should presume to look upon thy image, who art ever a Virgin, ever chaste, in body and soul equally pure and uncontaminated [. . .] but I have heard that He whom thou didst beget was for this end born into the world [. . .] that He might call sinners to repentance [. . .]. O shut me not out from beholding that life-giving wood, on which God, whom thou didst beget according to the flesh, was crucified, did give His own blood as a ransom for me. [. . .]" Thus was I brought into the holy of holies, and I was counted worthy to behold the wood of the life-giving cross [. . .]. Having prostrated myself on the ground and adored that holy pavement, I went out and hastened with all speed to her [. . .] and having bent my knee before the immaculate Virgin the Mother of God, I used these words: "[. . .] Now direct me whither thou wilt [. . .]." And while I was yet speaking, I heard the voice of one crying out from afar, "Pass over Jordan, and there thou shalt find a blessed rest" [. . .]. I cried out with tears and called aloud upon the Mother of God: "O Mother of God, my Mistress, forsake me not"; and having said this, I went immediately from the porch of the church, and have continually wandered ever since.[33]

This lengthy narrative comes toward the end of a series of sanctioned anecdotes taken from saints' lives and other sources that delightfully describe divinely fashioned images, acheiropoieta, that marvel and inspire believers and gentiles alike. In these stories, vindictive images are just as likely to work miracles as they are to seek revenge, taking, literally, an eye for an eye.

In this context, the narrative of the intervention of the image of the Virgin Mary in the life of Mary the sinner serves two purposes. First, it underlines the ways in which the holiness of images has the potential to speak to everyone, from venerable clergy to the greatest sinner. John, Legate of the East, responds to Peter's reading of Mary's conversion thus: "A similar image I have seen in the holy city of Christ our God, and have often worshipped it."[34] The image—read as an allegory of God's grace—is potentially available to all, from sinful nymphomaniacs to theologians, but the viewer must be open to recognizing it, to opening their eyes to see and their mind, soul, and body to be moved. Second, Mary's conversion story marks a transition in the structure of the proceedings of the Fourth Session from the exposition of specific and colorful examples of how holiness works through images to its final section dedicated to the recitation of letters, sermons, and other apologia that directly dispute the objections of iconoclasts. I want to suggest that

Peter the Reader's recitation of Mary the Egyptian's conversion prepares the audience to accept the final argument of the session in favor of the worship of images, and in doing so, the story of Mary of Egypt offers an alternative image theory to the dream of immediacy, to the conviction that mere seeing will lead seamlessly and necessarily to belief.

At least three mediating factors coincide to effect Egyptian Mary's famous change of heart. First, the prominence of "the life-giving wood" attracts the pilgrims whom Mary will, in turn, attempt to follow inside the church. This cross, however, is not just any wooden artifact. The story refers to the thing itself: the True Cross, recently found by Helen of Constantinople in 326. It is a relic, not just a symbol. Second, an icon, presumably a human-made representation of the Virgin Mary, intervenes, visible to all in the narthex of the church, that liminal space in early churches dedicated to those who were not yet full members of the church, catechumens, energumens, or penitents. Last, the loquacious sinner's exaltation of the incarnation recognizes the mystery of God's dual nature as the source of the life-changing power of both the icon and of the cross. A close reading of Mary's conversion brings to life the ultimate conclusion of the iconophiles at Nicaea: "And we confess that [. . .] even our Lord Jesus Christ the true God, did in these last days for our salvation become incarnate and was made man, and by the saving dispensation, both of His passion, His resurrection, and ascension into heaven, did save our race and deliver us from idolatrous error."[35] The record of the council does not spell out how exactly the mystery of the incarnation delivers the believer from idolatry, and this omission would result in subsequent intense misunderstandings in the Western reception of its teachings.[36] However, Mary of Egypt's story of conversion models a possible answer to the question.

Not historical relic, not human-made icon, not doctrine alone is responsible for the miraculous conversion of the promiscuous sinner. Instead, the story of Mary of Egypt shows in its shuttling from prayer, to cross, to icon, to vision (and aural revelation), and later to sacraments (confession, penitence, and baptism), that mediation matters. In other words, if images are to be a form of "silent preaching," it is not because symbol and referent are perfectly sutured thus actualizing the dream of immediacy and the confirmation that seeing is believing. On the contrary, because every ugly stitch of mediation is visible, images pave the way not to a transcendent elsewhere but rather to a manifestation of the divine through grace *here*—amid the imperfect world of stones, wood, dripping paint, and even ambiguous words, as Thomas Pfau's reading of the iconoclastic debates at Nicaea highlights.[37]

This gnarled vision of images is already present, albeit in a subtle way, in the peculiar response to the narration of Mary's conversion story that another participant of the council, John the Legate of the East, had. As mentioned above, immediately after the excerpt from Mary's vita was read, he noted: "A similar image I have seen in the holy city of Christ our God, and have often worshipped it."[38] Similar? The legate's admission that what he worshipped in Jerusalem may or may not have been the same miracle-inducing image of the Virgin Mary that the penitent sinner saw shocks modern sensibilities attuned to the value of authenticity. Conditioned by the image theory outlined by Leonardo and his intellectual and artistic descendants, a modern audience wants a coincidence of image-referent on intellectual and affective levels. It is not enough that the image should represent properly the Virgin Mother of God (the concern of decorum); there is also the expectation that the material icon itself should correspond to the "authentic" one in the story. Approximation is not good enough. Modernity asks that the image be true, if not Truth itself, all while fearing idolatry, the too-close-for-comfort appreciation of base matter to "that which should be adored" in the words of Pope Gregory.[39] In contrast, image theory according to Mary of Egypt bypasses the fixation with certainty that belies the emphasis on realism and authenticity in order to focus on vision as a visceral encounter with the jolts, surprises, and even detours that nonetheless make conversions possible. These conversions, however, operate according to a different temporality than that of the immediate and the inevitable.

WHEN SEEING IS NOT ENOUGH, OR THE SURPRISE OF HOLINESS

Holiness catches people by surprise. In all versions of the legend of Mary of Egypt, monk Zozimas leaves the monastery during Lent for the desert hoping to find a guide, a holy father, who could teach him how to reach the highest rungs of the ladder of saintliness. He finds instead "the shadowy illusion of a human body," a female penitent sinner who turns out to be God's treasure.[40] In the New Testament, startled disciples had a whole day's worth of walking dust on their feet before they realized that the stranger who joined them on the road from Jerusalem to Emmaus was none other than the resurrected Christ (Luke 24). As these stories suggest, holiness proves difficult to see because of humans' misplaced expectations that it should appear in predetermined bodies, places, and time—rather than because holiness hides from view or dwells in a mystifying realm inaccessible to the senses.[41]

And yet, even while present and walking beside believers, holiness remains to an important degree conceptually invisible. Jean-Luc Marion argues that "the saint remains invisible, not through an empirical coincidence, but in principle, and by right."[42] According to Marion, attempting to discern the limits of the holy through definition, can easily veer into an idolatrous fallacy, where the comprehension of specific words, images, or actions is mistakenly conflated with the capture of holiness itself. Holiness is, literally, not a property. It is not an attribute that can be described and possessed. That desire for definition and subsequent custody is Zozimas's problem. He thinks he knows what holiness is, what it looks like, how to seek it, and how to attain it. That hubris, however, is laid low by the figure in the desert who does not recognize herself as holy even as the monk demands her blessing. In a similar way, the two disciples on the road to Emmaus think they know Christ's story and its meaning.[43] In spite of witnessing Christ's story and narrating its details to the stranger, the apostles' "eyes were kept from recognizing him" (Luke 24:16). It is not until the unknown man breaks bread with them that their eyes open. The sacramental gesture, which reenacts the Last Supper where Christ announced his passion and resurrection, pokes through the veil of the disciples' certainty that they and other believers can immediately know and understand what is set before their eyes.

As a lesson in how holiness surprises the eye, this almost-missed recognition scene became a popular motif in the meta-pictorial genre now known as "inverted still life."[44] Pioneered by Dutch artist Pieter Aertsen (1508–75), it was fashionable from the middle of the sixteenth to the seventeenth century in the Netherlands and elsewhere in Europe. These works, typically large-scale paintings, feature a scene from everyday life—a butcher's stall, a kitchen—prominently in the foreground in a highly realistic, almost illusionistic manner, aiming to convince that the space of the painter is coterminous with the space of the viewer. In the background of these same paintings are small religious scenes, such as the Supper at Emmaus or Christ in the house of Mary and Martha. Architectural features of the foreground such as a door or window, or the beams of the market stall, often frame the inset religious images in a way that enhances the ambiguity of whether the historic religious scene is contiguous or not with the mundane foreground. Following Ingvar Bergström, modern art historians describe these paintings as "inverted" because stylistically they pay more attention to the realistic depiction of the inanimate elements proper to the minor genre of still life, to the detriment of the smaller religious painting in the background. Contrasting the perishables of the foreground against the spiritual gravity of the background, these paintings also ask viewers to toggle between literal and symbolic frames of reference. The dynamic these canvases solicit is thus more accurately described as conversion—an active learning to see—than inversion. These paintings go beyond "silent preaching" in the Gregorian sense: they do more than illustrate previously known biblical stories for didactic, emotive, or persuasive ends. Instead, they engage viewers in an exercise of reflection, inviting them to reassess the world in its visibility and our position in it.

The inverted still life disturbs the certainty that the spiritual is a simple contrast to the creaturely and that creatures are above mere created objects. Importantly, the surprise of the outsized role of the still life elements does not cancel the spiritual. On the contrary, the creaturely animates the holy. No longer confined to its frame and to the certain knowledge of where holiness belongs, the collision of holy and profane becomes the ground for revisiting what had previously seemed decidedly fixed, such as the ontological hierarchy that places human action above kitchen pottery. The planes of the sacred and profane intersect and infuse, rather than contradict, one another. For example, Jacob Matham's (1571–1631) engraving, after a painting by Pieter Aertsen, combines a kitchen scene with the motif of the Supper at Emmaus (figure 4). A large table displaying a dozen fish at different stages in the preparation of a meal occupies half of the foreground; the largest fish teeters at the edge of the table, its belly offered up for the viewer's inspection. Furthest away from the viewer but still on the table, sits a lobster on a platter. Two human figures, a kitchen maid who is about to fillet a small fish and a young man who interrupts her holding out yet another fish, take up the middle ground. A cat waits for scraps on the lower left corner. This is a scene of abundance, if not opulence, but the cat, a symbol of treachery and carnal need, reminds the viewer that this wealth is illusory.

Three small scenes fill the engraving's background. On the right, and in domestic continuity with the foreground, another woman tends to a fire. On the left, somewhat incongruously, a male servant hangs or draws a curtain while another woman stands nearby holding a platter. In the middle, framed by the curtain, appears the scene of the Supper at Emmaus. Once viewers catch sight of the surprising disciples in the background, the still-life objects in the foreground no longer only represent flesh in its transitoriness. The

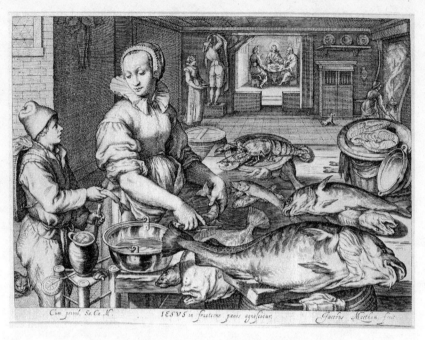

FIGURE 4. Jacob Matham, *Kitchen Scene with Kitchen Maid Preparing Fish, Christ at Emmaus in the Background*, from *Kitchen and Market Scenes with Biblical Scenes in the Background* (ca. 1603). Engraving. Metropolitan Museum of Art, New York. Source: Wikimedia Commons.

disciples' holiness imparts a symbolic dimension to the fish. They recall the ancient acrostic *ichthys*, meaning "fish" and also "Son of God, Savior." Moreover, in the kitchen context of butchering and preparing to transform dead flesh into sustaining life, the fish—and especially the large one offered up to the viewer's visual consumption—also become a symbol of Christ's sacrifice. The kitchen maid's right forefinger steadies her knife, but it also points to the large fish on the table, drawing viewers' attention to its sacrificial death and imminent transformation. Resting on the vertical axis between the religious scene on the background and the engraving's title, the lobster emerges as central to the image. Previously only a sign of conspicuous consumption, it now also represents, in the yearly molting of its shell, Christ's resurrection. The engraving's title—in Latin, "Jesus can be recognized in the breaking of bread"—outside the frame of representation invites viewers into the act of recognition. The transformation that the engraving accomplishes is therefore not only that of foodstuff into spiritual sustenance, the lesson of the Eucharist, but also one of vision. It is an invitation to recognize that we, too,

FIGURE 5. Diego Velázquez, *Kitchen Maid with the Supper at Emmaus* (ca. 1617–18). Oil on canvas. National Gallery, Dublin, Ireland. Photograph from *Velázquez y Sevilla: Monasterio de la Cartuja de Santa María de las Cuevas, Salas del Centro Andaluz de Arte Contemporáneo, Sevilla del 1 de octubre al 12 de diciembre de 1999* (Sevilla: Junta de Andalucía, 1999), 179.

can be surprised by holiness in the midst of a mundane task such as preparing a meal, or viewing an image.

This engraving circulated throughout Europe, and it served as inspiration for an early painting by Diego Velázquez, *Kitchen Maid with the Supper at Emmaus* (ca. 1617–18). The Spanish painter intensifies the engraving's dynamic cycling from holiness to quotidian and makes it his work's main theme by eliminating from the painting the eucharistic echoes sung by the food in the foreground of Matham's engraving (figure 5). The focus shifts instead to the Black kitchen maid, the lovingly crafted objects laid on her table, and, more poignantly, to question of what she sees. This movement is beautifully captured in a sonnet by the modern American poet Natasha Trethewey that responds to Velázquez's painting:

> She is the vessels on the table before her:
> the copper pot tipped toward us, the white pitcher
> clutched in her hand, the black one edged in red
> and upside down. Bent over, she is the mortar
> and the pestle at rest in the mortar—still angled
> in its posture of use. She is the stack of bowls
> and the bulb of garlic beside it, the basket hung
> by a nail on the wall and the white cloth bundled
> in it, the rag in the foreground recalling her hand.

She's the stain on the wall the size of her shadow—
the color of blood, the shape of a thumb. She is echo
of Jesus at table, framed in the scene behind her:
his white corona, her white cap. Listening, she leans
into what she knows. Light falls on half her face.[45]

Trethewey's interpretative ekphrasis of Velázquez's take on the tradition of the inverted still life traces the almost imperceptible transformation of a nameless woman, the kitchen maid of the title, through the repetition of the phrase "She is." The kitchen maid's ontological status shifts from the thingly ("She is the vessels [. . .] the copper pot, the white pitcher [etc.]") to the spectral ("She's the stain on the wall the size of her *shadow*"; "She is *echo* / of Jesus"). Trethewey's poem operates as an extreme example of chremamorphism, the attribution of thingly characteristics to a human. Through relentless metaphor, she extends the logic of the inverted still life to humans. In a similar vein, Tanya Tiffany interprets this painting in light of treatises circulating on the spiritual capacity of African slaves to receive Christian grace contemporary to Velázquez and available to his intellectual circle in Seville, and she argues that Velázquez offers in this canvas a visual argument for seeing slaves as "image and likeness of the Lord" fully capable of experiencing spiritual illumination.[46] The kitchen maid melts into the objects surrounding her, but in Trethewey's poem as much as in Velázquez's canvas, the communion with the objects surrounding the kitchen maid animates her rather than dehumanizes her. Partaking in both light and darkness, presence and absence, spiritual and material planes, the woman—at once a background laborer, foreground visual figure, and "echo / of Jesus at the table"—becomes a powerful figuration of grace's reach. Much like Mary of Egypt at the moment of her conversion, the kitchen maid is not just the "object" of grace, an example that holiness reaches beyond the confines of the foreseeable. "*Listening*, she leans / into what she knows," writes Trethewey about the kitchen maid; "*remembering* [. . .] she [Mary] raised her eyes to an image" Pacheco writes about Mary of Egypt. Grammar helps us see this point more clearly, for the Spanish "acordándose" (remembering) is a reflexive verb, which highlights the doubling of consciousness as self meets and calls self into account. In both cases, the female figures' capacity for conversion seems to emerge as much from unforeseen grace as from the refractive power of self-reflection—the recollection of past selves, the vision of potential future selves, but also the participial, nonfinite image of a self in the midst of transition.

OF TRANSITIONS, OR CONVERSION
ACCORDING TO MARY OF EGYPT

In the legend of Mary of Egypt, when encountering the image of the Virgin Mary, it is the reflexive act of remembering that allows her to visualize her sinful past and to see it as a contrast to the exemplary image and icon of the Virgin. She understands herself in relationship to what she was and what she is not. In the desert too, she shuttles from remembering her licentious life in Alexandria to the memory of her prayer to the Virgin asking the Mother of God to serve as guarantor for her uncertain future. Always in movement yet connected to the world she left behind (she inquires about its people, its kings, and the church), Mary of Egypt figures spiritual conversion in the precariousness of its transitional form rather than in its presumed finality. In other words, the creature Zozimas finds in the desert is still coming into her own; she is not the unified, happy self, recognizable from a modern understanding of conversion.[47] Moreover, the monk Zozimas's inability to recognize her—as a woman and as holy teacher—when he encounters her in the desert is not only because of the fundamental invisibility of holiness. Also at play here is that in the case of Mary the Egyptian, split between the memory of her past life and the future promise of salvation, her holiness is unrecognizable even to herself.

By contrast, Jean-Luc Marion poses the problem of the recognition of holiness from an external perspective. He is interested in exploring whether the beholder can know holiness. According to him, holiness is "undecidable," first and foremost because it defies a definition that claims to know from the outset what holiness is. But there is a second reason that the recognition of holiness is difficult to ascertain: It is obscured because the interiority of others, in matters both profane and holy, remains inaccessible to a prying gaze from the outside. Holiness, in other words, underscores a problem that is already present in every intersubjective situation. Marion writes:

> If I already have the greatest trouble knowing for sure what my neighbor (that is to say my unreachable alter ego) thinks, desires, wants, is capable of, and really is worth, how shall I determine his or her holiness (obviously assuming that I myself would know what that is)? The aporia of intersubjectivity, at least of intersubjectivity understood according to intentionality, applies above all to the judgment regarding the other's holiness or sanctity. [. . .] Anyone's holiness thus remains for us (quo ad

nos) undecidable, the saint consequently remains for us formally invisible.[48]

As philosopher, Marion is concerned above all with decentering the willful and knowing subject from the scene of revelation in order to make room for a subject that is called into being in the very act of receiving the gift of revelation. No surprise, then, that he does not pay much heed to the foundational insight of psychoanalysis that, before subjects can puzzle at the interiority of another, they must recognize that they, too, are strangers to themselves.[49]

The legend of Mary of Egypt teaches that the invisibility of the saint persists not only for the external witnesses who may fail to recognize the saint but significantly also for the self who dwells in an unsettled interior. This uncanny "foreignness within" permeates the legend of Saint Mary of Egypt: the very grounds that facilitated her conversion are home to the Holy Sepulchre that had been Temple of Venus. She insists on treating both her sinfulness and experience of grace as things simultaneously external to her yet paradoxically constitutive of her soul. Strange and stranger to herself, the legend of the Egyptian asks us to take seriously not just the accomplished turn but the participial turn*ing* within conversion. That is to say, she invites us to reimagine conversion as transit, transitional, as an intricate choreography in time rather than as journey with a predetermined destination.[50]

JUSEPE DE RIBERA AND THE RETRACTIONS OF PORTRAITURE

Jusepe de Ribera's hauntingly beautiful visual representation of Mary of Egypt—a half-length oil portrait, now hanging in the Museo Civico Gaetano Filangieri in Naples (figure 2)—provides a concrete sense of how this order of transition translates visually. This painting, signed and dated 1651, corresponds to the last period of the painter's life.[51] Ribera, a Valencian artist who worked in Italy from 1610 until his death in 1652, is perhaps best known for his naturalist "portraits" of martyred or ascetic saints, of philosophers dressed in contemporary pauper's garb, and—in keeping with the period's enthusiasm for curiosities—of characters such as Magdalena Ventura, a contemporary bearded lady. These works are characterized by Caravaggio-inspired play with shadows and dark hues that highlight the subjects' uncanniness—their numinous or anatomical otherness in tension with the hyperrealism of his draftsmanship.

Portraiture in the early modern period functioned primarily in terms of conservation, of drawing out (*protraere*) the sitter's essence and imprinting it on a surface, canvas, wood, or paper, with the goal of making the image available to viewers in perpetuity. Sebastián de Covarrubias, in his seventeenth-century dictionary of the Spanish language makes this clear in his entry on "retrato" when he describes a portrait thus: "the imitated image of any noble and important person whose effigy and likeness it is appropriate to remember in the centuries that follow."[52] The practice of artistic portrayal of individuals traces its origins to the death mask and funerary sculpture, and, as such, one of its aims is to freeze an image of the past. Its visual consumption, however, always takes place in the present, a "now" that the past nonetheless foresees—perhaps even orchestrates through the will to power shared by sitter and artist in what Harry Berger has famously called "the fiction of the pose."[53] The result is not exactly the visual impression of an individual but something closer to the visual representation of their exemplary self. What is more, that exemplary self is an example for the ages, in the sense of Alice Spawls's phrase: "each age thinks it reads a portrait fully, correctly, and finally."[54] Last, in the wake of the Council of Trent, the goal of religious portraiture is legibility—viewers should be able to quickly recognize the figure depicted—in order to guarantee its didacticism.

Coming face to face with the Filangeri portrait of Saint Mary of Egypt, however, viewers must wonder: What exactly is the essence, the exemplary moment, of this feminine figure portrayed in uneasy transition rather than in static self-possession? What does this portrait teach? Mary's body rests at a slight diagonal, coinciding with the light traversing the canvas from top left. Her eyes, however, turn up and away from the light source, as if slightly troubled, having been made aware suddenly of a presence outside the frame. A few strands of her dark hair escape the scarf that holds the rest modestly in place, testifying to the sudden upward movement of her gaze. She is fully clothed, though her garments have begun to fray, and a hair shirt peeks out from beneath her dress to cover her décolletage. Several feminine features— her dark hair, fair skin, plump coral lips—testify to her still-visible beauty, though the darker hue of her hands, the dirt under her fingernails, and the reddened outline of her eyes hint at the ravages that penance promises to bring to these lovely forms.

Writing about this painting in the context of visionary experience and its artistic representation in Spain, Victor Stoichita remarks, "without already knowing that this is Mary of Egypt, how can we be sure that the beatific woman portrayed is not one of the many mystics, illuminati, whose claims of communication with the divine through visions, were contested by the Catholic church?"[55] More polemically, I ask: Is the holiness of this female figure visible at all? How confident are viewers that she is not a kitchen maid, as those in the foreground of Diego Velázquez's paintings?

This question acquires urgency when one considers that Ribera's portrait represents somewhat of an anomaly, not only in his oeuvre, but also more generally in the tradition of representations of Mary the Egyptian. Eastern Orthodox and Western Christian iconography typically shows the saint unequivocally post-conversion, wearing her long wild hair as cloak. She is often receiving either a mantle or communion from monk Zozimas, whom she encounters in the desert after she has spent forty-seven years in penitence.[56] (Surviving medieval and early modern depictions of pre-conversion Mary as libidinous temptress of men are rare, but this may have more to do with censorship dictated by the changing mores of later centuries, especially after the Reformation, than an actual lack of interest in the motif.) In contrast to these norms, Ribera's portrait depicts Mary at an unspecified transitional moment, sometime after her stop in Jerusalem but before her time wandering in the desert has destroyed her famous beauty.

Scholars agree that the Filangieri *Mary of Egypt* represents a shift from Ribera's earlier more starkly tenebrist style; he has moved from highlighting a violent contrast between dark and light to reflecting a more delicate use of light. They disagree, however, on the meaning of this new style. Interpretations alternate between seeing "a new emotional and sentimental involvement [. . .] completely lacking in rhetoric" to the exact opposite, seeing the canvas as a technical triumph "carefully modulated to produce the greatest effect of naturalism."[57] In both cases, however, the implication is that the image speaks for itself. It either communicates a highly realistic exterior or the true emotion of the saint's interiority. The desire for a smooth continuity between visual representation and lived reality informs even the way most catalogs present this portrait. Art historians often mention the speculation that Ribera used his own daughter as the model for the holy harlot, even if only to characterize the story as spurious (in the most dramatic renderings of the rumor, she has been seduced and abandoned by an aristocrat or she is mourning the death of her husband and newborn child). And yet, the praise of realism in Ribera's rendition of penitent Mary is not unmerited. In technique and composition, the painting seems initially to align itself with the immediacy of perception of extreme realism. Ribera's unflinching brushstrokes, for example, beautifully capture the texturized continuum of skin-cilicium-linen enrobing the female figure. The chunk of bread teetering over the table's edge, as if about to tip into the world of the viewer, suggests a desire for a seamless movement from the world of the painting to the viewers. Some would say that the image of Mary of Egypt is touching, in no small measure because it asks the viewer to reach out and touch it as if the representation were contiguous with the viewer's space.

And therein lies the rub. In contrast with the famous anecdote about two competing painters Pliny records in his *Naturalis historia*, where the reigning champion admits defeat when he attempts to pull aside a curtain only to realize that he had been fooled by his competitor's lifelike drape, to compliment Ribera on his triumphant illusionism would only confirm his failure to move the viewer from the material to the spiritual. Or, as Pacheco might put it, Ribera would have succeeded as a painter *in general*, achieving glory for technical mastery, at the expense of earning the worthier acclaim of the *Christian* painter. Although certainly working within the grammar of pictorial realism, Ribera's portrait of Mary of Egypt ultimately bends its rules and moves the viewer away from the experience of immediacy's comfort to the jolts of undecidability and mediation.

The wayward chunk of bread, seemingly about to escape the surface that holds it and the canvas that represents it, provides an illustration of this point. Such a gesture, the aim of which is to convince the viewer of the reality of the representation by positing a common plane between viewer and canvas, is recognizable from tropes that characterize the still life genre. The magisterial still life canvases by the lay Carthusian painter Juan Sánchez Cotán (1560–1627), for instance, often feature objects protruding from a clearly defined window frame that serves as orderly conduit from one world to the other (figure 6). Mary's bread also tantalizes the viewer—but from a discontinuous space. Instead of a window frame to guide the eye from the plane of reality to the plane of representation, the painting vertiginously negates the parameters that would make space intelligible. Viewers get but a hint of the surface where the bread lies; the rest is cut off from view, making it impossible to ascertain its dimensions. Moreover, while luminously painted, austerity characterizes the canvas, perhaps most evidently in the exclusion of all background detail. Such abstraction obscures even the possibility of determining whether the saint is inside (a cave? an inn on her way to the desert?) or outside. In turn, this undecidability inflects the very perception of the surface holding the bread: Mary is absorbed in prayer at a rustic

FIGURE 6. Juan Sánchez Cotán, *Still Life with Quince, Cabbage, Melon and Cucumber* (ca. 1602). Oil on canvas. San Diego Museum of Art, San Diego. Source: Wikimedia Commons.

table (if she is inside) *or* a makeshift stone altar (if she is outside, as in the Montpellier canvas). Viewers' difficulty in situating the image in space or time inflects the perception of the figure herself. Stoichita remarks that, rather than represent the ineffable through paradox (as in Ribera's portrait of Saint Andrew, where holiness is present in the figuration of "light darkness," for example), this painting turns to ellipsis or what he identifies as the representation of doubt as the palpitating heart of belief. He writes, "[Mary of Egypt] is scrutinizing the horizon. Does she see something, or nothing? The question remains unanswered."[58] Unanswered, that is, in the grand language of portraiture.

Rather, holiness in this image is entrusted to the humble objects on the table/altar: bread and a skull facing away from the viewer and the saint—objects perfectly suited for a very particular type of still life painting, the *vanitas*. Deriving both from the minor ancient genre of rhopography (the depiction of insignificant nonhuman objects) and interpretations of the biblical Ecclesiastes, the genre of *vanitas* introduces to still life a moral dimension: a world subject to time and change, in all its apparent glory is in the end but "vanity and chasing after wind" (Eccles. 2:11). But in a radical condensation of the surprising contiguity of holy and profane in the inverted still life canvases of Aertsen and Velázquez, Ribera's unusual portrait of Mary of Egypt activates allegory to trouble the preference of *vanitas* for transcendence over transience. Here, viewers cannot discard insignificant bread, harbinger of carnal need, as it also speaks of eucharistic promise; similarly the skull's reminder that flesh will turn to bone and dust also signals, according to Jordan and Cherry, the hope of redemption.[59] The canvas's vibrant oscillation between immanence and transcendence, between literal and allegorical, sinfulness and holiness animates it: not because it reproduces in the viewer the vision of the mystic (following the logic of immediacy), but because it forces us to confront matter—bodies in the world, pigment on canvas—as mediation, as always already potentially holy.

That images should teach through asking the viewer to pay attention to the medium of painting itself, by taking their time (and ours!), by making us stop and question what it is that we see and how we see it, that is image theory according to Mary of Egypt. Such an understanding of images as subject to mediation rather than transparent immediacy lies latent in the example of Mary's conversion, as we have seen in this chapter. Similarly, it is central to the experience of viewing Ribera's representation of the saint. In the following chapter we shall see how mediation matters when what is at stake is the act of painting with words.

THE SEDUCTIONS OF HAGIOGRAPHY

> The rest of us, somewhat superficial Catholics, we need the picturesque to reach religious feeling.
>
> THÉOPHILE GAUTIER, *Voyage en Espagne*[1]

THE MYTH OF A DOUR MIDDLE AGES corseted by ascetic religious values endures in spite of decades of scholarship that has brought to the fore a more luminous understanding of the period's engagement with pleasure, the sensual, and the ludic. As Dorothy Severin's *Religious Parody and the Spanish Sentimental Romance* and Ryan Giles's *Laughter of the Saints* argue, this playfulness is foremost present in texts that modern readers would recognize as profane, lay, or parodic, where subversive laughter finds validation.[2] However, even religious and earnestly didactic texts partake in playfulness and profitable ambiguity when readers attend to rhetorical practices, as work by Mary Carruthers on medieval *varietas* (weaving different styles judiciously within a single composition), Jill Ross on *allegoresis* (allowing more than one interpretation for one text), or Catherine Brown on the dialectical *sic et non* (Peter Abelard's call for learning through contradiction) has shown.[3]

Scholarly recognition of these compositional and interpretative medieval modes has contributed, in turn, to a more nuanced view of the interactions of sacred and profane in the production of literary works. As Barbara Newman argues, in the Middle Ages the sacred was the default category, but it was always present in relation to profane forms, topoi, uses, and contexts.[4] Awareness of this entwinement implies that the task of the present-day scholar consists in identifying the ways in which these profane echoes resonate in religious writing (or vice versa), sometimes in simple harmony, sometimes polyphonically, sometimes in judicious silence. In the case of hagiography, scholars' awareness of this mixture has resulted in studies that consider the debts and contributions of this narrative form to other popular genres such as epic (*chanson de geste*), courtly poetry, or chivalric romance. What role beauty might play in vernacular hagiography with a focus on female holiness remains largely unexamined.

To speak of beauty in the context of hagiography may initially seem counterintuitive, but the question of the value and function of elegant speech, of eloquence, is, for practical and philosophical reasons, a central concern of vernacular hagiography throughout the Middle Ages. Most often associated with martyrdom or asceticism, the record of the life and deeds of God's chosen would seem to treat beauty at best as irrelevant to holy heroism and at worst as a distraction from the intended didacticism of the text. But there is a more fundamental reason that both hagiographers in the writing of stories about holiness and the scholars who interpret them tend not to think about beauty. The narratives exalting asceticism and martyrdom often run into a fundamental problem. The writing of holiness, like all human communication, is only intelligible through the senses that mediate the material aspects of language, from the engagement of the eyes and mouths that read and the "fleshly ears" that hear to the rhetorical devices that give form to thought. This fleshed-out discourse, in turn, risks drawing too much of the readers' attention to its charming surface, to the detriment of the redemptive substance it aims to communicate. It is no surprise, then, that hagiographical accounts, especially of holy women, record an anxiety that proper persuasion will turn into seduction.

The formulation "fleshly ears" refers, of course, to Augustine's analogy of the mystery of Christ's incarnation to the relationship of thought to speech.[5] Augustine and the early church fathers inherited from Plato and Quintilian a suspicion of rhetoric's troubling attentiveness to form and appearance over content and truth—a suspicion that mapped onto gendered tropes that align showy, elaborate discourse with effeminacy and fleshiness. However, the paradox of the incarnation, of the divine and human natures coinciding in Christ's person, problematizes a straightforward contempt of the flesh. This conundrum opened the way for a validation, albeit limited, of the sensory and the sensual aspects of language and rhetoric, as Jill Ross traces in *Figuring the Feminine*.[6] Still, such a legitimation does not upset the hierarchy that places spirit over matter. Augustine's acceptance of sensory-bound experience occurs, after all, within a carefully delimited context, which grants it, at best, the provisional status of useful means toward a greater end (knowledge of God).

This chapter and the next focus on the anonymous thirteenth-century Spanish verse retelling of the life of Saint Mary of Egypt, the *Vida de Santa María Egipciaca* (*VSME*). Multiple forms of beauty converge in this poem, from the physical beauty of its protagonist and the beauty of the words employed to tell her story to the beauty of an icon of the Virgin Mary that will produce the miraculous conversion of Mary of Egypt and the beauty of her ascetic, aged body. Beauty here is dense and polyvalent. In this chapter I will show how in contrast to the stories of virgin martyrs such as Catherine of Alexandria or of holy harlots like Mary Magdalene, beauty in *VSME* is not simply synonymous to holiness, nor does it need to be iconoclastically destroyed or sublimated in order for holiness to appear. This implies that the poet of *VSME* imagines the possibility of language at ease with its fleshiness and with the appeal of surfaces, all without falling prey to idolatry.[7] The exact ways in which the poem performs an iconophilic form of hagiography is the focus of chapter 3.

"HERE IS MY TREASURE"

A pivotal moment in *VSME* brings my first question—about how religious writing deals with the tension between sacred and profane—into relief. A young Mary, proud of her beauty and bored with the men she has already seduced in Alexandria, approaches a group of young male pilgrims about to set sail for Jerusalem. Her speech to the pilgrims ends with the following proposition:

> I swear to you by the true God
> That I have with me only one coin.
> Behold, here is my treasure,
> All my silver and gold.
> If you will agree to let me board the boat,
> I will serve you gladly.[8]

What exactly is Mary offering the pilgrims here? The expression "el mió tresoro" (literally, "my treasure") could easily refer to Mary's own body—a body whose beauty the poet cataloged in detail some hundred lines earlier (lines 205–52; 123–24) and whose desirability her lovers' bloody feuds evidence (lines 171–80; 122). However, this utterance is also a subtle rhetorical performance on the part of Mary, who had earlier been rebuffed by another pilgrim when she bluntly offered her body in exchange for passage to Jerusalem. Her forthright declaration, "'I have a good body' she said; / 'I will give it freely'" (126), was received with laughter and horror as the stranger ran away from Mary's sinful "madness," her "follía" (line 315; 126).[9] In contrast, the second time she approaches the pilgrims, she takes measure of her audience and addresses them as "good men" (127) who should respond to her distress on account of their Christian duty toward the unfortunate.[10] She also takes on a more demure disposition than in her previous exchange by casting herself in this speech no longer as a footloose temptress but rather as a damsel in distress. Thus, as a lonely, miserable female stranger in the city, she asks the pilgrims to take her onboard as an act of charity, an alternative form of almsgiving that will in turn assure them a swift voyage.

When Mary delivers the crucial line "fevos aquí el mió tresoro" (behold here my treasure), readers can imagine her finger pointing at her breast and metonymically to her body, her treasure. But she is also trying to convince the pilgrims that she has no money, nothing other than her words to pay her way. With this persuasive goal in mind, her speech takes full advantage of the deictic function of the adverbial "fevos aquí"—the expression's dependence on a shared perspective. Its meaning is empty in a referential sense since the phrase does not point toward a definite object the way the word "apple" would name both the category and the specific instance. Instead, "fevos aquí" becomes meaningful only in the context of the relationship established through words between a speaker and her interlocutors. In other words, this turn of phrase focuses as much on the incidence of communication itself as on the content being communicated. The emphasis on the scene of enunciation, on the here and now of the exchange between particulars, is palpable in the pleonastic combination of "fevos" and "aquí," a juxtaposition that twentieth-century lexicographer Joan Corominas notes was rarely found in medieval texts before the fifteenth century since both words basically mean "here."[11] I translate "fevos" as "behold," but it is not a verb; it is instead a word that calls out for the listener's attention.[12] This is why Hugh Feiss, the recent translator of *VSME* into English, settles for a single "here" instead of the more literal "Here (*fe*), you (*vos*), here (*aquí*)," which would capture Mary's unusual emphasis on the relational and highly contextual nature of her speech crafted for *these* men, at *this* particular moment, in response to *this* particular situation. Mary's invitation to the pilgrims to behold her treasure highlights, then, a self-assured reference to the value of *both* her body and her words. Consequently, the success of Mary's speech depends largely on maintaining the ambiguity of her gesture, which points to but does not spell out the nature of her treasure and of the services she so willingly offers. The confluence of words and bodies that she enacts, like a profane performance of the Word becoming flesh, proves also in her case to be effective.

I underscore Mary's rhetorical savvy to suggest that Mary's body, Mary's beauty, Mary's words, and the Christian legacy of incarnational poetics all converge here but not in easily resolved ways. Mary's *tresoro* is not simply a degraded, malignant version of the incarnation; after all, the insistence on the *tresoro* reappears at the end of the poem when Mary of Egypt becomes God's very own treasure (line 938; 144). The transformation of Mary's corporeal and rhetorical treasure into God's own, however, does not pass through a simple sublation of the physical or literal into the spiritual or figurative: God's *tresoro* still refers directly both to Mary's body *and* to its potential temptations. The seductiveness of her word-body cannot simply be ignored or rejected. What is at stake here, I suggest, is rather a matter of thinking through the permeability of the boundary separating legitimate persuasion from illicit seduction. This question, however, is not limited to Mary's beautiful words and body. It is an issue that concerns the poet's own use of language and which therefore colors the relationship of the text to the audience. As I argue in the rest of this chapter, the poem is deeply concerned with mediation, that is to say, with imagining a way to communicate religious content using and celebrating everyday words rather than hoping for a transparent language. In other words, parallel to the retelling of a legend about the forgiveness and transformation of a sinful woman, *VSME* also examines the powerful convergence of words and bodies, of rhetoric and the erotic, of profit and pleasure, of what is holy and what is profane.

The question at the outset about the nature of Mary's *tresoro* is but an instance of a broader issue at stake in the poem: What role, if any, should beautiful words, bodies, and images play in a didactic, religious text extolling holiness? This is a long-standing question, to which the poem offers a surprising answer. In contrast to other hagiographic works—especially those that foreground the beauty of a female protagonist, but which aim to bracket, destroy, or sublimate the heroine's beauty and hagiography's animating sensual energy—*VSME* embraces both the beautiful body and the desires it arouses.

IN THE BEGINNING WAS THE
WORD: *RAZÓN* OR *FABLA*?

The question of the efficacy of words frames the poem's reception from the very beginning. The poet addresses the audience directly and confronts readers with a contrast between truthful, profitable words that yield salvation, on the one hand, and false, vain words, on the other:

> Listen, disciples, to a *story* [*razón*] ˷
> Which contains nothing but the truth.
> Listen with your heart,
> Thus you would have God's mercy.
> It is all truth,
> There is no falsehood at all.
> [. . . . .]
> If you listen to this story
> It will do you more good than any *fable* [*fabla*]. (117)[13]

Feiss renders *razón* in his translation as "story," but that is only one of its nuances. The word is, of course, related to reason, and according to Kasten and Cody's *Tentative Dictionary of Medieval Spanish*, it refers to the faculty of discourse, to argument, persuasion, and doctrine—in other words, to what would be recognized in the Middle Ages as honest speech, what is appropriate and credible.[14] *Fabla*, on the other hand, has its roots in the Latin *fabula*. Isidore of Seville's discussion of rhetoric in the *Etymologies* follows a distinction drawn by pseudo-Cicero in the *Rhetorica ad Herennium* where *fabula* refers to untrue narratives, *historia* to ancient and true matters, and *argumentum* to fabricated stories that are nonetheless believable.[15] *Fabula* thus refers not only to the faculty of speech in general (the root of the Spanish verb *hablar*, to speak) but particularly to storytelling and speechmaking, often carrying the connotation of a made-up story.

The prologue of *VSME*, in its emphatic repetition of *verdat* (truth) throughout the opening of the poem (three times in the course of six lines), certainly indicates a desire to distinguish this true and beneficial tale from other kinds. The *razón* of the poet-hagiographer, along with the salvific content and didactic intent of his words, stands in the poem's prologue in contrast to the vanity of the *fablas*, epic tales and romances told by the poet-entertainer. The awareness of distinct types of speech, and especially of a hierarchy of value between them, falls in line with Ramón Menéndez Pidal's description of the poetic ecology of the late Middle Ages:

> the singer of saints' lives declares his art as more dignified and worthy than that of the other jongleurs, including those who sing of historical matters. Religious subjects allow him to disdain the lies of King Arthur [. . .] and to dismiss the stories of Ogier and Roland. [. . .] The singer of holy lives grounds his superiority on the moral profit it provides his listeners.[16]

Similarly, Manuel Alvar, *VSME*'s twentieth-century editor, remarks that the Spanish poet seems to show an increased disdain of heroic poetry when compared to earlier French poems that tell the life of Mary of Egypt. Alvar focuses particularly on the interpolated couplet present in the first stanza of the Spanish poem but absent in the French poems, "If you listen to this story / It will do you more good than any fable" (117).[17] He argues that the Spanish poet clearly grounds his work on the right side of speech by focusing on the subject matter of his poem. His *palabra* is spiritually profitable storytelling linked to the truthfulness and propriety of the *razón* of the opening line in contrast to the fabrications of vain, counterfeit *fablas*.[18]

Indeed, the poet's pride in the spiritual profit his work promises his audience appears again in yet another interpolation to the prologue, where he makes the bold declaration that listening to the poem is nothing less than a way to God's forgiveness: "Listen with your heart, / Thus you would have God's mercy" (117).[19] The logic of the exchange of God's favor for the listeners' attention becomes intensified and rather circular in the following stanza where the poet asserts that

> All those who would love God
> Will listen to these words.
> [. . . . .]
> This account will be heard with ready heart
> By those who would love God.
> These who would love God
> Will receive great benefit from it. (117)[20]

And yet, the very forceful, almost obsessive insistence on a difference between *razón* and *palabra* makes one wonder if the poet doth not protest too much.

Razón and *fabla* would initially seem to institute the first of a long list of dichotomies that arguably structure the poem: *razón/fabla*, male/female, clerical/lay, virtue/sin, and finally, honest speech and its concomitant effects (remembrance of religious duty, good actions, and salvation) versus the distraction and pleasure offered by false song that may in turn result in spiritual damnation. Nevertheless, this very insistence on the distinction calls attention to the ways in which *razón* borrows from *fabla*. First, at the level of content, the reference to *fablas*, to the popular stories dealing with the courageous feats of knights performed on behalf of the beautiful ladies they served, does more than simply serve as a foil to the poem about to begin. At their core, these stories are tales about adventure, desire, love, and lust, thus topically not terribly different from the exploits of a wandering, wanton woman that our poet offers up to replace them. Second, despite protests to the contrary, the means by which the poem aims to fulfill its promise of redemption borrow heavily from the *fablas* the poem wants to keep at a distance. The prologue of *VSME*, for example, emphasizes its oral qualities in an attempt to establish a more intimate rapport with the audience through direct address. It intensifies a gesture, already present in the French versions that inspired the Spanish poet, when it replaces the seigniorial addressee of "listen Lord" with a less hierarchical appeal to a general public of male listeners, "varones" (*VSME*, line 1).[21] Additionally, while the French poem draws attention to its oral performance through the occasional repetition of listening verbs such as *oiez* and *escouter*, the Spanish text's references to orality occur no less than six times in the first fifteen lines. This number, in itself, is not remarkable, given that the poem was most likely recited by memory or read aloud to an audience. However, the accentuation of the act of listening as a way of setting the stage for the poem is very much in line with minstrel conventions, and as I showed earlier, it is also of a piece with Mary's emphasis on the scene of transmission in her speech to the pilgrims.

The insistence of the poet in demarcating a distinction between *razón* and *fabla*, then, is symptomatic of a certain unease in the efforts to separate speech supposed to function as a path to God's forgiveness from vain or deleterious speech. In a more blatant instance of this ambiguity, when Mary finishes her persuasive plea to the pilgrims, the poet surprisingly refers to her speech as her *razón* (*VSME*, line 359). Typically, the poem reserves the use of *razón* to denote acts of speech associated with prayers, such as the one that the monk Zozimas utters at the start of his Lenten sojourn in the desert (line 928; 144). Mary's final prayer to God, when she asks for her reward after forty-seven years of penance, also appears under the guise of *razón*, significantly in the context of a couplet where the rhyme *razón/galardón* (lines 1277–78; 154) echoes the key terms of the prologue *razón, corazón, perdón, galardón* (reason, heart, forgiveness, reward). Moreover, on two other occasions (lines 1040 and 1101; 147, 149,), the poem links *razón* to prayer through rhyme, although the word itself refers to a just and reasonable action rather than to an utterance.

These examples underscore the distinctive way in which profane and religious elements share the same poetic space in the poem. The specter of *fabla*—of the possibility that even this earnest hagiographic poem may be beholden to fiction's pleasures, dangers, and temptations—haunts the prologue and the poem as a whole. Importantly, *fabla* and *razón* are not fixed terminals at opposite ends of a spectrum. Instead, this poem insists that they are modalities of the same phenomenon engaged in an always surprising dance with each other.

The impulse to delineate a distinction between *fabla* and *razón*—and the difficulty in doing so—is not just a medieval concern. It inflects modern scholarship on *VSME*, too. Echoing the terms of earlier theological debates, scholars ask, is the poem a hagiography engaged in competition against popular epic songs (Menéndez Pidal), or is it instead an uncomfortable mixing of the two, an example of "religious jonglerie" (García López)?[22] Most radically, Aldo Ruffinatto compares *VSME* to the hagiographic model of the thirteenth-century poet and cleric Gonzalo de Berceo and concludes that, at best, the anonymous poem is pseudo-hagiography. Ruffinatto notes that, with the exception of the prologue and the epilogue, which bear the brunt of the poem's didacticism, *VSME* is characterized by an adventurous plot and a dynamic structure, which according to him is "exquisitely literary."[23] Implicit in Ruffinatto's argument is the assumption that "literariness"—the poetic attention to form and the pleasures derived from the story and its telling—is incompatible with didactic intent.[24] At the opposite end of the spectrum from Ruffinatto, we find Lynn Rice Cortina's symbological reading of the poem, which as we shall see in the next chapter, attempts to neutralize what appears to be the poet's problematic delight in the description of Mary's sensual body.[25]

The careful mapping of the prologue's key terms *razón* and *fabla* shows that the medieval poem resists readings that would see in *VSME* a profane form that trumps its didactic and spiritual aspirations. Conversely, approaches that would deny the pleasures of the text fail to account for the literary, philosophical, and theological complexities of the poem. To do justice to the relationship of *razón* to *fabla*, we need to turn to a third central concern in the prologue: beauty.

BEAUTY AND THE SAINTS

In a poem that purports to exalt penitence and asceticism, it is surprising to see beauty as a central concern from the very beginning. The poem introduces its topic (Mary of Egypt) and theme (God's forgiveness), but the focus is patently on the former and especially on the beauty of Mary of Egypt:

> About a lady of whom you've heard
> I wish to tell you her whole life:
> Of Saint Mary of Egypt,
> Who was a lady of great beauty,
> And of her beautiful body,
> When she was a girl, a child.
> Our Lord gave her great beauty,
> Although she was a comely sinner.
> The mercy of the Creator
> Later bore her great love. (118)[26]

There is no doubt that beauty is Mary's primary attribute; in ten lines the poet mentions her beauty at least four times, although at this point it remains rhetorically underdeveloped, less described than gestured at through the use of abstract adjectives like "lively" (loçana) and "lovely" (fermosa). Such an emphasis serves a titillating function, stoking the curiosity of the poem's audience, and yet the poet also presents this particular beauty as a gift from God ("beldat le dio Nuestro Sennyor"). This detail stands in significant contrast to the initial presentation of beauty in the legends of other holy harlots, such as Pelagia or Thais. Both of those saints are described as beautiful, but in neither case is the beauty directly attributed to God. Instead, beauty is the seductive lure that attracts men to sinfulness.

Mary of Egypt does not stand alone as a recipient of divinely sourced beauty. Beauty and noble birth are conventional attributes in hagiography focused on female saints, particularly in the case of martyred virgins. In those legends, however, feminine beauty serves as an index for the spiritual goodness of the protagonist: the gracefulness of their bodies points to their holy disposition. That is the case of the other celebrated Egyptian convert, Catherine of Alexandria. Her legend details the struggles she waged against her own kin and the torments she suffered at the hands of the tyrant Maxentius on account of her steadfast commitment to the Christian god that made her refuse both the sexual advances of the emperor and his request that she adore pagan idols. In some versions of Catherine's life, physical beauty not only makes manifest her spiritual pulchritude, but it also functions as a sign that reveals a special relationship to Christ. That is the case, for example, in William Caxton's translation (ca. 1483–84) of the thirteenth-century compilation of saints' lives by Jacobus de Voragine. There, Caxton describes Catherine as "so fair of visage and so well formed in her members that all the people enjoyed in her beauty."[27] The text implies that it was fitting that she yearned for a husband "so full of beauty that angels have joy to behold him."[28] Closing the circle of beauty, Christ, in return, "desireth her beauty and loveth her chastity among all the virgins on the earth."[29] This circular structure recalls the special grace of the Virgin Mary: beautiful because holy. To step outside of this circle, that is to say, to ask for beauty to be meaningful on its own terms, would be to court sinfulness (the lasciviousness and idolatry of the emperor).[30] In tales of virgin martyrdom such as Catherine's, beauty plays handmaid to goodness.

Catherine's situation stands as a significant contrast to that of Mary of Egypt, whose beauty does not immediately signal holiness but instead serves her own ends. The description of Mary's early years makes this explicit: her licentiousness results from her excessive faith in her own youthful charms, which makes her impervious to any thought of a spiritual reckoning at the end of her days. Catherine, from the beginning, had her eyes set on the end, and, as Sarah Salih argues, the beautiful and wise Alexandrian will plot her way to martyrdom and spiritual marriage to Christ in the afterlife. In contrast, Mary's energies concentrate on the pleasures of the here and now that her beauty guarantees:

> Since she was so beautiful and affectionate
> She put great faith in her youthfulness.
> She so loved to follow her fancies
> That she gave no thought to other things
> Beyond spending and having a good time,
> For she was not mindful of death. (120)[31]

Mary's most important attribute in the poem after her beauty is lust, as expressed in her description as "so full of lewdness" (120).[32] This particular turn of phrase clearly places the Egyptian's lustful plenitude, her *luxuria plena*, in contrast to her virginal namesake's epithet: Mary, full of grace, *gratia plena*.

The Spanish poet harnesses Mary of Egypt's beauty to sinfulness directly when he identifies her as "beautiful sinner" (117) (fermosa pecador [line 24]) at the beginning of the poem. As Andrew Beresford points out, this characterization of Mary the Egyptian attempts to universalize her as archetypical sinner, importantly, without focusing on the particularity of her transgression—lust.[33] Beresford puts weight on the noun *pecador* as a demure description that distinctively avoids naming and condemning Mary as a prostitute and presents her instead as a gender-neutral example of sin. In this light, the adjective in the poem's chosen epithet for its protagonist, "*fermosa* pecador," is equally significant. On the one hand, *fermosa* carries the inflection of gender that the rhyme scheme required be erased from the noun *pecador*. On the other, *fermosa* also reveals the thematic preoccupation of the poem with, to echo Augustine, the question of the good use of beauty: how can beauty be divorced from sin, prevented from becoming idolatrous, an end in itself, and instead become a meaningful sign pointing back to God? Returning the emphasis on the adjective is not necessarily at odds with Beresford's point about the importance of Mary's characterization in the poem as paradigmatic sinner rather than common prostitute. On the contrary, embracing the specificity of Mary's attribute *fermosa* as a qualifier for *pecador* allows for a better understanding of *how* her sinfulness is representative. The common challenge faced by our protagonist, the men and women she meets—and, significantly, also the poem itself and its audience—is the possibility of putting beauty to good use.[34]

The anxiety that underlies the difficulty of separating *fablas* from *razones* finds a parallel concern in the debates pertaining to the role of images in Christian worship. More precisely, it is found in the troubling similarity of icons (visual or material artifacts that point to a divine referent) to idols (human-made objects that short-circuit the access to the transcendence promised by representation and ask instead to be meaningful in and of themselves). Ultimately, this common apprehension harks back to a more general distrust of poetic and artistic creations: the material and corporeal aspects of composition and performance link them, on the one hand, to feminine guile and the Fall and, on the other, to the commandment against making images. Augustine famously understood humans' inability to communicate without the mediation of material words (whether as sounds through air or words on paper) as a consequence of the expulsion from paradise. Per Margaret Ferguson's reading of a key passage in book 7 of *Confessions*, this expulsion into a theological, epistemological, and linguistic "region of unlikeness" threw mankind simultaneously into the shamefulness that accompanies sexual awareness and into the gap separating spiritual from phenomenal matters.[35] Language as such is, thereby, carnally implicated in the sensuality of signs. Humans must hold this sensuality in check so that what is loved and what brings delight is the truth expressed by words and not the pleasures brought about by the words themselves.[36] Similarly, the fleshiness of the work of painters and sculptors who fashioned images from base matter compromised the position of the medieval artificer. For one thing, the liveliness of the representation risked leading believers astray in worshipping a thing created rather than that which it represented. This was of particular concern regarding representations of the Virgin Mary, which, without proper contextualization, could be mistaken for a pagan goddess.[37] Furthermore, because creation was the domain of the divine, artifice in general and the plastic arts in particular, served as reminders of humanity's fallen state. Artifice, the result of manual work, was itself sometimes understood theologically as divinely inflicted punishment following the expulsion of humans from paradise.[38]

The figure of Mary of Egypt featured in *VSME* embodies beauty gone awry on account of both her dangerous eloquence and her alluring, desired, and desiring body, characterized in the first half of the poem as a sort of idol. Before studying the association of Mary of Egypt with idols (the focus of the next chapter), let us examine the origins of the fear of textual idolatry implicit in the conflation of bodies and words. In other words, what happens when the Word needs flesh in order to be persuasive?

ELOQUENCE AND SENSUALITY

The perils of eloquence and idolatry share a common source: the misguided love of beauty, an undue appreciation of the superficial, crafted, and material rather than the substantial and transcendent. In "On the Apparel of Women," Tertullian distinguishes, for example, between whatever is born and thereby aligned with the work of God and the artificial—that which is "plastered on"—which he equates with the work of the devil.[39] And yet, even as it pained his contemporary Augustine to acknowledge it, in that post-lapsarian "region of unlikeness," human communication demands "fleshly ears" and the imperfections of a sensory-bound language. As I mentioned in the opening to this chapter, the formulation "through fleshly ears" appears in *On Christian Doctrine* in the context of an analogy of the mystery of Christ's incarnation to the paradoxical relationship between thought and speech. For Augustine, thought depends on sensory means to manifest itself, all while maintaining its autonomy and integrity separate from being expressed. Augustine writes:

> It is as when we speak. In order that what we are thinking may reach the mind of the listener through the fleshly ears, that which we have in mind is expressed in words and called speech. But our thought is not transformed into sounds; it remains entire in itself and assumes the form of words by means of which it may reach the ears without suffering any deterioration in itself. In the same way the Word of God was made flesh without change that He might dwell among us.[40]

The foundational mystery of Christianity, of God being at once fully human and divine, also played a central role in the adaptation of pagan rhetoric to Christian purposes. Augustine and the early church fathers inherited from Plato and other writers of antiquity a suspicion of rhetoric's troubling attentiveness to form and appearance over content and truth. In fact, as Rita Copeland perceptively points out, the accusation that rhetoric possesses no content of its own is, ironically, "the stigma that has ensured its [rhetoric's] survival" and, importantly, makes rhetoric readily available for adaptation by Christianity.[41] Moreover, the perceived distance between rhetorical discourse and its subject matter maps onto the gap separating eloquence and virtuous ethos. Together, these disjunctions put into question the Socratic ideal of speech as a mirror of the soul. The orator's dependence on the external stratagems of make-believe (through the performance of a speech "in character" or through the deployment of figures of speech and of thought that give body to elegant stories that can convince the audience regardless of truth-content) makes his art suspect. As Jill Ross has shown, rhetoric's dependence on the artifice of figuration and impersonation in order to give an impression of truth and thus win the audience over earned it the disdain of moralists and philosophers from Plato and Quintilian down to the church fathers and modern philosophers such as Friedrich Nietzsche. Crucially,

that scorn passes through gendered tropes that align truth and rightful eloquence with natural masculine virtue while showy, elaborate discourse falls
to unnatural corporeality—read effeminacy—and sexual deviancy associated with the practices of homosexuality or prostitution.[42]

The association and condemnation of effeminate excess with ostentatious ornamentation in words, appearance, lust, and idolatry is often a topic
in the works of early Christian writers. Indeed, Howard Bloch uses Tertullian's account of Eve to demonstrate this logic: for Tertullian, the creation of
Eve metonymically from Adam's rib, her submission to the serpent's temptation, and her own subsequent seduction of Adam together expose artifice
(from the literary to the sartorial) as a reenactment of the Fall, in so far
as it implies prideful criticism of God's original work.[43] And yet, the doctrine of the incarnation, of the Word made flesh, rendered problematic the
unambiguous contempt of the body, thus tempering the ascetic impulse and
opening the way for a validation, albeit limited, of the body and the bodily
aspects of rhetoric. Indeed, Augustine's analogy between speech and the
incarnation quoted above makes possible an appreciation of the materiality
of words, which render immaterial thoughts perceptible for an audience
through sound without corrupting them. In this light, bodies matter, but
only insofar as they serve as an integument—a covering—that paradoxically reveals what otherwise would remain imperceptible.

Many readers of Augustine have pointed out that such a legitimation of
the bodily does not necessarily upset the hierarchy that places spirit over it.
In fact, for those scholars, Augustine's acceptance of sensory-bound experience (including that of human communication) occurs within a carefully
delimited context, granting it, at best, provisional status: that of being useful
"means" toward a greater "end." In this vein, Margaret Ferguson writes that
"for Augustine the incarnation does not redeem language itself; rather, the
incarnation guarantees the *end* of language because it promises the possibility of an ultimate transcendence of time. Augustine's rhetoric is ultimately a
'rhetoric of silence.'"[44] Similarly, though from a less deconstructive starting
point, Joseph Anthony Mazzeo concludes that many of Augustine's works
chronicle the saint's learning of the meaning of silence, where "the mind is
in immediate contact with reality."[45] Such a view does not discard the body,
beauty, or the arts, but it does place them in a hierarchy where these external
expressions will eventually give way to the "intelligible, the eternal, and the
'silent.'"[46]

The emphasis on the end of language in a rhetoric of silence implies
ultimately that communication is *best* achieved in a disembodied way. An

alternative to the subordination of the use of material means to spiritual ends can be found in Rowan Williams's sensitive reading of *On Christian Doctrine*. Rather than interpret the Augustinian concept of use (*uti*) as the strict opposite of enjoyment (*frui*)—and thing (*res*) opposed to sign (*signum*)—Williams finds a dynamic relationship between each term. This means that neither term alone can contain God or our relationship to divinity. More precisely, he works out the consequences of the humility implicit in the incarnation for Augustinian sign theory and ethics. As Williams writes, "the scope of Christ's love lies precisely in his own gratuitous acceptance of the limits of history: what is uniquely *res*, the eternal wisdom of God, becomes uniquely and entirely *signum*, a worldly thing meaning what it is not."[47] Seen this way, striving for possession of unmediated knowledge of God represents an act of un-Christian hubris. Moreover, the metaphoricity inherent to the realm of signs—the understanding that on a human level finality of meaning is always deferred—calls for believers' humility of spirit. That is to say, they must accept their own position—and that of the world—as incomplete signs, incapable of bearing or conferring fullness of meaning once and for all. The recognition of this fluidity thus liberates believers from "the threat of an idolatry of signs," from believing that signs afford direct possession of knowledge, of the world, of each other.[48] Instead, this recognition delivers believers to dialogue and to a relationship to language and to other human beings as ongoing processes driven by desire, "not a triumphant moment of penetration and mastery, but an extended play of invitation and exploration."[49] This model of incarnational language, focused on process, desire, and the *usefulness of pleasure*, makes possible a poetics that does not seek its own end in silence, but rather depends on the continuation of conversation; or to quote Jean Leclercq's beautiful conclusion to his study of monastic culture, believers can come to understand "literary style as an act of homage to God."[50]

This insight, however, is not restricted to theology: James J. Murphy, coming to Augustine from a rhetorical angle, makes a similar point when he reads *On Christian Doctrine* as more ambitious than a "mere rejection of the Second Sophistic."[51] Augustine, for Murphy, does no less than provide an influential justification of the integration of pagan learning to Christianity by identifying and responding to two distinct forms of "rhetorical heresy."[52] The first corresponds to the "sin of the sophist," or the accusation that rhetoric neglects moral content in favor of beautiful form. This concern, as I have shown, carried within it the seed for a more pernicious problem: a slide into idolatry.

The second rhetorical heresy is a subtle inversion of the first, though no less pernicious. *On Christian Doctrine* seeks to rebuke what Murphy terms a "Platonic rhetorical heresy," namely, the folly of imagining that an author could convey a message without paying any attention to form. I examined this failure earlier, at the discussion of Mary of Egypt's unadorned offer of her body to the pilgrims. Only when she dresses up her request with attention to audience, emotion, and ambiguous language can her word be effective. Murphy argues that Augustine's response to the Platonic heresy was *not* to turn away from rhetoric but instead to seek an agreement of matter and form, of doctrine and eloquence in Christian hermeneutics and preaching. This perfectly proportionate equivalence, or decorum, is what allows Mary Carruthers to claim Augustine as the "patron saint of the pleasures of style."[53] This patron saint sanctifies rhetoric, in all its complexity, as long as it remains justly decorous: attentive as much to the particular context as to the ultimate goal of making proper use of it. The *VSME*, however, presents a limit case: Is indecorous eloquence possible? The poem raises that question when Mary's second, more rhetorically sophisticated supplication to the pilgrims proves persuasive but, boldly, does not give rise to a moral condemnation on the part of the poet, in contrast to her first, rhetorically bald attempt, which was clearly aligned with sinful madness.

HAGIOGRAPHY AND THE DREAM OF
A REDEEMED LANGUAGE

The balance sought by Augustine—making sure that the superficial, sensory, and sensual aspects of rhetoric do not mask deleterious content—is difficult to achieve. This difficulty lies at the heart of the ambivalence regarding eloquence in medieval texts. On the one hand, when the speaker employs words judiciously, the art of speaking well can serve as a marker of virtuous and heroic character. In the case of the paradigmatic epic hero, Rodrigo Díaz de Vivar earns praise in the opening of the *Poema de mio Cid* (mid-twelfth century) for his prudent speech: "The Cid spoke well and wisely" (fabló Mio Çid bien e tan mesurado).[54] On the other hand, eloquence for its own sake, or when divorced from ethical content becomes seductive, deceitful, and meretricious. Fernando de Rojas's *Tragicomedia de Calisto y Melibea* (1499) perhaps best exemplifies this darker, more negative perception. In that work, Celestina, a procuress of cosmetics and nubile girls, becomes the very embodiment of eloquence-as-pandering. What is more, as Charles Fraker notes, her noxious eloquence bleeds into the ethos of other characters such that "rarely does a character become eloquent and moralizing without some sort of malice aforethought, broad or discreet."[55]

The question of the value and function of eloquence is, for practical and philosophical reasons, also a central concern of vernacular hagiography. Pragmatically, by the thirteenth century, saints' lives became one among many other forms of expression in courtly circuits and in the marketplace, and there was a greater need for poets, performers, and lawmakers to distinguish between proper and improper stories. As I have discussed, when the poet of *VSME* insists on distinguishing his *razones* from vain *fablas*, he is making a claim for its superiority based on the spiritual profit that the listener may reap from his song. These claims place the poem along the lines of the contemporary self-conscious declarations found in other *mester de clerecía* (clerical arts) works, such as the anonymous *Book of Apolonio*, the only surviving Spanish version in meter appearing in the same manuscript as *VSME*. These works emphasized the novelty and great care of their poetic craft, and they presented themselves as mediators between bookish authority and their lay audience. More formally, canon 16 of the decrees of the Fourth Lateran Council (1215) singled out public entertainers, including those who trafficked in dishonest songs, and threatened them with nothing less than excommunication while instructing the clergy not to associate with them.[56] In Castile, Alfonso X's statutory code, *Siete partidas* (ca. 1265), also distinguished legitimate entertainers who sang for their own pleasure or to bring joy to kings or other noblemen from those jongleurs who sang wanton songs for money.[57] Similarly, Thomas Chabham's early thirteenth-century penitential noted that only those who sang of saints and princely deeds ("gesta principum et uitas sanctorum") to bring solace to men's souls were to be considered honest singers.[58]

On a more philosophical level, hagiography tested the tenet of Christian epistemology that the concept of God as *logos* encompasses "both the knowledge of God and the process by which human beings arrive at that knowledge."[59] Central to the question of the efficacy of words in relaying a spiritual message is the ekphrastic function of language, that is to say the capacity of language to create vivid mental images. This creative force is behind language's persuasive power, but its effectiveness is inseparable from the danger of creating the equivalent of textual idols. Medieval and classical manuals of rhetoric encouraged the use of vivid language, especially to present an argument *visually* in order to persuade the listener. Indeed, as

Nicolette Zeeman notes, medieval grammarians use the word *imago* to refer to rhetorical tropes, and commentators speak of narrative texts as "mentally seen."[60] However, this passage through the senses—conceived etymologically as sensual and pleasurable (*suadere*, in the sense of "to advise," is understood literally as making something pleasant or sweet to someone)—is not without its problems.[61] Foremost, too sharp a focus on the poetic craft and its dependence on the sensory risks turning the poem itself into a "creature" or an idol, a human-made artifact that goes beyond persuasion and seduces its audience without actually fulfilling its promise of transcendence.

The fear of creating textual idols helps explain why medieval hagiographic texts often opt for a sublation of eloquence along the lines of the Augustinian dream of a transparent language, the rhetoric of silence. Similarly, Brigitte Cazelles's study of French hagiographic poems of the thirteenth-century notes that the path to holiness for both men and women passed through "estrangement, abnegation, *quest for silence* and solitude, [which] serve, in their case, as shields that protect them from temptation, thereby guaranteeing their access to God."[62] A more optimistic version of the quest for transparency emerges in the works of the thirteenth-century Spanish cleric Gonzalo de Berceo (ca. 1198–ca. 1264). Mary Jane Kelley's "Ascendant Eloquence" traces, for example, the hagiographer's aspirations to a redeemed language, a language where words and things, ethos and eloquence coincide. Holiness, she argues, is recognizable in Berceo's works through the characters' proper use of language, and conversely, the poet-hagiographer often presents proper speech—whether it be the saints' divinely inspired words or the cleric's learned, didactic, well-crafted poems—as a pathway to heaven. This is evident in Berceo's portrayal of a character's good words (*buenas razones*), which are good on religious and stylistic grounds and just as easily qualified as true (*verdadera*) and as beautiful (*fermosa*). Conversely, bad characters do not simply speak falsehoods and incite sinful behavior but do so in particularly corrupt language.[63] Thus, Berceo extends a verbal dimension to what Harriet Goldberg has described as the style of Christian literary portraiture where physical features are filtered through an "ethically didactic screen."[64]

In this linguistic ecology, where the goal is to redeem language, so to speak, by attempting to suspend the ambiguity of signs that resulted from the expulsion of humans from paradise, success entails either falling into meaningful silence (Saint Oria) or being divinely inspired through nonlinguistic intervention (Saint Aemilian of Cogolla's dream vision). Although, as Kelley notes, silence and visions are not the exclusive privilege of any one gender, not all silences are equal. Silence is a feature of the future Saint Dominic of Silos's childhood; it is a preparatory stage for his later eloquence and efficient prayers. In contrast, Oria's silence is associated with the withholding of speech, indeed, the clenching of her lips, and it remains in effect even after her devotion has been rewarded with heavenly visions. Julian Weiss's reading of Berceo's *Poem of Saint Oria* takes into consideration the gendered inflections of her story, focusing on how her silence and extreme cloistering serve as "metaphor for the victory over disorderly fleshliness and the recovery of the transcendental unity of body and spirit" that makes possible "a voice untainted by carnality."[65] This cleansed language then serves as the point of departure for the transformation of Oria's particular vision into scripture (first by her confessor, then by Berceo himself) that partakes in her holiness as it makes it available to the community.

Female asceticism and silence, however, are not the only paths to sainthood. So-called female preaching saints, such as Catherine of Alexandria or post-conversion Mary Magdalene, present interesting models of female eloquence, which while still beauty-bound, work toward Christian ends. This beauty, as many critics have noted, serves both to attract and distract their listeners, and it is in both cases linked to their rhetorical prowess.[66] Significantly, in the late fourteenth or early fifteenth-century vita of Mary Magdalene found in Escorial manuscript h-I-13, the saint is introduced as both beautiful and prudent as she arrives in Marseilles just in time to interrupt the pagans' idol worshipping:

> And that morning, the town's bad people came to make their sacrifice
> to the idols. And when they got there, the Magdalene had already been
> up. She was very beautiful and graceful, and very prudent and eloquent
> and very firm. And she began to preach words of life and salvation. And
> everyone was in awe of her beauty and of her prudent words and of how
> she displayed them prudently.[67]

Her beauty attracted the villagers' attention, the same way it had once attracted the attention of men, but this time instead of inciting lustful thoughts or actions, it delivers prudent words of salvation in a prudent or pleasurable manner. Tradition ascribes the Magdalene's congruence of beauty and prudence to her penitent contact with Christ: "And do not be surprised if the mouth of the Magdalene spoke well and prudently for it had kissed the feet of Christ."[68] Importantly, this etiology did not serve as a blanket justification of female preaching, or indeed of female speech in general, but scholars such as Claire M. Waters and Karen Winstead have shown that male preachers used it as a way to validate their own use of potentially seductive rhetoric.[69]

I will close this chapter's consideration of physical beauty and eloquence by returning to the legend of Catherine of Alexandria. When the virgin confronts the idolatrous emperor Maxentius, he falls silent, in awe of her beauty and eloquence. In the words of a fourteenth-century Spanish prose version of Catherine's legend, "He fell silent and listened carefully to her and was enchanted by her beauty and semblance and of the resolve of her words."[70] As a pagan idolater, however, he is unable to see past the surface of Catherine's words and body, and instead he attempts to win her over by deploying his own good speech aimed at flattering her. Catherine remains impervious to his sweet talk, and throughout the multiple debates with the emperor and his gang of philosophers she remains true to her message, delivering it at each moment with greater conviction and in words inspired by God. She pleads to God for eloquence thus:

> Lord, be with me and put in my mouth *good speech, prudent and beautiful*, so that those who seek here to bring down your name shall not have power over me and instead their wits shall recede and they shall be conquered by the virtue of your word or be converted and give Glory to your holy name.[71]

Catherine leaves nothing to chance, and she glosses exactly what she means by good speech. In contrast to the superficially sweet words of the emperor, she wants speech that is both prudent ("sesuda") and beautiful ("fermosa"). The "goodness" of this speech consists in being sensually sweet and morally good; it is pleasing in both content and form, not only in execution but also in its effect.

Although her verbal persuasion coupled with the goodwill of her audience brought about by her beautiful demeanor converted the philosophers, the empress, and countless witnesses to her disputations and her martyrdom, the legend makes clear that even love of Catherine's holy beauty for own its sake would be no different from idolatry. This is evident in an exchange between the pagans of Alexandria and the soon-to-be martyr. On her way to decapitation, the townspeople urge the virgin to ply her will to

THE SEDUCTIONS OF HAGIOGRAPHY · 71

the emperor's and thus protect "the wonder of your beauty" (la maravilla de tu beldat), to which she responds: "Dismiss your vain mourning over my lost beauty for it is worthless."[72]

Not incidentally, the target of these beautiful saints' preaching is in each case a pagan governor whom they must persuade of the vanity of his idols. Tertullian famously denounced idolatry as synonymous with all other sins, such as murder, adultery, fornication, fraud, and vanity. Idolatry is thus made to encompass "the concupiscences of the world," including lasciviousness but also "the circumstance of dress and ornament."[73] Significantly, then, in the case of Catherine, her resistance to the idolater is at once a rejection of his pagan gods and of his sexual advances. Thus, in this model of female sainthood, the virgin martyr must resist the temptation to adulterate her faith or her body if she is to achieve glory defined by heavenly nuptials.

Omitted from the Spanish version of Catherine's legend quoted earlier (Escorial ms. h-I-13) but present in other versions of the saint's life collected in *The Golden Legend* is the moralizing conclusion drawn by Jacobus de Voragine, where he praises her eloquence, chastity, constancy, and wisdom:

> It is to be noted that this blessed virgin S. Katherine seemeth and appeareth marvellous in five things: first, in wisdom, secondly, in eloquence, thirdly, in constancy, fourthly, in cleanness of chastity, and fifthly, in privilege of dignity. [. . .] For there be five things in which chastity may perish, that is in pleasance of riches, convenable opportunity, flowering youth, freedom without constraint, and sovereign beauty. And among all these things the blessed Katherine kept her chastity, for she had great plenty of riches as she that was heir of rich parents; she had convenable leisure to do her will, as she that was lady of herself, and conversed all day among her servants which were young of age [when the urges of lust are strongest]; she had freedom without any that governed her in her palace, and of these four it is said before, and she had beauty [which in and of itself is provocative], so much that every man marvelled of her beauty.[74]

As Claire M. Waters has convincingly argued, this conclusion picks up Tertullian's association of idolatry with femininity, lasciviousness, eloquence, and beauty to show how female preacher-saints deploy "feminine allure with similarly beautiful speech the better to destroy the idolatrous attraction to verbal or physical beauty for its own sake."[75] In other words, empowering the beautiful, eloquent female martyr-to-be results nonetheless in her ultimate silencing, in what amounts to yet another version of what could be called hagiography's iconoclastic tendency to sacrifice rhetorical or feminine beauty in order to achieve holiness.

What does the *VSME* contribute to this legacy? The poem is clearly concerned with working through the difficulty of distinguishing profitable *razones* from vain *fablas*. But, as I have shown in this chapter, by explicitly thematizing the connection of words and bodies, the poem opts on the side of humility, not claiming any prelapsarian or redeemed language for itself. Its didacticism is of a piece with the beauty of its protagonist and the literariness of its execution. In the next chapter I shall examine exactly how the poem sketches an alternative to the iconoclasm of hagiography. By embracing the carnality of discourse as sanctioned by the mystery of the incarnation, the poem exemplifies the ways in which persuasion is possible only through an engagement of the senses and the body, thereby making possible what I call an iconophilic hagiography, as we will see in the next chapter.

THE SHOES OF THE SINNER AND THE SKIN OF THE SAINT

> Visible beauty becomes properly visible precisely when it speaks to us and we question it.
>
> JEAN-LOUIS CHRÉTIEN[1]

THE PREVIOUS CHAPTER SHOWED HOW THE fear of textual idolatry, of beautiful words being sought for the pleasures they provide (seduction) rather than for the lesson they may convey (persuasion), led to a tendency in hagiography to seek a language so transparent that it becomes ultimately contemplative silence. The *Vida de Santa María Egipciaca* (*VSME*) takes a humbler turn by not claiming for itself any prelapsarian language; it embraces instead the carnality of discourse as sanctioned by the mystery of the incarnation. The humble embrace of carnality is not exclusive to the Iberian version, although it is central to that text. The first surviving complete account of the life of our holy harlot, dating back to the seventh century and attributed to Sophronius, already shows awareness of the necessity and risk inherent to communication among humans. The legend begins with a preface that insists that "it is good to keep the secrets of a king, but it is honorable to reveal the works of God."[2] Moreover, keeping silent about the miraculous works of God constitutes a form of spiritual poverty and betrayal.

Importantly, the text makes clear that the author must obey the imperative to make public the wonders worked by God, all while being aware that there is a chance of meeting with disbelief:

to have mean thoughts unworthy of the majesty of the incarnate word of God, as well as to disbelieve what has just been said, does not seem to me sensible. If there are some people who happen to read this account and, allegedly because of their amazement at the extraordinary <aspects> of the story, refuse to believe it readily, may the Lord be merciful to them, because they, too, thinking in terms of the weakness of human nature, find it hard to believe the extraordinary tales told about human beings.[3]

Defending his text, the author makes what seems a surprising parallel between doubting the "majesty of the incarnate word of God" and doubting his tale. The association of the paradox of the incarnation with the extraordinary tale of a radical transformation from sinfulness to holiness highlights the important distinction between truth (what is) and verisimilitude (what can be conventionally believed). That the thirsty, tired, time-bound, and suffering body of Christ shares in the divine nature of God the Father is doctrinally true and well established by the church in Sophronius's time, even if it exceeds what might be reasonable to expect. Similarly, Mary the Egyptian's tale of radical transformation, her excessive acts of penitential love, and her walking on water and levitation upon prayer do not fall within the reasonable bounds of human nature as normally manifested. Yet, to doubt these marvels is to be insensitive to the truth of the boundlessness of God's grace toward his flawed creatures.

Significantly, the defense of the truth of the extraordinary in this version of the tale does not discard wonder as a surface that the audience must penetrate in order to arrive at truth. Neither does the text present marvel as a distraction or false appearance *hiding* the truth. Such interpretative strategies and metaphors, dismissing surface in favor of depth, certainly would have been available to the author from the exegetical work of contemporaries, such as Gregory the Great, or directly from a hermeneutics present already in the Bible. A paradigmatic example of this strategy is the parable of the mustard seed, present in three of the four Gospels. Not only does it teach that the appearance of the insignificant-looking, tiny seed hides within itself the very figuration of the Kingdom of Heaven, but its explicitly pedagogic context reinforces the same message. Jesus instructs his disciples to be aware of the distinction between (superficial) seeing and hearing, on the one hand, and (substantive) perceiving and understanding, on the other. Rather than turning to a model of interpretation that would look through

THE SHOES OF THE SINNER AND THE SKIN OF THE SAINT   75

the superficial, the author of this seventh-century vita, significantly, does something different: following the model of the incarnation, he insists on a hermeneutics that upholds the integrity of the union of surface and substance in the story of Mary of Egypt in order to speak a truth that defies easy belief.

Maintaining the inseparability of surface and substance becomes all the more important in later versions of the legend of Saint Mary of Egypt, especially in the Western branch of the legend, to which *VSME* belongs. In those versions of the story, the body of the sinner-saint takes center stage—in the form of a detailed portrait of her desirably beautiful body—and thus raises the question of what to do with the sensuality of such a description. This tradition developed in France in the last quarter of the twelfth century as a response to an increase in Marian devotion. The versions of the life of Mary the Egyptian that belong to this tradition invert the narrative structure of the seventh-century story. The legend that in the account attributed to Sophronius began with monk Zozimas's quest for the perfection of holiness, in which the Egyptian's life serves as a model of humility and perfect asceticism for the monk, becomes by the twelfth and thirteenth centuries truly Mary's story. These versions begin with her life, told chronologically in great detail from sinfulness to sainthood, and they consign Zozimas to the role of privileged witness to the Egyptian's holiness. This innovation entailed two notable amplifications. First, Mary's pre-penitent adventures now include the meticulous portrayal of her beauty and the representation of her seductive actions as if they were happening before the audience's eyes, thereby engaging their imagination cognitively and affectively. Second, what was in the seventh-century vita a brief mention of her penitent body after forty-seven years of ascetic residence in the desert becomes in these later versions the site of a lovingly specific portrait.

As we saw in the previous chapter, one of the fears of eloquent diction is that it may create textual idols. How is the audience supposed to take in the evident delight in the text's description of *both* the seductive beauty of pre-penitent Mary *and* in the decrepitude of that same body after four decades of ascetic practice? In this chapter, I propose that—rather than represent a simple proto-makeover, where the before of superficial beauty gets left behind for inner holiness to emerge—the poem recuperates the value of surfaces, whether it be the skin of the saint or the leather of her shoes, as a site of love. Such a recuperation is all the more striking because of the poet's awareness of how easily created objects can become idols.

CONSORTING WITH IDOLS

The first portrait of Mary the Egyptian appears in *VSME* after she has left her home for Alexandria, "in order to better to do her will" (121).[4] The poet emphasizes Mary's desire to follow her own will through the repetition of the word *voluntat* (will) at the end of lines 128 and 133. Moreover, in a perverse echo of Jesus calling the apostles to leave behind their loved ones to live according to the will of God, Mary's will consists of enjoying the present moment without being mindful of, or more literally without remembering, her own mortality. Mary's obliviousness is apparent first when, settled comfortably in Alexandria, she is in the lap of luxury and has no thoughts beyond the immediate present:

> In drinking and eating and lewdness
> She passed day and night.
> When she rose from eating
> She went to have sport with them.
> So much did she want to play and laugh
> That she forgot she had to die. (122)[5]

More shockingly, she displays the same abandon to pleasure in the midst of a storm aboard the ship that takes her to Jerusalem, inviting her fellow pilgrims to romp with her instead of attending to their bodies and souls in danger.

Mary's life, released from any filial and societal claims on her, and in its lack of concern for past or future, represents an enthusiastic emptiness. Coupled with the emphasis on the enthralling nature of her beauty and the people of Alexandria's response to her, the text presents her as a sort of idol. Repeatedly, Mary's beauty is reified and emptied of its capacity to point back to its original source in God. First, the prostitutes of Alexandria receive her with great fanfare on account of her beauty. Then, the young men of the city, upon seeing her displayed, fight for the right to be with her. Her beauty so bewitches them that, torn from their civic and religious duties, they do not hesitate to shed blood:

> The young men of the city
> She so delighted with her beauty
> That each day they came to see her

From whom they could not keep away.
So many companions came there
That the games turned to hard feelings.
At the gates, in the doorways,
There were great sword fights;
The blood which flowed from them
Ran down the middle of the street. (122)[6]

These effects are not unlike those described by the fourteenth-century Dominican preacher Robert Holcot, whose *Commentary on the Book of Wisdom* warns:

"Turn away thy face from a woman dressed up, and gaze not upon another's beauty" [Ecc. 9]. These women are creatures of whom the letter says [they are turned into an abomination] "and [are] a temptation to the souls of men, and a snare to the feet of the unwise." For in this mousetrap David was caught, and this idol also seduced the wisdom of Solomon to the worship of idols as we read in 3 Kings 12. These idols are to be fled, and not sought out through curiosity, for as the letter says [Wisdom 14.12], "the beginning of fornication is the devising of idols." For it is impossible for a curious and lascivious man associating with these idols not to be corrupted by them; indeed, a man, diligently seeking out and considering in his thought the beauty of women so that he makes idols for himself, necessarily prepares for his own fall.[7]

Michael Camille quotes this passage in *The Gothic Idol* in order to argue for the existence of an iconographical and ideological connection between the sins of lust and idolatry since both imply the construction of an image that subsequently becomes the viewer's object of desire and worship.[8] In the context of Tertullian's warning that idolatry encompasses all other sins, the Spanish poet too presents the young men of Alexandria as guilty not just of lust but, more gravely, of idolatry. In their actions, they are not all that different from King Solomon, whose lust for foreign women led him to make sacrifices to pagan idols, an act that finds a gruesome counterpart in the poem's description of the blood flowing through the street, shed for Mary's sake. The text completes its representation of Mary as an idol by noting Mary's tepid response to the mayhem her presence has brought upon the city. Much like a hollow, insensitive statue, she remains perfectly unmoved: "When the wretch saw the situation / no compassion gripped her."[9]

Immediately after the description of the chaos caused by the Egyptian's beauty, the poet turns his attention to a physical depiction of the Egyptian temptress. Often recognized as the first full rhetorical portrait of female beauty in medieval Spanish literature, this rhetorical set piece follows compositional conventions, as Peter L. Podol has shown, and it offers the reader a top-to-bottom image of Mary.[10] Yet, the elaborate description of Mary's beauty is surprising on two accounts. First, given that its immediate context is a graphic report of the moral deterioration of Alexandria's young men on account of Mary's beauty, the description of this beauty risks enticing the audience to *imagine* her and create an "idol in the mind." This imaginative act would put the listener in the position of her unhappy male suitors. Second, and more significantly, the poet does not frame the portrait with explicit moralizing warnings about Mary's beauty. What is more, the poet flaunts the fact that the description to follow is a digression, a textual resting place where the poet diverges from the poem's main purpose:

> Of the beauty of her appearance
> As it is described in writing
> *Before going further*
> I would say something of her appearance. (123)[11]

How to account then for the poetic portrait of the sinner? The hermeneutic model based on the biblical distinction and separation of surface from depth gave rise to a series of very productive tropes (bark/pith, chaff/ wheat, husk/kernel) used throughout the Middle Ages by both writers and readers as a way of accounting for strangeness within a text.[12] Turning to this model, modern scholars have accounted two ways for the uncomfortable presence of Mary's beautiful portrait in a religious and didactic poem about penitence and asceticism. Both options eschew the troubling surface description of beauty in favor of a truth that more easily fits the didactic purpose of the poem.

Most critics justify the presence of the ekphrastic digression by reading Mary's external beauty—the dark eyes, rose-like complexion, apple-like bosom, and so on—as the seductive mask covering up the truth of her corrupt inside, a structure that the text flips when it turns to the description of a penitential but decrepit body housing a holy soul. Alan Deyermond, in his *Literary History of Spain* notes, for example, that "the poem is built on a double contrast: María's outward youth and beauty is a mask for inner corruption, whereas later her aged, roughened, and hideous body houses

FIGURE 7. *Frau Welt*. Sculpture. Cathedral of Worms, Germany, ca. 1310. Source: Pilettes (https://creativecommons.org/licenses/by-sa/3.0/legalcode).

the purified soul of a saint; appearance and reality change places."[13] Similarly, writing about the portrait of penitent Mary in a prose vita of Saint Mary of Egypt, John Maier notes that "as in the picture of Dorian Gray, Mary becomes externally what she had been internally: corrupt, repugnant, and vile [...] the external now serves as a mirror for what the internal had been but which is now rejected."[14] A visual analogy to this interpretative mode is to see Mary's statuesque perfection as a textual manifestation of the personification of vanity, *Frau Welt* (Lady World; figure 7). This sculpture, found in the Cathedral of Worms (ca. 1310), Germany, shows on the front an idealized feminine figure, smiling alluringly while her backside teems with snakes, toads, and other creatures signifying the ultimate rot of death.

There is a second approach to understanding the troubling presence of beauty in *VSME*. It, too, assumes the dispensable value of beauty's surface.

This time, however, instead of seeing beauty as a false appearance hiding the truth of mortality, each surface element becomes assimilated into a symbolic scheme that ultimately negates the actuality of the literal. Thus, Lynn Rice Cortina reads the ekphrastic digression in the poem within the context of the epideictic tradition where the orator uses description to shower praise or cast blame. The pause in the narrative, then, becomes a way for the poet to "achieve symbolic depth without disrupting the narration."[15] She argues that, although the description follows rhetorical conventions (i.e., the vertical head-to-toe organization of body parts, apostrophes to the audience framing the description, as well as the individual descriptions of her features), the portrait's primary function is symbolic. Moreover, the poet's comparison of Mary's body parts to natural elements, according to Cortina, also correspond to Christian images. For example, Mary's ears are described as white and round and compared to ewe's milk (lines 213–14; 123). In the scholar's account, this original detail would point to the image of Christians as a flock of sheep, to the representation of Christ as the Lamb of God, and of heaven as the land of milk and honey.[16] Similarly, she traces parallels between the conventional beauty of Mary and the mystical attributes of the eponymous Virgin Mary.[17]

Although it is difficult to deny the power of allegoresis and the extent to which it permeated medieval interpretative communities, "it is simply incorrect to claim, as some have supposed, that every single scriptural passage had assigned to it four distinct 'senses' or levels of meaning, i.e. the literal, the allegorical, the tropological (or moral) and the anagogical (whereby the mind is lifted up to the celestial goals of the Christian life)."[18] Not every word in a text (scriptural or secular) needed to dissolve into allegory in order to be meaningful. While it may be possible to map almost one to one Mary's physical attributes to Christian symbols and to conceive that an audience of male clerics (or more widely of lay pilgrims) would have been able to decode this mapping, the allegorical process cannot do without the literal body. To approach the description of Mary's beauty simply as a mask that must be penetrated in order to reach the meaningful core risks not only to explain the text but to *explain it away* in pursuit of thematic coherence.[19]

Rather than seek ideological coherence—expecting a religious text to always *only* speak religiously, eschewing the letter for the spirit—I take seriously Sophronius's suggestion that the wonder of the text resides in the fact that those elements that do not easily fit in with our preconceptions of holiness still must be told. Seen this way, the representation of Mary's beauty in the poem is, at the very least, ambivalent. The text recognizes the dangers of representation (by positing the possibility that pre-conversion Mary is idol-like), but as I shall show, the poem is less than clear in its condemnation of the delights it creates.

THE BEAUTY OF THE SHOES

Mary's portrait in the poem appears framed on one end by the violent chaos that the worship of her beauty caused in Alexandria and on the other by an elaborate description of her clothing:

> The worse day of the week
> She did not wear clothing of wool.
> It took much silver and gold
> for her to dress according to her desire.
> She wore expensive gowns
> Over which she wore an ermine mantel.
> She never wore shoes
> Unless they were made of cordovan leather.
> They were decorated with gold and silver
> And cords of silk with which she fastened them. (124)[20]

The portrait itself might be allegorized away as a strategy of the poet to turn Mary from idol of beauty to Christian symbol, as Cortina proposes, but it is more difficult to explain the purpose of the detailed description of her clothing. The Spanish poet amplifies this difficulty by severing the explicit connection between Mary's profession and the luxury goods it affords her by omitting four lines that in the French poem present a transition between the description of her body and that of her clothes:

> She received great presents
> she bought herself expensive clothes
> she had good and agreeable bed linens
> to better please her lovers.[21]

The poet's silence on Mary's attire as the result of prostitution separates her from her holy-harlot sisters, such as Pelagia, in whom superlative beauty and the ostentatious display of wealth in the form of rich garments point directly to prostitution.[22] That silence also makes it more difficult to agree with Patricia Grieve's interpretation that, following Averil Cameron's study of Christianity in late antiquity, proposes to see in the description of the clothing a "signal of corruption."[23]

Instead of providing a narrative transition between the two parts of Mary's description by alluding to the wages of prostitution, the Spanish poet passes from body to clothing through an appeal to the *topos* of inexpressibility. Unable to give an accurate representation of her beauty, he tells us that he will move on to the clothing:

> We have to leave her beauty now —
> It is not possible to portray it to you —
> To say something of her clothes
> And of her adornments. (124)[24]

Taking as a cue Alice M. Colby's study of literary portraiture in the works of Chrétien de Troyes, where she notes that the inclusion of a description of a character's clothes is not unusual in the tradition of chivalric romance, I suggest that the significance of dressing up the naked body here emerges through a comparison to another example from the romance tradition.[25] The physical description of Mary of Egypt shares some traits with the Pygmalion episode in the *Roman de la Rose*, where the sculptor first carves Galatea's body and, as his love for her grows, indulges in dressing up her naked body with luxurious fabrics. Michael Camille's reading of Pygmalion's actions highlights that "Jean's poem inverts the convention and sees the dressing not as covering shameful nudity but a titillating ritual of pure pleasure."[26] In the *Roman de la Rose* as in *VSME*, the act of clothing the female naked body, rather than serve to conceal what should not be publicly seen, engages in a compensatory action: the poet offers the delight in textual and textile artifice as a substitution for not being able to fully seize the beauty of the represented object, or indeed to possess it. In *VSME*, the poet's delight in decking out Mary's beautiful body with his beautiful words manifests in the choice of amplification: while he erased the association of prostitution with clothing, he added four lines on Mary's exquisite shoes.

Grieve interprets the description of Mary's luxurious shoes as yet another example of the poem's conflation of the feminine body with currency and corruption, based on the association of footwear with female sexuality.[27] That iconographic association, however, need not be negative. Unlike the representations of female vanity that also demonstrate its ultimate and fundamental corruption (the image of *Frau Welt*) or corruptibility (Saint Catherine's disdain of her perishable beauty), the digressive descriptions of Mary and her clothes do not yet point to a moral teaching. Indeed, these signs are incapable of signifying beyond themselves because the image of Mary until now is still too empty to signify. She is beautiful and brought forth through beautiful words, almost as if the poet were too enthralled with the frontal side of the statute to turn his gaze toward the rot it may hide. When the poem expresses concern with the effects of her sinful life, it is not in relation to the potential loss of her soul but rather to express sorrow at how low a woman of high social standing (*paratge*) has come. Those around her would say: "'It is such a shame / About this woman of noble lineage.' / She seems learned about all things. / Why does she live such a life?" (124).[28] The concerns of the poet are very much in the here and now.

The shoes in particular stand out as a stubborn remainder. A symbological interpretation cannot account for their delicate presence in the poem. Neither the Cordoban leather nor the silk laces serve as figurations of some future redemption. Moreover, the description of Mary's exquisite shoes does not lean on figurative language in order to convey the richness of Mary's attire to the audience. Instead, the description lingers lovingly on the surface, noting the artistry of the well-cut, crafted, and painted luxurious leather and the silkiness of the delicate laces. While the point here is less to transport the reader through metaphor to other realms of signification, the description remains intensely and intricately moving and effective. The poet involves his audience by sliding from texture to texture, wrapping the reader or listener in luxurious word-fabrics. Importantly, sight is not the only sense to be activated. The audience is not only treated to the sight of the fabulous clothes, but instead is also moved to touch them, figuratively, with the finger of the mind. Likewise, the audience is affected acoustically as the predominance of the vowels *a* and *o* required by the Spanish rhyme scheme resound in the audience's ear as exclamations of delight, if not wonder (ah! oh!). Sartorial elegance here meets its linguistic match in the poet's eloquence.

What is then the purpose of the dazzling exhibition of Mary's attributes and of the poet's skill? When the goal of ekphrasis is to move the audience by producing appropriate emotion upon witnessing the scene linguistically painted before them, one must ask what is the nature of the emotion aroused here. Lust is an obvious answer. That is, after all, the reaction of the young men who fall all over themselves to please and pleasure Mary (158–64). Similarly, Michael Solomon's reading of the poem as a hygienic text posits that reading or listening to the poem is meant to stir sexual passion in its male listeners, although ultimately in order to function as a *pharmakon* to those impure thoughts.[29] The young and lusty Alexandrians have as their ultimate goal possession of Mary: "They all went there to court her / and to *possess* her body" (122).[30] In Solomon's account, the audience's reaction also depends on a goal-oriented relationship to desire (to incite or to restrain passion). And yet, full possession or full control of desire—like the full knowledge Augustine yearned for—is not possible in the creaturely realm humans inhabit.

A less apparent and more complex emotion aroused in the poem's display of beauty is admiration or wonder. Encompassing simultaneously splendor, astonishment, attraction, and dread, *maravilla* appears no less than six times in the poem, often as the poet's commentary on the expected reaction from the audience to his narration. The poet comments, for example, after the description of Mary's tempestuous travel to Jerusalem with the pilgrims that "one can wonder greatly, / That one woman had such an impact" (128).[31] Wonder arouses the audience, it serves the purpose of maintaining their interest in the narrative through memorable descriptions, and, crucially, it produces desire and delight. It does so, however, without seeing the fulfillment of desire as the end, without the presumption of ultimate possession, whether of bodies, words, or meaning.[32]

In the figuration of delight without possession, the anonymous poet of *VSME* differs from poets who also indulged in the textile-textual play of describing the body and clothing of the Virgin Mary. As Jill Ross has beautifully shown, both King Alfonso X of Castile (1221–84) in the *Canticles of Holy Mary* (*Cantigas de Santa María*) and thirteenth-century hagiographer Gonzalo de Berceo in his collection of *Miracles of Our Lady* (*Milagros de Nuestra Señora*) seek to legitimize their authorial practice through an appropriation of Mary's creative power as the womb that issued forth Word having become flesh.[33] For those poets, the act of composing songs or narratives in praise of the Virgin is intimately tied to clothing her statues in finery (Alfonso's Cantiga 295), or to a miraculous cloth that the Virgin herself offers to those who do her honor through the use of a language that appropriately represents her (Berceo's Miracle 1). The poet of *VSME* also assimilates words to bodies, as we saw in the previous chapter, and to sartorial appreciation, but he speaks from a position of humility, of someone who is ultimately *unable* to convey the beauty of the Egyptian sinner because she is too much. While those poets who sing the glories of the Virgin imagine themselves as participants in her corporeal plenitude and integrity, the poet of *VSME* composes compensatory verses that result in digressions and, as we shall see, in yet another excessive portrait when he turns his attention to the body of the penitent.

BEYOND ICONOCLASTIC READINGS

It would be tempting to see in the description of Mary's penitent body a transformation of Mary from idol of concupiscence to symbol of repentance. Her body, now almost reduced to the proverbial dust, no longer points to itself but seems to give witness to the creaturely truth that, in the end, all is vanity and that true beauty is to be found in the love of God. The poem, however, undermines such a neat transformation in its exuberant and loving celebration of Mary's penitent body and acts of asceticism.

The second description of Mary's body is remarkable because it does not simply offer a new and more truthful vision of Mary, her degraded outside and beautiful inside the inversion of the first and dangerous image of profane external beauty and internal moral corruption. In fact, the poem does not even offer to its audience the discrete portrait of a single sitter. Rather than simply list Mary's features transformed by time and penitence, the poet recalls her alluring attributes in their former glory before describing them in their present state of decay, giving the audience two portraits instead of just one. Thus, her gleaming white ears, once compared to lamb's milk, are now black and oily, and her previously lily-white complexion is now sunburned and wrinkled:

> Her appearance had changed completely.
> She had neither clothes nor vesture.
> She lost weight and her color,
> which had been white as a flower.
> Her hair which had been blond
> Turned white and grimy.
> Her ears which were white
> Became very black like tar. (138)[34]

Scholars often understand the recollection of the first description of Mary's body in a context that underscores its transformation into what Podol termed an "anti-portrait," that is to say, the depiction of an unappealing woman, in iconoclastic terms.[35] Mary's beauty is presented again to the audience in order to produce a righteous satisfaction in its destruction, a demise that ultimately makes possible her spiritual growth. E. Ernesto Delgado argues, for example, that the detailed description of the penitent's body represents a clear manifestation of its essential corruption. For this critic,

Mary's holiness can only be visible when her body has suffered a progressive "auto-destruction."[36] Focusing on the description of penitent Mary, Connie Scarborough suggests that "the utter lack of luminosity of Mary's physical features [in the second portrait, in contrast to the first] would have struck the poem's audience as a deliberate attempt to destroy utterly the previous description of her."[37] For his part, Julian Weiss focuses on the response from both Mary's male admirers and the poem's male audience. Weiss follows Simon Gaunt's reading of the French version of the legend where "the men reading this text can enjoy both the titillating spectacle of the adventures of the comely and sexy harlot, and then the physical degradation of that very same body as it is punished, largely for the desire it aroused in them."[38] Taking that analysis a step further, Weiss writes, "[the] 'double pleasure' in watching both the operations of female libido and its degrading consequences [. . .] can be developed by resituating the portrait of physical degradation back into its full narrative context. This makes it plain that Mary's body, even after it has become shriveled, sunburnt, and emaciated, remains an object of a highly ambivalent male awe and desire."[39]

While working from different perspectives, all these interpretations fall in line with what I call iconoclastic readings of hagiography. The false idol of Mary's beauty must be destroyed in order to replace it with the chaste symbol of her repentance and the proper beauty of the poem and its message of penitence and asceticism. And yet, the signs of artistic prowess, of the poet's pride in displaying his rhetorical skill to create images both beautiful and repulsive, emerge in the sheer excess of two portraits where the audience expected just one. Recognizing this excess allows for an alternative to iconoclastic readings: the poet's knowing display of the power of words to move and arouse wonder and desire identifies the poet with Mary, rather than with her suitors or even with Zozimas, for that matter. In other words, while the poet acknowledges feminine beauty and rhetorical artifice as potentially dangerous on account of the precariously thin line that separates seduction (Mary's loveliness) from persuasion (the task of the hagiographer-poet), the poem does not disavow them—not even when the subject turns to ascetic ground.

First, the second portrait (of Mary's penitent body) is slightly longer than the portrait of Mary in Alexandria and of her clothing combined, suggesting that rhetorically there is as much skill, if not delight, in the representation of ugliness as of beauty.[40] More importantly, Mary's metamorphosis does not necessarily imply an opposition between body and soul, external appearance and internal substance. Patricia Cox Miller's study of the conceptual paradox of "holy women" in early Christian hagiography points out how even the seventh-century depiction of Mary of Egypt combined masculine and feminine elements into what she calls the grotesquerie of the harlot-saint. Mary of Egypt's penitent body combines "in the very same sentence" features that recall the Christ of the Apocalypse whose hair was white as wool, while at the same time "she is also cast as the 'black but comely' bride of the Song of Songs 1:5–6, with her 'body black as if scorched by the fierce heat of the sun.'"[41] These same grotesque features of white hair, burned black body may be found in the description in *VSME* (lines 954–59; 138).[42] Mary emerges thus as the very embodiment of paradox, of holding two opposing beliefs at the same time.

A second important detail that reveals how the poem does not neatly fit an iconoclastic reading has to do with the power of memory. One of the demonic temptations Mary suffered early during her stay in the desert is the remembrance of pleasures past:

> The devil tried to tempt her
> And to remind her of all
> That she used to love:
> The big dinners and good beds
> Where she used to commit her sins.
> But she was fortunate
> That she had forgotten it all.
> All her life long
> She did not remember her sin. (140)[43]

Mary's previous inability or unwillingness to remember her own mortality, which had once been responsible for her dissoluteness, is now a blessed forgetfulness that allows her to wander the desert unaffected by the devil's temptations.[44] Although in this the poet follows his French source, the detail stands in contrast with other versions of the legend, such as Hildebert of Lavardin's early twelfth-century Latin poem. The ninth canto consists of Mary's confession to Zozimas, and after accounting for the loss of her clothing and beauty to age and the ravages of the elements, she elaborates on her transformation:

> I exchanged hymns for jests,
> I purged loud
> laughter by sorrow,
> Punishment atoned for pleasure, thirst for drunkenness,

Poverty for luxury, toil for leisure, juice for honeyed-wine,
Torture for a soft couch, holy devotion for guilt.[45]

Instead of the torture, punishment, and purgation described by Lavardin's
Mary as the rightful corrective to her morally lax past, the poet of *VSME*
states in a surprising couplet not found in any French versions that "it is not
to lament her sin / Of the body that she goes about so afflicted" (140).[46] Within
the logic of the poem, Mary's suffering body is decidedly *not* the punishment
dictated by poetic justice for her "sin of the body" (*pecado del cuerpo*).

In fact, a few lines later when the poet describes the routine of the holy
men of the monastery of Saint John, the details of their penitence echo
Mary's. She survives on loaves of bread initially so hard that they resemble
stones (line 763; 139), while the monks "ate barley bread and no other / For
certain they added no salt" (141).[47] She slept on the ground with no other
covering than what a tree could provide (line 695; 137), while the monks
"were not found on beds or cots" (140).[48] Finally, and perhaps most startling
is the monks' reenactment of Mary's joyful treading on thorns: "When a
thorn wounded her, / One of her sins was expiated / And she was very glad /
to suffer such a hard thing" (139).[49] The reader is also told that the monks go
barefoot "to be cleansed of their sins" (141).[50] Although each act of penitence
is consistent with conventional descriptions of asceticism, the careful set up
of this network of correspondences becomes significant. On the one hand,
it prepares the ground for the competitive humility that will characterize the
encounter between Zozimas and Mary later in the poem. On the other, it
provides an answer to why Mary would pursue the path of asceticism when
her sins have not only been forgiven but, as we saw, also forgotten (lines
781–89; 140). In this poem, deprivation and suffering are the currency of
love or, as the poem describes the monks' ascetic regime: "They did so for
the love of God" (141).[51] Suffering is not necessarily equated with degrading
punishment. Mary's wrinkles and her withered body emerge then as more
than just signs of punitive destruction, they point to living and to loving
and, I would argue, to a kind of beauty capable of encompassing suffering.

INCARNATIONAL TRIPTYCH

This chapter shows that finding a rightful place for beauty in ascetic, didactic texts is a central preoccupation in the early thirteenth-century Spanish

rhymed version of the life of Mary the Egyptian. I have argued that the poet of *VSME* is well aware of the traditional associations of the female body with eloquence, beauty, and artifice, as well as with manifestations of lust, pride, and idolatry. Nonetheless, he forges an alternative to what I name the iconoclastic tendencies of hagiography that interpret the surface (bodies and literal meanings) as irrelevant or contrary to spiritual depths. To the fear and distrust of rhetorical prowess, beauty, artifice, and the body, the poem offers the paradox of the incarnation as a model for accepting human imperfection and embracing creatureliness, including the creaturely in language.

This spirit of humility and love unites Mary's, albeit extreme, physical degradation and the ascetic practices of the monks of Zozimas's order. Mary's abject image then, rather than representing the destruction of illicit beauty and the toppling of a dangerous idol, indicates its acceptance. This equivalence is not to say, however, that both portraits are somehow "the same." They are not. But neither are they wholly the reverse image of each other, "as in a photographic negative" that Robertson imagines, nor do they hang as the opposing yet interrelated panels—the "before" and "after" images of a diptych—as Delgado and Weiss argue.[52] I suggest a more nuanced understanding of the relationship of the two portraits emerges by creating a triptych out of the poem's diptych. This central third panel features the pivotal scene in the poem where the Egyptian encounters an image of the Virgin Mary in the narthex of the Church of the Holy Sepulchre. Here, too, the centrality of the mystery of the incarnation to Mary of Egypt's lyrical prayer to the Virgin, allows for a recuperation of beauty and sensuality.

Mary's conversion occurs when, once in Jerusalem, she follows the crowd filing into the church, but she is supernaturally denied entrance by forces invisible to others, described as angelic sword-yielding knights (lines 446–53; 130). Iconographically, the image of the fierce great knights holding swords to protect an entrance harks back to illustrations of the expulsion of Adam and Eve from Paradise, a transgression brought about by deceitful eloquence and linked to shameful sexuality. The movement of Mary's life up to this point had always been forward, away from her family, away from Egypt, always in search of new experiences, but the vision of the angels immune to her charms forces her to turn back for the first time in her life. This shock makes possible a self-reflection that is both cognitive and affective: "Then she began to ponder / And to cry from her heart" (130).[53]

As I have shown, the poem presents Mary as an object of vision, be it as the object of the gaze of the poet and his audience, or, within the text, of the young men that fall in love with her. The external vision of divine retribution, the apparition of the knightly angels, prompts in Mary an internal vision of herself mediated, significantly, by the external image of the Virgin Mary. This new image makes visible to Egyptian Mary all that she is not but could yet become through grace. She exclaims, "You and I share a name, / But you are very different from me. / You are Mary and I am Mary / But the two of us have not the same life" (132).[54] Wandering Mary finds salvation in what should be a logical contradiction, that is to say, in the claim that she is both like *and* unlike the Virgin Mary.

It is easy to see how the two Marys differ. In the words of the Egyptian, "You always loved chastity, / And I, lust and evil. [. . .] / You are a most humble lady, / I am poor and haughty / and lustful in my body" (133).[55] And yet, as Matthew's Gospel makes apparent, Joseph initially understood the incarnation of Christ through Mary as adultery.[56] Biblical exegesis and popular tradition saw Mary's virtue crystallized in her willingness to accept the shame of an adulterous reputation, while Joseph, described in Matthew as a just man, "received the title of cuckold as a blessing."[57] Of course, the taint of sexual defilement in the case of the Holy Mother (punishable by stoning according to Deuteronomic law) was, from the limited human perspective, a misapprehension cleared up by an angel who will bid Joseph not to repudiate his chaste-but-pregnant wife. Nonetheless, Mary of Egypt addresses herself to the Virgin as the figure of God's chosen lover, and it is on the basis of that unmerited and extravagant love—a love that is as much physical as spiritual—that she asks for mercy: "Our Lord loved you, / And since he loved you, / Lady, have pity on me. [. . .] / In you the King of Heaven took flesh" (133).[58]

The similarities between virginal Mary and the sinful Egyptian are not only figurative but also physical. In the portrait of Mary of Egypt before conversion, the poet describes her as well proportioned: "Her figure was well proportioned; / She was neither fat nor very thin. / She was not tall or short, / but just the right height" (124).[59] Manuel Alvar, editor of *VSME*, glosses *tajada* as modeled according to specific measures or canons, as in sculpture. Outside the temple, after being refused entry, Mary turns her head and sees an image of the Virgin: "She saw an image of holy Mary. / The image was well fashioned / And crafted in good proportion" (131).[60] While the ideal of a canonical, well-proportioned figure may be a commonplace in the description of a feminine body, in the context of a poem so aware of the importance of images, it is not accidental that the poem uses similar formulations to describe both the idol (Mary in Alexandria) and the icon (Virgin Mary), stressing in both cases their significance as the handiwork of a loving creator. Indeed, the heavenly hand that crafted both female figures appears once more in the poem to write on the ground the inscription around Mary's corpse at the end of her life that gives monk Zozimas the instruction to bury her: "He saw some letters written on the ground. / They were very clear and well crafted / Because they were formed in heaven" (157).[61] But there is more. Rooted in the Latin *taliare*, to cut, *tajado*—which Kasten and Cody's dictionary of medieval Spanish defines as "carved (as in stone)"—the description of both Marys as *tajadas* recalls the pattern on Mary of Egypt's shoes, "de cordobán *entretalladas*" (line 242).[62] A continuum is thus suggested from heavenly crafted words and bodies down to their worldly counterparts.

As these examples show, paradox is the central device of the Egyptian's prayer to the icon of the Virgin Mary. On the one hand, paradox describes Mary of Egypt's own relationship to Christ's mother (both similar and different), and, on the other, paradox defines the Virgin's role in the incarnation. Mary begins her prayer thus: "O Lady, sweet mother, / Who in your womb carried your father" (131).[63] A few lines later, she repeats, "I believe, by my faith, / That God was in your giving birth. / From you he took his humanity, / But you did not lose your virginity. / It was a great miracle: The Father / Made his daughter his mother" (132).[64] Using more flowery language, she describes the incarnation thus, "That from the thorn budded the rose; / And from the rose blossomed the fruit / By which the whole world was saved" (132).[65]

The rose that springs from the thorn is clearly the Virgin Mary who will in turn give birth to the saving fruit that will atone for original sin, but the Egyptian's conversion also rises as an unexpected rose from the thorns of her previously sinful life. Writing about the Old French poem, Duncan Robertson notes that "what Mary of Egypt calls upon in the name of the Virgin is not merely a person but an incarnate formal principle, the universal reconciliation of contraries—nothing more and nothing less than poetry itself."[66] I add: the reason the Virgin can function as an incarnation of poetry is that she was the vehicle that made possible the incarnation of Christ, which rather than dissolve oppositions such as human/divine, body/spirit, sign/thing, embodies them. Mary of Egypt recognizes this generous logic, and she appeals to the Virgin in her prayer, recognizing herself also as a living paradox of divine love.

NEITHER VENUS NOR VENERABLE OLD MEN

> Beauty is really as obvious as blue: one does not have to work at seeing it when it is there.
>
> ARTHUR DANTO, *The Abuse of Beauty*[1]

THERE IS NO BEAUTY WITHOUT AN appeal to the senses. But does this make beauty immediately apparent? Is beauty pornographically recognized upon seeing it, available directly to any and all, ultimately "really as obvious as blue"? Does it purvey the sort of attractiveness "with a power of pleasing quickly and without much thought or effort," an expectation on the part of viewers accustomed to traditional art experiences that Arthur Danto lamented interfered with the appreciation of twentieth-century art?[2]

I paraphrase above, with modest polemical intent, Supreme Court Justice Potter Stewart's notorious declaration in 1964 that while the defining characteristics of pornography are difficult to pin down, there exists a consensus that makes the declaration "I know it when I see it" meaningful and valid. Danto's much-quoted blunt assertion about the immediacy of beauty masks a more subtle understanding, yet it shares Justice Stewart's conviction that beholders will ultimately come to a consensus. In contrast, the particular beauty of Jusepe de Ribera's portraits of Saint Mary of Egypt is far from being transparent and easy to agree upon. Whereas in chapter 1 we explored the connection between temporality and the inherent invisibility of holiness, in this chapter I argue that untimeliness—stepping outside of straight chronological time—is a feature of the paradoxical characteristics

NEITHER VENUS NOR VENERABLE OLD MEN

and temporalities of the grotesque, that is to say, of a beauty that is perceptible just on the horizon, a beauty that remains a promise, so to speak.

"Beauty is only the promise of happiness," Stendhal (1783–1842) mused in a famous footnote in a chapter from the essayistic *De l'amour* (1822). The aphorism appears in the context of a vignette that purports to describe "beauty dethroned by love," as the chapter title puts it.[3] However, a closer look at the anecdote and its footnote reveals that it is not love that occupies the throne that beauty held; rather, it is time that conquers all. The story is simple: Stendhal describes the case of a young man who finds himself so attracted to a woman whose face suffers the marks of smallpox that he proves immune to the charms of a flawless woman he encounters one evening at the theater. How is this possible? Importantly, it is not that love makes him blind to the beloved's flaws. On the contrary, Stendhal seeks to explore how beauty arises directly *from* the imperfection not in spite of it. The novelist is interested in the likelihood of the scars breaking the lover's scansion of the beloved's face; he imagines scars as the punctuation on her countenance, turning the otherwise blank canvas of beauty into a legible mark. The beholder must pause; the interruption slows perception down and allows him to be filled with wonder, so that in the end the lover comes to experience "a thousand sentiments in presence of that small-pox mark, sentiments for the most part sweet, and all of them of greatest interest."[4] The pattern of break/repetition that works the miracle of turning ugliness into beauty is itself repeated when Stendhal recounts how three years after the ugly lover died the young man came to befriend two ladies, one beautiful, the other too thin and pockmarked. He is cognizant of the ugliness of the one, and yet, Stendhal writes, "I see him love [her] at the end of eight days which he has spent erasing her ugliness with his memories."[5] The revelation of the beauty of ugliness is subject to time, a nest of experience where love may hatch.

But there is more. The sentences that follow the quotable aphorism rarely get attention, but the comparison Stendhal dares his readers to make is relevant for understanding the sort of beauty that concerns this chapter:

> Beauty is only the *promise* of happiness. The happiness of a Greek was different to that of a Frenchman of 1822. See the eyes of the Medici Venus and compare them with the eyes of the Magdalene of Pordenone (in the possession of M. de Sommariva).[6]

Taken in its entirety—as content, as typographical convention, and as metaphor—the famous footnote emerges as a scar on discourses about beauty in so far as it forces us to confront the continuities, disruptions, and contradictions that undergird three sets of transformations. First, we have the discursive and conceptual transition from women's bodies (the subject of the main text) to works of art (the comparison in the footnote). Second, the male lover's gaze looking at a real woman gives way to the eyes of chiseled female figures—the Venus and the Magdalene—that are recognizable as both desirable and desiring female subjects and objects of art. Finally, the very juxtaposition of the goddess of Love and a Christian holy harlot blurs the outlines that distinguish the categories of pagan/Christian and secular/religious. Rather than attempt to smooth away the coarseness of the stitches that bring these terms together, this chapter studies their texture as they emerge in Ribera's representations of Saint Mary of Egypt. This chapter shows, in particular, that Ribera best gives shape to an aspect that is latent in other manifestations of the legend: Mary of Egypt embodies a new type of beauty, neither Venus-like in seductive voluptuousness nor venerably holy and masculinized.

A different Stendhal than the writer who exalted love (and time) as the balm that could turn ugliness into beauty will introduce the sort of beauty and holiness that Mary of Egypt embodies. This Stendhal stood in the galleries of the newly established Musée Fabre in Montpellier, contemplating a Ribera portrait of the Egyptian saint (figure 8). The three-quarter length representation of a penitent Mary, her athletically ascetic body front and center of the canvas, faces the viewer in an almost defiant way, daring them to turn their gaze away. The French writer clearly would not avert his eyes and meets the challenge with an equally direct judgment as recorded in his travel journal: "Horrible old woman; all the more horrible since we can see that she has been beautiful."[7] The writer's acute awareness of the untimeliness of beauty—that one can see the past in the present—allows us to pose the central question of this chapter: does the depiction of the consequences of time and penitence on Mary's aged body result in unintelligible deformity, or does it embody the possibility of the grotesque to emerge as a form of beauty just on the horizon?

DECORUM, OR IS THERE A SAINT IN THIS FRAME?

Not one to follow neoclassical rules blindly, Stendhal's judgment of Ribera's portrait of Saint Mary of Egypt nonetheless depends on a theory of decorum

FIGURE 8. Jusepe de Ribera, *Saint Mary of Egypt* (1641). Oil on canvas. Musée Fabre, Montpellier, France. Source: Courtesy of Oeuvre du Musée Fabre.

to make sense. As Kathy Eden's *Hermeneutics and the Rhetorical Tradition* traces it, the notion of decorum dates back to antiquity and to a rhetorical understanding of what is a proper manner of representation, that is to say, acceptable according to convention but also to what is fitting in its attentiveness to context.[8] Broadly, Stendhal was horrified by Ribera's painting in part because the image did not conform to the expectations of how art should depict an old woman, much less a saint. Leonardo da Vinci crystallizes the contradiction of having the same body represent "old woman" and "saintly" in a telling image when he recommends that old women "should be depicted as bold and alert, with furious movements, like hellish furies and the movements of their arms and head should appear livelier than those of their legs."[9] No room for sainthood there. In the following section, the Renaissance master recommended that women, in general, should be depicted modestly in a way that makes their bodies take up as little visual space as possible (legs closed, arms folded, head tilted downward and to one side); Ribera's Montpellier canvas does quite the opposite. Mary's head is high, her face and gaze tilted upward, and while her arms come in front of her chest, hands in prayer pose, the V-shape that her left arm makes highlights her exposed breast, whose smoothness contrasts with the wrinkled skin of her hands. This is not a decorous woman, old or young, but is she a saint?

To answer that question, let us first consider the words dedicated to the topic of decorum in the course of the Council of Trent and then the different local ways in which clergy and artists interpreted the short decree on the utility of images. In chapter 1 we saw how a central tenet from the eighth-century Council of Nicaea still held sway at Trent: for images to find their proper place in a religious context, they must be instructive and move to virtue. The importance of decorum follows from this pedagogical imperative. After all, an image will fail to teach, appeal to emotion, and persuade if viewers cannot clearly recognize what it represents:

> Moreover, in the invocation of saints, the veneration of relics, and the sacred use of images, every superstition shall be removed, all filthy lucre be abolished; finally, all lasciviousness be avoided; in such wise that figures shall not be painted or adorned with a beauty exciting to lust; nor the celebration of the saints, and the visitation of relics be by any perverted into revellings and drunkenness; as if festivals are celebrated to the honour of the saints by luxury and wantonness.
>
> *In fine*, let so great care and diligence be used herein by bishops, as that there be nothing seen that is disorderly, or that is unbecomingly or confusedly arranged, nothing that is profane, nothing indecorous, seeing that holiness becometh the house of God.[10]

To put it simply, what is at stake in the creation of religious images is their legibility: saints and their stories should be recognized easily and painted in such a way that they represent their subject matter accurately and in a dignified manner. Faithfulness to the truth of scripture defines accuracy in this context and thus discourages the representation of apocryphal stories. In the case of postbiblical representations, such as those drawn from *The Golden Legend* or those that depicted local, recently canonized saints, preceptists promoted adherence to a verisimilar principle by which saints and biblical characters should not appear dressed in modern garments and care should be taken to avoid dressing female saints in ostentatious apparel.

Alfonso Rodríguez G. de Ceballos's introduction to *Sacred Spain* details the importance of decorum in the wake of attacks on religious images by various Protestant thinkers, and he concludes that "lack of decorum was understood to be the tendency to mix the religious and the profane, such as covering sacred images in modern dress, jewelry, and all manner of adornments, thereby reducing respect for them and confusing them with secular portraits."[11] He notes in particular that the representation of female saints and the Virgin often received meticulous treatment in many diocesan synods and in various treatises, such as the 1654 Synod of Salamanca, which specified that the head of Our Lady "is not [to be] adorned profanely with curls or other hair embellishments . . . but is [to be] covered by her wimple, with all possible decency and reverence."[12] Elsewhere, and more explicitly, Father Bernardino de Villegas (1592–1653), a Jesuit preacher, complained that the finely decked out images of female saints and the Virgin contributed to the pursuit of frivolities by the female faithful, who would seek to imitate the finery they saw portrayed rather than follow the holy example of the saintly model.[13] Moreover, sartorial imitation had the potential to go both ways. Art historians have examined, for example, the polemics over the use of sumptuous clothing borrowed from the laity to dress religious statues for processional purposes. Palma Martínez-Burgos García notes that the apprehension over this clothes swap was not so much on account of modesty and humility, such as we find in the criticism launched against clergy wearing luxurious robes. Instead, at stake when it came to clothing the holy statues was an attempt to carve out clear distinctions between sacred and profane realms and avoid any "excessive familiarity" that would blur those boundaries.[14]

We can see then that the question of whether there is a saint in Ribera's multiple portraits of Mary of Egypt is not just a modern question but would have been asked by patrons, artists, and viewers of his own time. In fact, the question gets to the heart of a long-standing anxiety surrounding the representation of sacred matter in general, which increases when coupled with female beauty. An old exemplum going back at least to the eighth century tells of a sculptor who makes two statues perfectly identical except for the label: one reads "Venus" and the other "Virgin Mary." Which one should the believer adore? A similar concern echoes in Erasmus's *Opus orandi Deum* (ca. 1524), where he defends the use of images in churches, if "nothing be in evidence but that which is worthy of Christ."[15] However, even that low standard seems hard to meet. The humanist, who counted Albrecht Dürer among his friends, nonetheless laments that "the saints are not depicted in a form which is worthy of them—as when a painter, commissioned to portray the Virgin Mary or St. Agatha, occasionally patterns his figure after a lascivious little whore, or when he, commissioned to portray Christ or St. Paul, takes as his model some drunken rascal."[16]

Even more troubling, and closer to the medieval Venus-Mary problem of the medieval exemplum quoted above, was the common practice of the pictorial translation of pagan models into Christian images. Dürer approvingly refers to the analogy of Venus to the Virgin writing that "just as they [artists from antiquity] employed Venus as the most beautiful woman, so will we chastely present the same lovely figure as the most pure Virgin, mother of God."[17] With significantly less alacrity Erasmus condemns the practice in the *Dialogus Ciceronianus*. He wonders, "What if someone today were to render the Virgin Mary in the same manner as Apelles had painted the Venus Anadyomede [Venus, rising from the sea, as in Botticelli's famous *Birth of Venus*], celebrated by all writers, or St. Thecla in the form in which he had painted Laïs [a famous Roman courtesan]? Would you say that such painter was similar to Apelles? I don't think so."[18]

In Spain, the Jesuit preacher Bernardino de Villegas, partisan of asceticism, would also advise against excessively luxurious representations of female saints. He makes his case by positing an innocent viewer who could be drawn astray by the lavishness of the saint's clothing:

> What more indecent thing than an image of Our Lady in a long gown with a train, *copete*, Walloon collar, ruff, choker, and similar things—and virgins dressed so profanely and with so many jewels and finery, worn only by the most splendid ladies in the world! So much so that sometimes one doubts whether to adore Saint Lucy or Saint Catherine or to avert one's gaze in order to avoid seeing the extravagant profanity of their attire because in their clothes and accoutrements they do not seem to be heavenly saints but rather worldly ladies, and if Saint Catherine does not hold her sword in her hand and Saint Lucy her eyes on a platter, from the dress and fancy clothing they are depicted wearing, no one would be able to tell that they were the saints or the modest virgins that they were.[19]

The conventional identifying attributes of each saint save the innocent viewer from foolishly mistaking the image of a saint for a beautiful lady of the world as we saw was the case with the Ribera portrait of Saint Mary of Egypt now in Naples (figure 2), where the three loaves of bread allude to the miraculous way she survived for years on meager fare. Yet, given the inflation of the civic, political, and economic value of holiness in the sixteenth and seventeenth centuries, the proper valuation of saintliness, inside and outside the frame, would still have been an issue worthy of debate.

PENITENCE AND THE PROLIFERATION OF PAINTED SAINTS

If asceticism, mysticism, and other forms of experiencing holiness proliferated in the sixteenth century, the same could be said about the representation of saints, especially penitent saints. As Alain Saint-Saëns, historian of the early modern period, puts it, "rare were the painters of the period who failed to depict the penitent Magdalene."[20] The Council of Trent's reaffirmation of the importance of the sacraments, especially penance and the Eucharist, partly explains the surge of what Palma Martínez-Burgos García calls "a veritable inflation of penitent saints," but the image of the penitent saint touched a cultural nerve that went beyond the details of Tridentine sacramental ideology.[21] The narrative arc from sinfulness to repentance and redemption of many saints' lives resonated not only with literary characters like the popular theatrical figure of the repentant bandit but also with the lived experience of the authors and the audience.[22] Significantly, the life and works of the notable and notorious playwright Lope de Vega oscillated between erotic dalliance and religious fervor. What's more, the attractiveness of the narrative of sinfulness followed by repentance and salvation coincided with a rising popularity of spiritual manuals that recommended sustained meditation on Christ's Passion and one's own death thus increasing the desirability of penitential life.[23] Together these factors resulted in a new iconographic trend that stressed the penitential episodes in the lives of saints such as Jerome and Mary Magdalene and even turned many saints who previously had not figured obviously among the ranks of repentant desert dwellers into ascetic penitents.[24] In the case of Jerome, for example, art historians identify a shift from early Renaissance representations of the church father as a proto-humanist surrounded by books in his study to baroque images of a penitent in the wilderness, often depicted striking his naked breast with a rock in order to atone for his sins. Similarly, the Magdalene—always a popular figure in the history of Christian art—also underwent a pictorial transformation. Before the Counter-Reformation's focus on penitence, she appeared primarily in scenes that placed her in relationship to Christ (washing his feet, witnessing the Crucifixion, at Christ's empty tomb, etc.); after Trent, scenes of her renunciation of sinfulness and penitence in the French wilderness proliferate.[25]

The high esteem for the motif of eremitic saints meant that lay and ecclesiastic patrons often commissioned these images as part of a series. Among the most impressive is the set of thirty-five anchorite paintings by an unknown Dutch artist for the Convent of the Descalzas Reales in Madrid, one of the richest in Europe when it was established in the sixteenth century by Philip II's sister, Juana of Austria. According to Ana García Sanz, curator of the royal convent, and historian Juan Martínez Cuesta, the decoration of the Descalzas Reales had initially consisted of dramatic episodes from the life of Christ or the Virgin Mary, but these eventually gave way to a series of meditational landscapes with eremitic saints, among whom Mary of Egypt is the only female. The painting focuses on the end of the saint's story, depicting her receiving communion from the hand of monk Zozimas in the foreground, while in the background he buries the saint aided by a lion.[26]

The saintly gathering was not limited to convents or churches. The cycle of hermit saints at the Descalzas Reales was likely inspired by the drawings of eremitic figures by Maerten de Vos (1532–1603), which circulated widely throughout Europe in volumes of engravings of his work produced by Jan and Rafael Sadeler.[27] In Milan, Archbishop Federico Borromeo, author of the treatise *De pictura sacra* (1624), owned several volumes of the Sadeler collections of de Vos's prints, which inspired him to commission a series of anchorite paintings from Jan Brueghel and Paul Bril. These images later hung at the Ambrosiana Library and Gallery, which the cardinal established. Their purpose was to incite viewers—theologians, scholars, and other artists—to create an internal spiritual landscape through meditation.[28] Similarly, Tintoretto flanked the altar of the first floor of the Scuola Grande di San Rocco in Venice (1582–87) with large twin landscape paintings. On one side Mary of Egypt, still sumptuously dressed already carrying a book hinting at the meditative work ahead of her, stands at the edge of the Jordan river, and on the other wall a reclining Mary Magdalene already reads a book.[29]

Back in Spain, a 1658 inventory of the property belonging to Don Jerónimo de la Torre, a high officer in Flanders, reveals that he owned no less than eight paintings of desert saints by Jusepe de Ribera. The number alone is not surprising. In a monograph on the work of Ribera, Javier Portús notes the predominance of religious themes in his oeuvre (300 out of the 364 paintings attributed to the Valencian artist concern religious topics), and many of these works, especially portraits of saints, were meant for private

FIGURE 9. Jusepe de Ribera, *Saint John the Baptist in the Desert* (1641). Oil on canvas. Museo Nacional del Prado, Madrid, Spain. Photograph from Alfonso E. Pérez Sánchez and Nicola Spinosa, *Ribera, 1591–1652* (Madrid: Museo del Prado, 1992), 356.

collections.[30] What does stand out in de la Torre's collection is that of those eight portraits, three were of female saints: Saints Mary Magdalene, Mary of Egypt, and Agnes. The others included Paul the Hermit, John the Baptist in the desert, Bartholomew, Sebastian, and Onophrius. The series of eight was dispersed in the eighteenth century, and only four remained together, owned by the Museo Nacional del Prado in Spain.[31] These four depict a youthful John the Baptist (figure 9), an elderly masculine saint possibly identified as Bartholomew (figure 10), a beautiful contemplative Mary Magdalene (figure 11), and an aging Mary of Egypt (figure 12) sitting on a rock also caught in in mid-prayer. Each of the four canvases depicts its protagonist in isolation and mid-ground; the landscape is craggy with meditation-inducing caves, unimposing trees, and imposing skies in the background. Writing about these paintings, Javier Portús highlights the monumentality

FIGURE 10. Jusepe de Ribera, *Saint Bartholomew* (1641). Oil on canvas. Museo Nacional del Prado, Madrid, Spain. Photograph from Alfonso E. Pérez Sánchez and Nicola Spinosa, *Ribera, 1591–1652* (Madrid: Museo del Prado, 1992), 358.

of each portrait and of the series taken in at once, where the painter displays his virtuosity in depicting "a variety of anatomies and ages" all with the same devotional and emotional power.[32]

Ribera's cycle of saints nicely represents many of the artistic trends mentioned above. It inducts Saint Bartholomew among the ranks of the ascetics, even though he is normally not associated with contemplation or penitence.[33] His pose—body facing the viewer, enveloped by a flowing grayish cloth, and sitting on a diagonal with one leg extended in front of him—visually inverts that of his younger counterpart, an almost adolescent John the Baptist. The baptist's shepherd's staff in his raised left hand echoes Bartholomew's knife, thus strengthening the connection between old and young male saints, but it also calls to mind Mary of Egypt's pose, sitting with legs a bit askew, one leg in front of the other. Mary Magdalene is not part of

FIGURE 11. Jusepe de Ribera, *Penitent Magdalene* (1641). Oil on canvas. Museo Nacional del Prado, Madrid, Spain. Photograph from Alfonso E. Pérez Sánchez and Nicola Spinosa, *Ribera, 1591–1652* (Madrid: Museo del Prado, 1992), 355.

this positional repetition-with-a-difference since she is clearly on her knees, but the red of her cloak echoes the younger male saint's—a color sanctioned by Francisco Pacheco in his *Arte de la pintura* who associated it with future martyrdom—and she holds her hands in prayer the same way as her older female counterpart. Taken together, all four portraits create the visual equivalent of a corona sonnet cycle where repetitions move a story forward, give

FIGURE 12. Jusepe de Ribera, *Saint Mary of Egypt* (1641). Oil on canvas. Museo Nacional del Prado, Madrid, Spain. Photograph from Alfonso E. Pérez Sánchez and Nicola Spinosa, *Ribera, 1591–1652* (Madrid: Museo del Prado, 1992), 359.

it greater depth, playing off differences and similarities in age and gender. Moreover, in creating a tight iconic system of visual cross-references across couplings, Ribera also calls attention to the bold pairing of male and female saints on equal footing, a remarkable choice. As we shall see, "female" and "sanctity" were not concepts that always found their way together.

PENITENCE, THE GROTESQUE, AND THE QUESTION OF FEMININE HOLINESS

The representation of penitent saints, as we have just seen, was all the rage in Catholic countries after Trent. This coincided with a rising number of women professing their faith in unorthodox ways as mystics or anchoresses. According to Alain Saint-Saëns's estimate, of approximately eight thousand people living as hermits in various shrines and caves in the Iberian Peninsula at the beginning of the sixteenth century, one in nine were women.[34] These high numbers troubled authorities who found reason to return to the question of the proper role women should play in Christianity in general and, more precisely, to reconsider the ways in which female bodies could align with holiness. Although the Council of Trent's support and preference of conventual life for women religious (as opposed to following an uncloistered spiritual life) was unambiguous, it did not always mean that royal and ecclesiastic authorities worked actively to suppress untraditional practices. It did contribute, however, to a general waning of support and respect of freelance hermits, unattached to any particular recognized order, in favor of a new model of sanctity largely based on obedience, communal living, and enclosure for women.[35] And while the public sometimes regarded both male and female hermits with skepticism, Saint-Saëns has shown that hermitesses (*ermitañas* or *santeras*, local shrine keepers) faced prejudice twice over: first as "theoretically holy but in fact ever suspicious [qua] hermits" and second as undeniable daughters of Eve.[36] This double affliction resulted in particularly aggressive derision from villagers, parish priests, and satirical writers who charged *ermitañas* with promiscuity, vanity and pride, drunkenness, and hypocrisy—vices, not surprisingly, associated in misogynist literature particularly with femininity.

One way for female religious to express their devotion without opprobrium was to disguise their femininity in favor of a neutral maleness that would grant them an exception.[37] That was the case, for example, of the cross-dressing eremitism of Catalina de Cardona (1519–77), a historical figure initially admired by Teresa of Ávila. Cardona was born into a prominent Catalan family as the illegitimate daughter of Don Ramón de Cardona, general of the Spanish troops in Naples. She was cherished as a mother figure by Don Juan de Austria, Philip II's illegitimate half-brother, and she served as governess to the king's son Don Carlos and to Rui-Gómez de Silva, Prince of Eboli. In 1562, aided by Father Piña, himself a hermit attached to the royal palace, she procured herself the rough, brown cloth of a hermit and had her hair shorn in preparation for living in a cave in what is today the province of Castile–La Mancha. In the version of her life told to Italian friar and painter Juan de la Miseria, she specifies that her cloak should be cut "in the manner of Saint Francis of Paula's," referring to an Italian hermit and founder of the Order of the Minims in Calabria, canonized in 1519, thus establishing her wish to enter a lineage of holy *men*.[38] Cardona lived an ascetic life in La Roda until she established her own monastery in honor of Our Lady of Perpetual Help. And yet, for all her male identification, Cardona allows one female figure as model, even if only implicitly: Saint Mary of Egypt.

Juan de la Miseria's manuscript specifies the apprentice anchorite's extreme acts of penitence, which echo almost directly those of the legend of Saint Mary of Egypt. The sustenance of the Egyptian at the beginning of her penitence in the desert consisted of three loaves of bread that miraculously lasted her years. Miseria writes that Cardona survived on three ounces of bread. Once she had finished her loaves, Mary of Egypt survived by grazing on wild herbs. Similarly, Cardona "had, like a lamb, grazed and eaten herbs with her very mouth; herbs she knew to be good to eat."[39] Cardona emulates and surpasses her legendary predecessor, surviving on only three ounces of bread (not three full loaves), and Friar Juan's account also highlights the humility implicit in eating like a lamb. But there is a difference: the tale of Mary of Egypt emphasizes the miraculous energy that the anchoress draws from the herbs she chews, which allow her to roam the mountains; Cardona's ruminations have her grazing, lamb-like, in full trust of what the Lord had provided. Cardona's story highlights *her* humble exemplarity; Mary of Egypt's testifies to the miraculous.

Scholars have studied the example of Catalina de Cardona largely as a foil to one particularly influential female early admirer: the future Saint Teresa of Ávila. Cardona's remarkable story so impressed and inspired Teresa that she speaks admiringly of Cardona in *El libro de las fundaciones* (1573–82). Teresa's attention to Catalina's eremitic calling, however, betrays both admiration and dismay. After all, Teresa was a strong advocate for the strict enclosure of nuns. Her ambivalence was ultimately resolved in a vision where the Lord tells her in no uncertain words: "Do you see all the penance she does? I value your obedience more."[40] Weber concludes that the homage Teresa pays to Catalina in the *Fundaciones* signals the end of an eremitic model of holiness and "contains an implicit warning to her nuns regarding the dangers of 'public' sanctity."[41] That same publicity, or visibility, earned Catalina explicit criticism and contributed to making her a controversial figure.[42] Efrén de la Madre de Dios, a later hagiographer of Teresa of Ávila, was unambiguous in his assessment of Cardona, suggesting that Teresa's initial enthusiasm for the rogue anchoress was not so much genuine admiration as her attempt to be kind. For his part, he did not mince words regarding Catalina, describing her as "a grotesque figure of a female hermit (*grotesca figura de ermitaño femenino)"* —a slight that, as Saint-Saëns remarks, studiously avoids the feminine form *ermitaña*.[43]

In his invective against Catalina Cardona, the male cleric does not simply seek to discredit her discrete qualities (intelligence, piety, authenticity, etc.). Instead, by flinging the adjective "grotesque," Efrén de la Madre de Dios does something more insidious: he repudiates the very concept of feminine holiness. The grotesque in the early modern period encompassed the ridiculous, extravagant, and of bad taste, as it does today, but it was not simply a synonym for "monstrous." The term "monster" was reserved for perceived scientific aberrations in nature such as hermaphrodites, multiple births, and bearded ladies, that is to say, for abnormalities that did exist, that could be *demonstrated*, and therefore called out for interpretation (*monere* in Latin, meaning to warn or counsel). The grotesque, on the other hand, was still deeply tied to the fifteenth-century rediscovery of fantastic decorative paintings of human-animal hybrids found in ancient Roman caves. The category expressed, for better or worse, an element of the unreal, of what did not exist in the world and could only be dreamed by artists. In his influential *Discourse on Sacred and Profane Images*, Cardinal Gabriele Paleotti dedicated several sections to the grotesque, worrying about the pedagogical impact of these unreal images. He wonders, "if art is the imitation of nature, then grotesques fall outside of the bounds of art. If pictures are meant to serve as books for the illiterate, what else will they learn from grotesques than fibs, lies, deceits and things that do not exist?"[44] The cardinal, therefore, did not consider them a legitimate form of art, and certainly, not one acceptable for use in churches.

The grotesque as an aesthetic category encompassing the barely thinkable is, however, useful for thinking about forms of feminine holiness that do not conform to virginal patterns. Strikingly, Patricia Cox Miller, scholar of late antiquity religious traditions, places the seventh-century vitae of Mary of Egypt and Pelagia in the tradition of artistic and philosophical grotesque. Combining Judith Butler's reading of Antigone as an anomalous figure that "remains somewhat unthinkable" with Geoffrey Harpham's theorization of the grotesque as a constitutive contradiction of art, Miller argues that the vitae of the holy harlots bring forth a "not-quite-coherent construct" of figures that are both holy and recognizably feminine (i.e., not spiritually or sartorially masculinized).[45] In the case of Mary the Egyptian, Miller stresses the fact that the narrator never describes her using the praiseful paradoxical phrase "female man of God," but neither are her femininity nor status as a *female* saint ever fully affirmed.[46] Instead, Mary of Egypt as *holy woman* appears in the text as spectral, as the ghost of a possibility.

Against this background, I argue that Ribera's portraits of Mary of Egypt contribute to a further delineation of a specifically female sainthood by grafting it onto another representational impossibility: the grace of the aged feminine body. In contrast to the grotesque animal-human hybrid that Catalina Cardona sought to imitate in deleting the distinction between male and female in a symbolic return to a prelapsarian nature, the image I want to recuperate for the Egyptian anchoress does not shy away from femininity or beauty yet remains, in its untimeliness, still grotesque.

Geoffrey Harpham identifies untimeliness as a defining feature of the grotesque, and he points back to George Santayana as the first to have analyzed the "purgatorial" capacity of grotesque works of art to condemn the viewer to a temporal suspension. For the nineteenth-century philosopher, the grotesque consists of the creative transformation of an ideal type into "a thing which nature has not, but might conceivably have offered."[47] Once produced, the grotesque begs to be considered according to its "inward possibility" rather than in light of the norm whence it has departed.[48] An encounter with the true grotesque (as opposed to the merely jumbled), Santayana argues, will open a window to unease as past categories fail to account for the new object and future norms are not yet set.

To return to Ribera's portraits, seen in relationship to the past, to the established type, the grotesque will always fall short of the ideal; Mary the Egyptian will never be the Magdalene, much less the Virgin. But considering what Santayana called the "inward possibility" of the grotesque from the perspective of the future, of an extension of acceptable forms, Ribera's portraits give rise to the novel beauty of the aged female body. But before approaching the horizon of the new, let us look at the paradigm that the grotesque will not achieve: Mary Magdalene, a Christianized Venus.

MARY MAGDALENE, OR THE MIRACLE OF A VIRGINAL VENUS

The legends of Mary Magdalene and Saint Mary of Egypt borrowed narrative elements and iconographical details from each other to the point that these two saints, more than any of the other so-called holy harlots (Pelagia, Thais, Abraham's niece Mary), found themselves coupled together in ritual celebrations and paired in literature, painting, or sculpture in a wide variety of contexts.[49] Hagiographic tradition paints both Marys in their youth as very beautiful, sexually adventurous (mostly Mary of Egypt), and attached to luxury (mostly the Magdalene). They both repent and leave civilization for the wilderness to atone for their sins (mostly Mary of Egypt) and meditate on the love of Christ (mostly the Magdalene). In the desert their long hair often covers what worn-out clothes no longer can (originally true of Mary of Egypt, then the Magdalene, too), and their sustenance is miraculously provided (long-lasting bread for the Egyptian; brought by angels to Mary Magdalene). Finally, at the end of their lives, their holiness is attested by male clerics (Zozimas for the Egyptian, Maximin for the Magdalene) who administer communion and final rites. And yet, despite this sorority, there is an important distinction between them: iconographically, Mary Magdalene's flesh rarely exhibits traces of the ravages of eremitic life.[50]

This apparent contradiction between the multiple decades that legend has her spend in the French wilderness and her beauty still in bloom was not lost on early modern viewers. It is in fact the topic of an often-quoted witticism by Titian, recorded by the influential politician and condottiero Baccio Valori (1477–1537). He recounts visiting the painter and stopping in front of a canvas featuring a penitent Magdalene by the master, identified by most art historians as the half-length 1531 portrait now in the Pitti Palace in Florence. The saint stands in front of a rock formation suggesting a cave; her gaze, wet with tears, is set raptly at the heavens above. The rugged rocks provide a contrast to the cascade of wavy, golden hair that she uses to cover herself, although it parts suggestively at her alabaster breasts, letting pinkish nipples peek out. Valori engages the painter in conversation with the observation that the saint "was too attractive, so fresh and dewy, for such penitence," then he recalls Titian's response thus:

> Having understood that I meant that she should be gaunt through fasting, he answered laughing that he had painted her on the first day she had entered [her repentant state], before she began fasting, in order to be able to paint her as a penitent indeed, but also as lovely as he could, and that she certainly was.[51]

Art historians have parsed this clever repartee for what it has to say about the reception of the painting by either of its two original recipients, the Duke of Mantua and poet and noblewoman Vittoria Colonna. However, what interests me here is that the beauty of the penitent Magdalene was a subject of discussion deemed worthy to record. Moreover, while Valori raises an objection to the decorum of painting beauty-in-asceticism, the painter's stated goal—to paint *a most pleasing penitent* figure—and the final assessment by his interlocutor that the product was indeed beautiful, confirm that by mid-sixteenth century, beauty had become a central feature of any representation of the Magdalene, even in the context of penitential asceticism.

In the following thirty years Titian would paint at least seven more portraits of beautiful penitent Magdalenes. The latter canvases follow more closely the injunction to dress female figures in religious scenes more modestly, but she retains the sensual pose of a *Venus Pudica* as well as the "freshness and dewiness" that had impressed Valori.[52] Most likely writing about one of these portraits, Giorgio Vasari writes approvingly of an image of a "disheveled" (*scapigliata*) Saint Mary Magdalene, painted down to her thighs, "with her hair falling around her neck down on her shoulders and on her breast, while she holds her head high with her eyes fixed towards the sky, showing remorse [compunction] in the redness of her eyes and, in her tears, sorrow for sins."[53] The compunction visible in the Magdalene's eyes condenses the spirit of the entire canvas: not merely regret or shame but rather the particularly pleasurable pain that accompanies spiritual cleansing.[54] Similarly, for Vasari, what makes the canvas truly remarkable is that "this painting would move anyone gazing at it in the most profound manner, and, what is more, although she is extremely beautiful it does not move the viewer to lustful thoughts, but rather to pity."[55]

As this quotation suggests, the meaning of the sensuality present in such "freshness in penitence"—lust versus pity—was up for debate even at the time, not least because humanists, theologians, and painters were concerned with being able to distinguish between pagan and Christian iconography. And yet, for all the anxiety surrounding improper mixture, Venuses cohabited peacefully with penitent Magdalenes in the cabinets of powerful patrons. What's more, the very translation of profane Venuses into saintly Magdalenes, Venuses of Divine Love, was not only practiced but sometimes even encouraged. A 1632 letter published by a group of Spanish influential clergymen unambiguously condemns the production and possession of profane mythological nudes.[56] It makes allowances, however, for turning Venuses into Magdalenes: "nothing would be lost, rather a great gain would be made from transforming a Venus into Mary Magdalene, and a Diana into Saint Mary of Egypt, and other female saints as best suited."[57] It would be tempting for modern readers to attribute the call for such transformed Venuses to unsophisticated prudishness or hypocrisy regarding female nudity. However, as Javier Portús shows in a critical article on the importance of historically sensitive "ways of seeing," nudity has never been transparent, and in order to fully understand those partially undressed Magdalenes (or more generally, how indecent or lascivious art was defined in the period) we need to consider not only how religious and sexual practices and attitudes may have changed through time but also what is meant by "seeing."[58] Drawing on existing elements of the saint's famous legend, it became possible to imagine that a Magdalene who both sinned and was saved "for having loved too much" (Luke 7:47) would become an icon of sacred eroticism. More surprising is the way in which this Christianized Venus would undergo a further transformation: a purification that iconographically brought her closer to the ideal of the Virgin Mary than to her fellow penitent saint from Egypt.

Such a transformation is perhaps most visible in the popular motif of Mary Magdalene's daily ascent to heaven, a mystical rapture described as a reprieve from her ascetic life with the purpose of either joining the choirs of angels to sing the glory of God or, more prosaically, to receive communion as her daily sustenance. Remarkably, the representations of this ecstasy, whether in painting or sculpture, recall the imagery of the Virgin's Assumption to heaven. Ribera's Assumption of the Magdalene, painted for El Escorial and now at the Academia de San Fernando (figure 13), is a great example of this motif. It was deemed by French art historian Émile Mâle as the most beautiful of its genre.[59] This large canvas features a youthful saint who wears her long auburn hair loosely, mingling with the hair shirt she wears beneath a flowing red cloak. Her hands, lightly crossed at her chest, signal prayer or contrition, a sentiment confirmed by her upturned eyes and faraway gaze. A flock of angels bears her kneeling figure toward a cloudy sky, carrying along the symbols of her solitary meditation (skull) and mortification (whips).

The painting, as a whole, does not differ much from Pacheco's prescriptions for the proper depictions of the Virgin's Assumption. First and foremost, he declares that the Virgin's full beauty should be visible and correspond to the body of a significantly younger woman than the seventy-two years Pacheco had calculated must have been Mary's age at her dormition. Second, she should rise to heaven amid a bevy of angels, though they are not to physically touch her to help her ascend, rather they should simply hover by to signify glory.[60]

After insisting that the Virgin's Assumption should not feature a sitting protagonist but rather one rising fully erect (cloud is optional), Pacheco returns to explain the preternatural beauty of the Mother of God. An obvious reason, he points out, is that Mary never suffered physical illness and

FIGURE 13. Jusepe de Ribera, *The Assumption of Mary Magdalene* (1936). Oil on canvas. Real Academia de Bellas Artes de San Fernando, Madrid, Spain. Photograph from Gabriele Finaldi, ed., *Jusepe de Ribera's Mary Magdalene in a New Context* (Dallas: Meadows Museum, Southern Methodist University, 2011), 107.

that she left this world not because she was old and her body frail but as a grace from God, to reunite her with her beloved Son. More mysteriously, Pacheco also credits Mary's eternal virginity as a verisimilar guarantee of her youthfulness in old age. While Pacheco does not go into theological detail on how virginity operates this miracle, he does offer a parallel drawn from his own observations as an example of the truth that living chastely preserves the flesh: "it is very reasonable that she should be depicted as very beautiful and much younger than her age on account of how virginity preserves external beauty and freshness, as can be seen in many elderly women religious (nuns)."[61]

Pacheco does not discuss in detail the iconography of Mary Magdalene, but his assertion that "virginity conserves external beauty and freshness" recalls those medieval legends and sermons that imagined in colorful ways how the sinner's redemption, effected through divine love and perfect penitence, also restored her pulchritude, a form of spiritual purity reflected in physical beauty. Theologians were quite clear about the distinction between spiritual virginity and the bodily sort, and the renewed purity of Mary Magdalene belonged unambiguously to the former. However, the metaphors used to convey the renewed purity of the Magdalene were unabashedly sensual and often traced on the model of the Virgin Mary. Tellingly, fourteenth-century preachers deployed Old and New Testament imagery of conversion as the recasting of a vessel to imagine "the fire of divine love" melting down the Magdalene and reshaping her into a precious liturgical cup. In turn, as Katherine Jansen has shown, the metaphor of the consecrated cup became literalized: the penitent saint was depicted bearing on her chest the very image of Christ's face, an iconographic twist that recalls the Byzantine tradition of the Virgin of the Sign, where at the moment of the Annunciation Mary opens her arms in prayer and the face of a grown Christ is imprinted on her chest.[62]

Other times the transformation passed through the language of horticulture, such as Dominican preacher Iohannes de Biblia's description of the Magdalene's conversion as the work of Christ the gardener, whose cares result in her "bursting into flower" and eventually becoming "a garden of pleasures just as if she were a sort of paradise of delights."[63] Late medieval hagiographic texts and sermons that focused on the Magdalene echoed the erotic poetry of the Song of Songs, with its long tradition of interpreting the Bride as a figure of the Church or the Virgin Mary, in order to give loving flesh to the sacrament of penance. If the doctrine of the incarnation affirms the full divinity and humanity of Christ, a dual nature made possible through the paradox of a virgin birth, then the miracle of a Virginal Venus—a freshly cleansed, rejuvenated, loved and lovely Mary Magdalene—is conceivable through the love of Christ and the power of true penitence.

The Magdalene's spiritual conversion and the conservation of her physical beauty in spite of eremitic rigors in post–fifteenth century painting gave rise to a composite: part Virgin, part Venus but certainly not a "Venus in sackcloth," in the pithy formulation of Marjorie Malvern.[64] However much the early modern Mary Magdalene came to represent the very image of penitence from the thirteenth to the seventeenth centuries, the Christianization of the classical ideal of beauty represented by Venus did not necessarily mean the repression of its sensuality, as early feminist readings of the sinner-saint par excellence would have it. When Marina Warner's 1976 groundbreaking mythography of the Virgin Mary touched on the legend of Mary Magdalene, she identified its roots in "Christianity's fear of women, its identification of physical beauty with temptation."[65] Similarly, thirty-two years later, when Margaret Miles's study of "the secularization of the breast" addressed the "frankly eroticized" breasts of the Magdalene (as opposed to the maternal and religious single breast of the Virgin), Miles traced the cultural function of the Magdalene back to masculine "fears, apprehensions and attraction to a beautiful and flamboyant woman."[66] In contrast, I argue that the image of Mary Magdalene emerges as the incarnation of a Renaissance ideal of female holiness: beautiful because holy, holy because beautiful.[67] Beauty is not simply a temptation for male viewers, nor is it a stumbling block for the beautiful female. It is instead both a marker of grace (in analogy to the Virgin's incorruptibility, a gift freely bestowed) *and* a badge of honor earned by the true penitent. As such, the Magdalene's beauty calls the viewer not only to gaze at a delectable female body but also to meditate on the miracle of beauty maintained in hardship.

From this perspective, the beauty of the early modern penitential Magdalene complicates Margaret Miles's secularization thesis where the body of the holy penitent as represented on canvas becomes objectified as art offered exclusively to one's sight and artistic judgment, no longer subject to the expectation that it touch the viewer. And yet, it should be stressed that this beauty remains conventional, adhering to canons that extol "freshness." *Freschezza* in Italian, *frescura* in Spanish, the noun designates what is youthful and pleasing. Filippo Baldinucci's 1681 *Vocabolario toscano dell'arte del disegno* associates "freshness" with foisoning flora, but it refers in particular to a life-giving force, to vigor, and vitality.[68] It is the beauty of a female body

A BREAST ALL HER OWN

Let us look again at the two paintings by Ribera that belonged together, the portraits of Saints Mary of Egypt and Mary Magdalene that are now at the Museo del Prado (figures 11 and 12). Painted in 1641, they belong to the painter's mature period: single figures at prayer, set in mid-ground, illuminated from the left and framed by a cavernous landscape that allows the viewer to glimpse a few trees, mountains, and clouds at a distance. The tone of the paintings is one of peaceful contemplation, exemplifying, according to Craig Felton, a "more restrained style and structurally controlled settings."[69] Both canvases feature the female saint in a prayer pose—the Magdalene kneeling, Mary of Egypt leaning on a rock—their faces turned slightly, as if responding to a call; their eyes, focused on the upper left corner of the painting, are attentive to something outside the frame.

And yet, despite these similarities, there is no mistaking one saint for the other. The Magdalene's features are soft and girlish with large liquid eyes and full mouth, her skin pearlescent, fingers long and elegant, and her long tresses golden. She wears a silky red mantle over a brilliant blue chemise. The luxury of the mantle may point to her earlier sinful life, but its vermilion color also signifies the self-inflicted "martyrdom" of her chosen penitential exile, similar to the cloth worn by the figure of John the Baptist that is also part of the series. The blue color, often associated with the Virgin, calls to mind her renewed pulchritude through penitence, a point that is highlighted by the blue garment that slips slightly off her left shoulder to expose the hair shirt underneath. As in the representations of the Magdalene in ecstasy just discussed, the sensuality of this painting, visible in the vibrant colors and loose brushstrokes, moves the viewer to wonder and tranquility rather than to the arousal of lust.

In contrast, Mary of Egypt's body (figure 12) shows unmistakable signs of age and penitence in her tanned complexion, wrinkled hands, and long graying hair pulled back in a disheveled bun. Decades of solitary penitence mark her body, but Ribera also depicts ghostly traces of her former beauty. Beneath her furrowed brow, years of crying have reddened the rims of a pair of dark, lovely, expressive eyes. The wrinkles around her mouth frame lips that have lost their crimson but retain some fullness. But the most jarring difference from the depiction of Mary Magdalene resides in two subtle details. First, a shadow falls softly on the right side of Mary of Egypt's face and following its flow downward toward the neck the viewer notices that unlike the impassive, perfect face of the Magdalene, hers bears the trace of a smile—a smile that seems to echo, albeit in a mellower key, the fuller expression on the young John the Baptist's face in the same series. Second, and again in contrast to the Magdalene's splendid colorful garb, the Egyptian's attire is a simple, dark, rough cloak. However, while the Magdalene's exposed soft, rounded shoulder marks a contrast to the hair shirt she wears under otherwise fancy garments, Mary of Egypt's plain cloak drops from her shoulder to reveal a dry décolletage, and the diagonal formed by the fallen cloth and her praying arm highlight the surprising detail of the saint's shrunken breast. There is no conventional freshness or dewiness here. Yet this aged female saint is not subjected to the derision typical of representations of older women, which skew toward the horrifying naturalism of the hag or the weird ugliness of the witches painted by Ribera's contemporary Salvatore Rosa. In contrast to these two well-known models for the representation of feminine old age, I argue that Ribera has lovingly painted as somehow still lovely the wizened body of Saint Mary of Egypt.

Virginal, adolescent beauty worthy of wonder and admiration or degraded, senescent deformity deserving laughter or pity: in poetry as in painting the female body rarely found an alternative to these conventional poles.[70] Margaret Miles closes her study on the "complex delight" of the representations of the female breast on a plaintive note. She observes that early modern artists seemed to recognize only two types of femininity: the attractive beauty of the nubile and soon to become maternal breasts or the terrifying flaccid breasts of the witch. Lamenting that even the symbolically rich maternal breast of the Virgin Mary is not immune to objectification, she turns to Augustinian psychology, and in particular the distinction he traces between use and enjoyment to identify the source of the cultural difficulty in imagining a non-objectified female body. According to Augustine's description, in the fallen world humans are fodder to one another; they "eat each other up."[71] In the City of God, however, the "*enjoyment* of the other *as* other" will be possible in part because, as Augustine writes, female bodies will no longer be "suited to their old use [for procreation], but to a new beauty [*decori novo*], and this will not arouse the lust of the beholder, for there will be no lust, but it will inspire praise of the wisdom and goodness of God, who both created what was not, and freed from corruption what he made."[72] I suggest that the shriveled breast of Saint Mary of Egypt, especially as depicted by Ribera, gives substance to the prospect of this new beauty, beyond possession and lust, yet very much carnal and still tied to sexual difference. For, while Mary of Egypt does not achieve the feminine ideal of beauty embodied by Mary Magdalene, neither is she just an avatar for venerable male saintliness.

As I demonstrated earlier in the case of sixteenth-century anchoress Mother Cardona, assuming the trope of what Carlos Alberto Vega termed "transformismo religioso" (religious cross-dressing) was one way to render comprehensible the choice to leave a life of courtly amusements for the rigors of prayer and asceticism.[73] Cardona's commitment to a life of chastity, prayer, and penitence aligned her with the virtuous elderly matrons and widows extolled by Juan Luis Vives. The humanist imagines these women past childbearing age crowned with the wisdom and equanimity that only their proximity to death and the realization of the vanity of the world can bring. The good widow or matron can "raise all her senses, mind, and soul to the Lord, and girding herself for that departure, she will meditate on nothing that is not suited to that impending journey."[74] Thus cleansed from the feminine vice of frivolity, the old woman can aspire to become a man's equal: her husband's friend, confidant, and counselor. Erin J. Campbell has studied the portraits of older women in Northern Italy as didactic examples of this virtuous religious masculinization, rightly arguing that the wrinkles painted on the face of Abbess Lucrezia Agliardi Vertova do not point to the cruelty of old age but are best understood as "the sign of a woman's masculine authority," of an individual whose life of rectitude in the past has rendered her "more spiritual than carnal."[75] But is this the image that Ribera presents in his portrayal of Mary of Egypt? Has asceticism turned Mary the Egyptian into a virile woman, a man of God? Campbell is careful to point out that the virtuous beauty of masculinized women in old age makes sense only within a patrilinear and domestic context where the wrinkles have been earned by the "good old *mother*" who patiently awaits her individual death, remaining chaste and faithful to her husband thus ensuring the continuity of his line.[76] To answer the question of whether the masculine, virtuous beauty of the old woman applies to a saint who was promiscuous in her youth and never motherly, let us return once more to the series of eremitic saints (Bartholomew, Mary of Egypt, John the Baptist in the Desert, and Mary Magdalene) that Ribera painted in the 1640s and are now at the Museo del Prado.

Art historians had initially imagined these canvases as a coherent quartet, where a young and an old male saint were paired off with the two female saints. The museum website of the Museo Nacional del Prado notes that since scholars now know that the series included eight saints and not just four, one should be careful about imputing an *intended* parallelism among the paintings.[77] Still, the fact that they offer the viewer examples of male and female ascetics depicted by Ribera at the same time allows us to make some comparisons. As mentioned earlier, the portraits of Saints Bartholomew (figure 10) and Mary of Egypt (figure 12) share the rocky, cavernous background proper to hermits, but whereas the sky in Mary of Egypt's canvas is bright and mostly blue, Saint Bartholomew's features clouds feebly illuminated by a setting sun.[78] Both saints are seated and their bodies partly covered: hers by a brown cloth that reveals her left shoulder and upper torso; his by a linen mantle (whose color is a similar shade of gray as his bushy beard and tousled hair) that, in spite of its generous folds, leaves the saint's left shoulder uncovered. His face is deeply wrinkled, and although the sharp cheekbones give him a slightly gaunt look, the muscular arm that defiantly holds high the instrument of his martyrdom contradicts any suggestion of frailty in old age. Although the Apostle Bartholomew is not normally associated with eremitical feats in any textual tradition, Ribera's deployment of the tropes of asceticism (solitary landscape, unkempt hair, partly exposed body) clearly identifies him with one of the many masculine athletes of God whose "herculean anatomy" has led cultural critic Pilar Pedraza describe it as "carne de Dios," sanctified flesh—unlike the body of a female past its prime, which "becomes suspect, witchy, Celestinesque; her body is not only assumed to be ugly but it is also horrifying."[79]

Bartholomew's raised arm and extended leg lend his pose such dynamism that the viewer can imagine his cloak slipped off his left shoulder and caused his right hand to clutch and cover the left breast that would have been otherwise exposed when he proudly lifted the arm to show the knife that will flay him. The almost girlish modesty in covering his chest contrasts with the full exposure of Mary of Egypt's breast. And yet, this is not a breast exposed to ridicule, as in Quentin Matsys's *An Old Woman* (*The Ugly Duchess*) (1513, National Gallery London), or in any one of the many anti-Petrarchan poems of the late Renaissance and baroque that scorned feminine failed attempts to maintain a beauty that nature no longer allows.[80] Mary of Egypt's breast—featured prominently here and in two other paintings by Ribera (figures 3 and 8)—is no longer voluptuous, but it is also not flaccid nor simply assimilated to the masculine torso of a holy man. In the Prado painting, the arm that frames Mary of Egypt's breast is cut of the same sinewy muscular cloth as Bartholomew's, but while his is flexed high in a pose of masculine prowess, hers bends in prayer, echoing visually the arms of the Magdalene in the same series. Her breast, bisected by the cloak, is similarly cleft between the representation of old age (its wrinkles) and youthfulness (its visible firmness), but it is clearly not the unmarked (and unremarkable) breast of Bartholomew or a Saint Jerome.

Ribera's depiction of Saint Mary of Egypt follows the same tropes of ascetic pictorial representation that confirmed Bartholomew's standing, but as I showed already in the comparison with Mary Magdalene, the Egyptian's face, while bearing traces of rigorous penitence, maintains a soft, feminine beauty, especially around the eyes and mouth. Similarly, by painting her breast without derision or erasure, Ribera declines a representation of female sanctity that dissolves femininity, and especially the feminine body, into a masculinized ideal. Instead, his portraits of Mary of Egypt incarnate *in this world* Augustine's assertion that the bodies of women will be redeemed as such, and not as a masculine and therefore improved, version of themselves. This, the bishop writes, is conceivable not because of God's omnipotence and ability to correct any and all imperfection but more fundamentally because "the female sex is not a defect, but a natural state."[81] Neither Venus nor venerable old man, Mary of Egypt's breast actualizes the subjective breast that Miles hoped for: a breast that is beautiful not because it is desired or conforms to a determined standard but because it embodies the fullness of *her* experience from youthfulness to old age, from sinfulness to sanctity.

This holds true even when Ribera's depiction of the saint veers toward the naturalistic, as it does in the 1641 three-quarter length portrait of Mary of Egypt, now at the Musée Fabre in Montpellier (figure 8), which had horrified Stendhal. Again, Mary is at prayer in a pose that seems familiar by now; her gaze is fixed beyond the frame, her hands gathered together at her breast and her mouth slightly open in prayer. A warm ray of light illuminates the saint from the left and together with the shadow it casts on her face serves to emphasize her gaunt demeanor, tracing the outline of every wrinkle on her hands, of sunken eyes, and hollow cheeks. Whatever suggestion of softness left in the Prado painting has disappeared here. Even the landscape has hardened, with greenery giving way to dramatic rock formations behind the saint that leave visible only a tiny sliver of early evening sky in the upper left corner. Writing for the 2003 catalog of the exhibition *Jusepe de Ribera, el Españoleto*, art historian Nicola Spinosa offers a description of this painting that jibes perfectly with Ribera's reputation in the nineteenth century as painter of dark and sinister subjects: "[Mary of Egypt] is depicted as a stiff, wounded, and sickly old lady with matted hair, a figure that could only be found in the lower-class districts and dark alleys of the Spanish viceroyalty of Naples."[82] As recently as 2012, María Cruz de Carlos Varona also painted an image of infirmity in her description of the Montpellier canvas: "a cadaverous figure whose enormous eyes bulge out of her bony, toothless face, while her threadbare cloak reveals an anatomy consumed by age and hardship. Her hands are wrinkled and dried by the sun, and her hallucinatory, empty gaze is that of an unhealthy person."[83]

And yet, a close look at the painting belies these descriptions of mere decrepitude: her hands are tanned and wrinkled but positioned in such a way as to draw a marked contrast to the smooth skin of her upper body, especially the lean and powerful muscles of her shoulder and arm. While her pose is not particularly dynamic, it is hard to argue that it signals illness or pain for her posture is erect and her eyes shine with intensity, but they are not the "hallucinatory, empty gaze" of the sick but rather the visionary, unearthly gaze of the saint.[84] Similar to the unforgiving stare of Diego Velázquez's 1620 portraits of Mother Jerónima de la Fuente (figure 14), founder of a convent in the Philippines, Ribera's painting is an image of resilience and determination, perhaps even heroism, and certainly not of an ailing body. In contrast to Velázquez's portrait, painted from life and adhering to decorum in the portraiture of an actual nun, Ribera's portrait of Mary of Egypt asks the viewer to accept an image of female holiness that shatters the spectrum of decorum. As Stendhal noticed rightly, what makes Ribera's paintings of Saint Mary of Egypt deeply uncanny in the history of European painting is that they straddle time: "All the more horrible because one can see that she *has been* beautiful." Her hair may be wild, but it is youthfully dark; her face may look gaunt, but it highlights the delicate features of a beautiful woman; and that breast again, it may begin to wrinkle but its outline is still discernibly rounded, nestled lovingly in the folds of her falling cloak. Most visibly here, but also true in the other paintings, Ribera's depiction of Saint Mary of Egypt is a highly original vision of a holy woman: neither erotic nor maternal nor holy virago. Most fantastically, Ribera envisions for Mary the Egyptian a twofold grace: she ends her days in holiness, and she escapes the narrow categories of the artistic representation of female bodies, structured by the binary logic of desire (coupled to beauty, youthfulness, and reproduction) and revulsion (associated with decrepitude, old age, and death).

FIGURE 14. Diego Velázquez, *The Nun Jerónima de la Fuente* (1620). Oil on canvas. Museo Nacional del Prado, Madrid, Spain. © Museo Nacional del Prado.

BODIES AND TEMPORALITIES OUT OF JOINT

In this chapter I have shown that three factors—age, gender, and holiness—render invisible the beauty promised by Ribera's portraits of Saint Mary of Egypt. Historically, the conventional expectation in portraiture has been that the female body worth representing as beautiful is young and that a holy woman will be either virginally youthful or a masculinized matron. At the opposite end of the spectrum stands the frightful body of the threatening, unholy witches of Salvator Rosa's repertoire, or the usually repellent depictions of old women that serve as an allegory of *cupiditas*. The naked body of an aged woman depicted in a positive light is a rarity—if not altogether taboo in the history of Western art, as Pilar Pedraza has argued. It would be tempting to attribute this lack of positive representations of old female bodies to the normalization of "the male gaze"—that is to say, a way of looking that places feminine bodies in the position of objects to be transformed through the masterful eye and hand of the male artist into art that is then offered up for the (male) viewer's pleasure and judgment. And yet, to stop our analysis there obscures the queering role that age plays in their particular invisibility.

As the only stage in life with no meaningful future on the horizon, medical and moral discourses from antiquity to the Renaissance depict old age under the aegis of decline at best; at its worst, old age condemns us to a stuttering repetition of the past. Aristotle explained the old person's tendency to reminisce about the past as the result of a lack of futurity: having only death to look forward to, the past acquires greater importance to the present. Philip Sohm goes one step further when, in his analysis of old age as reflected in the late style of Renaissance masters from Leonardo to Titian, he identifies senescence with a veritable existential crisis. Age, he writes, "turns us against ourselves [. . .] we look less and less like ourselves; we move and feel unlike ourselves. We lose parts of our individuality, our identity, and acquire attributes shared by every other old person."[85] A self-image wrought from a lifetime of experience is suddenly confronted with a body that no longer corresponds to the singularity of those experiences and has become instead a conventional litany of ailing and failing body parts.

Juvenal expresses this sentiment hyperbolically in one of his satires whose stunningly vivid imagery of infirmity influenced medieval representations of growing old:

"Give me a long life, Jupiter, give me many years." But just think of the many, never ending disadvantages an extended old age is full of! Take a look at its face, first of all—ugly and hideous and unrecognisable—and the ugly hide in place of skin and the drooping jowls and the wrinkles. The mother ape scratches wrinkles like those on her aged cheek in the extensive shady groves of Thabraca. There are so many differences between young men: he is better looking than him and he than another, he is much more sturdy than him. But old men all look the same: voice and body trembling alike, head now quite smooth, a baby's dripping nose. The pathetic creature has to munch his bread with weaponless gums. He's so disgusting to his wife and kids and to himself that he makes even Cossus the fortune-hunter feel sick. The delights of food and wine are no longer the same as his palate grows numb, and as for sex—it's now just a distant memory, or if you try to rouse him, his stringy little prick lies limp with its enlarged vein and will stay limp though you coax it all night long.[86]

The satire spares no detail of the decrepitude awaiting all—yes, including those "handsomer" and "stronger" men who in their prime do not see themselves yet in the portrait of the old person. Yet the influence of his particular version of the rhetorical topos of the abuse of old age (*vituperatio senectutis*) may be attributed as much to the context in which it appears as to the eloquence of the description. This satire takes as its organizing theme the suffering that pining for the wrong things (such as a long life) brings to the foolish. Such stoicism found resonance in ascetic strands of late medieval and early modern Christian discourses on vanity. There, the inevitable deterioration of the flesh came to be seen as a sign of humanity's intrinsic sinfulness, and the only attitude proper to living in a fallen world is to hold it in contempt, echoing the opening words of the Book of Ecclesiastes: "Vanity of vanities, says the Teacher, vanity of vanities! All is vanity" (Eccl. 1:2). This perspective turns the gross and finite materiality of the old person's body into a living memento mori for the self and for others. Contemptuous laughter is no longer the only response to exposed wrinkles, infirmities, and deficiencies. Instead, each ailment and foul body part becomes a Janus-faced sign: facing backward to finally see the vanity of all past earthly strivings that will have come to naught in death, and forward as reminder that the wise set their sights on God alone in his eternity.

The specific moral of the message may have changed from antiquity's emphasis on achieving a Stoic state of mind in this world to Christianity's meditation on the fragility of life and the preparation of the soul for the hereafter, but the signifying structure remains intact. In depicting an old man (as in Juvenal's satire) or an old woman (Quentin Matsys's *Ugly Duchess*), the status of old flesh remains the same: it is disposable, like Saint Bartholomew's skin, a sign that deceives one minute, appearing to be true (the equation of skin and temporal self), but which reveals the hidden truth ("all that is fair must fade") when it is finally sloughed off. Much like the structure of paranoia as Eve Kosofsky Sedgwick analyzed in her seminal article on paranoid and reparative readings, traditional depictions and interpretations of old bodies fear surprise above all: all old bodies are always the same and they speak the same truth, insisting that the matter of this world is unreliable (if not altogether deceptive), and truth lies in a spiritual elsewhere.[87]

Ribera's depictions of Saint Mary of Egypt brilliantly throw off the structure that requires the surface appearance of the now to give way to the depth and truth of the future. This is perhaps most readily visible in the painting now in the Juan Antonio Pérez Simón private collection (figure 3). This canvas differs in both genre and tenor from other well-known paintings by Ribera, usually half- or three-quarter length depictions of Mary in meditation. In this painting instead, the viewer sees a representation of one of the miracles for which she is known: her levitation during prayer. Instead of simply admiring the serene portrait of a discrete saint, the focus of this canvas is the drama and desire for narrative that characterize a history painting, the highest form of representation recognized by classical canons. The second remarkable difference from the other works discussed in this chapter follows from the first: Mary is no longer alone, but monk Zozimas lies prostrate at Mary's feet with his mouth open, staring out, possibly in disbelief. The monk's outstretched right hand, however, does not point to the miracle at hand. Instead, his index finger directs our view past the miracle of Mary's elevated feet, past the awe and wonder of the "present" moment, to a minuscule and hazy scene of the "future." This scene depicts the episode in the legend of Mary of Egypt when Zozimas will have returned a year later to discover Mary's dead body and will give holy burial to her corpse upon reading a command mysteriously inscribed on the ground. This tiny scene (figure 15), barely visible on the lower left part of the canvas, blurrily shows the monk as an indistinct shadow-like figure attending to Mary's luminous body on the ground. What is appearance and what is truth here? Is the miracle of her levitation a false appearance—exactly the mistake that the incredulous monk made in fearing that Mary was not human? Is the barely visible death of the anchoress where truth resides? Even taking Zozimas,

FIGURE 15. Detail from Jusepe de Ribera, *Saint Mary of Egypt in Ecstasy* (ca. 1640). Oil on canvas. Colección Juan Antonio Pérez Simón, Mexico City, Mexico. Photograph from Alfonso E. Pérez Sánchez and Nicola Spinosa, *Jusepe de Ribera el Españoleto* (Barcelona: Lunwerg Editores, 2003), 156.

witness to Mary's holiness, as a stand-in for the viewer, there is no clear answer. Whereas his hand points in the direction of a scene of narrative future, his attention is elsewhere. Not on the miracle itself, which frightens him and makes him doubt, his gaze is directed upward, like Mary's own, looking beyond the frame at the source of the miracle. This source is outside of the narrative logic of before/after where present is superseded by the future, that we should turn our attention.

Narrative untimeliness in this canvas accentuates what was visible already in the portraits examined earlier, where Mary of Egypt bears the marks of a body out of joint with itself. The painting is illuminated from the left so that a sharp light falls on half of Mary's body, highlighting the exposed parts. The left side of her face is smoother than in the Montpellier painting, though still betraying the passing of time. The fallen cloak reveals a shapely left calf, and the uncannily muscular yet wrinkled upper body recalls the athletic asceticism of other male saints (notably Jerome and Paul the Hermit) as depicted by Ribera, proclaiming her resilience and wisdom.

Evocative of the title of a late seventeenth-century prose retelling of the Egyptian's legend by Andrés Antonio Sánchez de Villamayor, *La mujer fuerte, asombro de los desiertos*, this depiction of Mary as *la mujer fuerte* (the strong woman) might lead one to place Mary among the ranks of "spiritual cross-dressers," those female saints who disguised themselves to be able to enter a monastery or live in the desert as anchorites (such as Mary/Marinos, Pelagia/Pelagius; in Spain Mother Cardona) or, as Erin Campbell has argued, matrons whose virtue makes them the spiritual equivalent of men. And yet, as I explored with Ribera's portraits of this saint, the Egyptian remains clearly a strong *woman*.[88] Her facial features, the delicate nose, large eyes, the curve of her neck, and so on, remain elegant and softer than those of her male counterparts. Even more remarkable, her hair—iconographically, an important attribute as it has been allowed to grow long enough to cover her nudity during her years of wandering the desert—is here depicted as both long and short. The illuminated part is gray and cropped short, close to her skull, evocative of those female saints who shear their locks as a sign of spiritual conversion and a first step toward cross-dressing.[89] From the shadowed right side, however, we can just make out a longer, dark mane of hair flow down her concealed shoulder. Her body shows signs of ascetic rigor, most dramatically in her shrunken breast, but that rigor has not erased the traces of her femininity, discernible still on her face, in her long dark hair, and most dramatically by her (taboo) shapely legs.[90] Thus, the figure of Mary contains the juxtaposition of manly and feminine features, earthly and ethereal elements, strength and frailty, asceticism and sensuality, youthfulness and old age; and as if to highlight this embrace of opposites, her body is positioned in equal parts exposure and concealment.

The surprising conjunction of decrepitude and youthfulness in the same body, a source of anxiety and horror from Stendhal to Sohm, maps on to the queerness of old age—that is to say, a time when one's body will no longer be recognizable as congruent to one's own sense of self, of a time when the folds of the skin seem to hinder the forward movement that lends meaning to life and living. However, as Ribera's depictions of Saint Mary of Egypt make clear, this incongruence and untimeliness need not be markers of an impending end; rather, they trace a choreography of transition—especially in the Pérez-Simón canvas, where penitent Mary is depicted in motion. Julian Carter, writing about the ways in which dance as an art medium that takes advantage of movement through space in time, offers a perspective on transgender experiences that bypasses the expected temporality of a clear *before* that must be erased for the truth of *now* to emerge. An important contribution of Carter's turn to dance as a way to represent the experience of gender transitioning is the emphasis it places on relationality—among dancers but also between bodies and space—which challenges at once narratives of transitioning that focus on the individual and a dualism that would see the body as inconvenient matter (a prison of the soul) to a true self.[91] This queer temporality and how it inflects the use of space is useful for understanding Ribera's representations of Mary the Egyptian. Choreography imbues the concept of transition with a dynamism that escapes the strictures of Albertian perspective, and by imagining "dancing in the folds of time" the *trans* of transition and transgender emerges as a pleat that multiplies possible positions, identities, and stories instead of a discrete phase to overcome.

The folds for Carter, like the wrinkles on the skin of Saint Mary of Egypt, find a place for the past and future in the present moment. This gnarled temporality where the past is not conceived in terms of loss and the future is not a preconceived goal is imprinted on Mary's grotesque body, but its lessons hold for those who behold her—from Zozimas to the viewers of Ribera's paintings. These canvases make visible for us the beauty of the queerness of old age, a beauty that, as the feminist scholar of religion Krista Hughes puts it, does not ignore "wounds and scars" but instead integrates them into a whole.[92] This whole, she reminds us, is not synonymous with perfection. Instead, the queer wholeness of the body of Mary of Egypt points to the fullness of experience, making room within its folds for paradox.

APPEARANCES ARE EVERYTHING

> The poet is to pay attention to the disposition of the matter so that even if it is necessary to do violence to the story, and even if the play should be about Saint Alexis or Saint Bruno, there must be room for courtships and profane love, else people will say that it is an anthology of saints' lives and not a play.
>
> IGNACIO CAMARGO, *Discurso teológico sobre los teatros y comedias de este siglo*[1]

AMONG THE MANY VICES OF MARY the Egyptian, medieval and early modern audiences may have been surprised to find that two are missing from the satirical catalogs of moral flaws typically associated with women: lying and the related corrupt devotion to cosmetics, a form of mendacity related to performance. While I have shown that in some medieval sources Mary of Egypt emerges as a powerful orator, one whose speech straddles the separation of persuasion from seduction, she does not at any point *lie* outright. Similarly, while she understands herself as an object of admiration, by men and women alike, nowhere does she ever appear preparing or using tinctures or cosmetics to attract men via deceptive makeup. In fact, the association with boudoir elements belongs to the iconography of Mary Magdalene, and it goes beyond the signature jar of oil she used to wipe Christ's feet. Caravaggio's gorgeous canvas *Mary Magdalene and Martha* (ca. 1598), now at the Detroit Institute of Arts, shows her standing by a vanity table that holds a convex mirror, a comb, and placed centrally, a ceramic vessel for powder with its puff sticking out, ready for use. No such accoutrements appear in visual representations of Mary of Egypt. And yet, the saint was no alien to baroque games of appearances. As we saw in the previous chapter, Jusepe de Ribera's images of Mary the Egyptian trouble our ideas of holiness and beauty because, instead of appealing to the desire for visual transparency, he painted Mary's likeness in its manifold appearances: holiness appears in the unexpected body of an old woman, beauty appears in the midst of the grotesque, and a sinner appears as a saint.

Ribera's portraits of Mary of Egypt and the peculiar drama that they embodied were, as far as scholars today know, displayed in the private collections of a cultured elite. In contrast, a seventeenth-century theatrical enactment of the transformation of Mary from sinner to saint would have most likely taken place in a *corral de comedias*—an urban, open-air, public theater where nobles, bourgeois, clergymen, and common people of all genders could enjoy almost three hours of dramatic performance with interspersed shorter pieces of music and dance. The Council of Trent had nothing to say about theater per se, focusing instead on upholding earlier decrees on the legitimacy of the use of images (painting and sculpture) to teach doctrine and model virtue. However, the debates surrounding decorum and didacticism intensified when the stillness of images became animated by bodies on a public stage. In such a context, how would the mixed audience of early modern theater have taken in the complexities of a figure such as Mary of Egypt? To what extent could the audience, especially the less well-educated men and women who filled the *corrales* comprehend the play's core doctrinal message of repentance and redemption when it was coming through the appearance of a seductive character played by an actress on stage. How did the play communicate the holiness of the protagonist to theatergoers used to profane plot twists and spectacular stage effects?

These questions mattered, for example, to the inquisitor who, in 1761, lamented that Juan Pérez de Montalbán's play *La gitana de Menfis, Santa María Egipciaca* (The gypsy girl from Memphis, Saint Mary of Egypt) (ca. 1621–25), concentrated its aesthetic efforts on the "before" of sinfulness. The censorship report of the play's printed edition writes disapprovingly that Pérez de Montalbán's play "paints through the mouth of the prostitute and her suitors every attractive aspect of vice in the most inflammatory manner, and although the author wants to counteract it by deploying Zozimas, he does it so faintly that it provides no antidote."[2] While it is true that more lines are spent on Mary's licentious lifestyle, the true wonders of the play—and, arguably, the reason people would have flocked to *see* it—all occur in the last act. Among these marvels are no less than four saintly miracles: characters levitate and walk on water; bodies fly; the Host reveals a luminous image of Christ as a child; and last but not least, a man comes back from the dead.

What the censor misses, in other words, is that a play is not just words on paper, it is also the creation of wonder through the presentation of bodies that are at once themselves *and* something else on a stage that is at once there *and* somewhere else, all for the benefit of others to see.

This chapter examines the character of Mary of Egypt in *La gitana de Menfis* as a figure of theater and theatrical allure that nevertheless keeps true to the legend in two important respects. First, she does not aim to deceive— and to deceive in a specifically *theatrical* way through costumes, makeup, stage props, dance, and other suggestive body language. Second, the play depicts her particular appeal as fully gratuitous, in both senses of the word: extravagant but also free from the taint of profit. More precisely, I argue that the figure of Saint Mary of Egypt, who is at once at home with appearances but distanced from dissembling, helps us understand the encounter on stage between what Jean-Luc Marion has described as the "ontological invisibility of sainthood" and the theatrical imperative to display. The dilemma of how to communicate holiness is central to the life of Saint Mary of Egypt, as we saw in chapters 2 and 3. It becomes a particularly important issue in the context of stage performance, for while moralists derided theater in general for its illusionism, for representing vice in ways so realistic that it could lead the audience to take falsehood for truth, its defenders often turned to hagiographic drama as an example of how the pleasures of imitation could be harnessed to teach its wide and diverse audience. According to moralists and neoclassical critics alike, theater could find legitimacy if it foregrounded its textuality to the detriment of spectacle (gesture, music, special effects). In Pérez de Montalbán's play, various characters call this word-centered approach *sermón*: literally *preaching*, but the concept is expansive enough to include the nuances of *logos*, of rationality and speech cleansed of "inflammatory" artifice, as the Inquisition report would have it. This purified speech would thus have the power to redeem the disturbing presence of unruly human bodies on stage and the awe-inspiring machines off stage that allowed those bodies to appear, disappear, fly, and otherwise defy nature and, in doing so, belief. Such a defense of theater, however, can hardly satisfy a theatrical audience since it effectively asks theater to stop being theatrical. To paraphrase the epigraph by Jesuit Ignacio Camargo that opens this chapter, theater as *sermón* asks the playwright to offer a devotional text, a *flos sanctorum*, to an audience that comes expecting the highs and lows of popular theatrical representation. As we shall see, the figure of Mary of Egypt in Pérez de Montalbán's play offers a way out of this impasse by presenting a conversion that does not require relinquishing the sensuous pleasures of appearances and spectacle. In fact, spiritual transformation in the play *depends* on them.

THEATRICAL *APARIENCIAS*

Hagiographic drama, as it developed in the seventeenth century, became a contested site in the polemics over the promise and risk that theater posed to what moralists called the Christian Republic. Central to this discussion is the question of appearances. At its most basic, an appearance is anything available to the senses. However, because those senses do not give a direct access to substance—as when human eyes perceive the sun and the moon as being the same size or when human artifice tricks viewers so that they take, for example, linear perspective in a painting as depth—appearances often took on a negative connotation for medieval and early modern religious authorities. Compounding the suspicion of appearances is that, on occasion, willful deception is at play, as when an intriguer's sweet words and kind gestures convince the audience of a falsehood.

Sebastián de Covarrubias's seventeenth-century dictionary lays out the range of this largely negative understanding of appearances:

> *Appearance*, what at first glance is attractive but belies essential and substantial qualities. *Attractive words*, those which move [the audience] precipitously, but when well considered have no effect and do not convince or conclude. *Apariencias* are those mute representations, which are shown to the people when a curtain is drawn and are then covered again.[3]

The breadth of lexical uses of the word covered by Covarrubias is worth unpacking. He begins considering the word "appearance" in the realm of sensory experience, "what is at glance attractive," but he immediately underscores the gap between perceived exterior and inherent substance, a gap heightened by the attractiveness of the exterior. This apparent beauty, the "buen parecer" of the appearance, however, far from guaranteeing its virtue, is as much a lure as alluring. The lexicographer turns to an example from rhetoric in order to better describe the deception at work in the coupling of beauty and appearance. According to him, flashy words, *razones aparentes*, catch the audience unawares; they appeal to the unsuspecting listener's emotions, which give in to a precipitous deception that true *razones*, honest words, will eventually set straight. After this disavowal of rhetoric's sensual appeal, the dictionary entry concludes with a description of a theatrical device that also depends on surprise, but this time of a visual and artificial kind—the revelation of a painting, a tableau vivant, or puppet scene previously hidden by a curtain—to create an emotional effect on the audience.

According to Hugo A. Rennert, in both England and Spain, a theatrical *appearance* referred to stage machinery used to reveal something (a painting, sculpture, or tableau vivant), but Spain's "silent representations," painted scenes, were not limited to the public theater stage.[4] (In this chapter, I use *apariencia* when referring specifically to stage effects and the English "appearance" where the wider meaning of the word is warranted.) The veiling and unveiling of paintings to heighten the effect of certain parts of a performance was also a device typical of what Emilio Orozco Díaz has called the "theatricalization of the temple."[5] A 1601 letter by Francisco de Luque, priest from Seville, provides a lively description of such a spectacular use of word and image. Writing about the sermons he had attended in preparation for the celebration of Christ's Passion, he was initially struck by the Madrileños' use of painting in contrast to his native Seville, where they used sculptures (*figuras de bulto*) to recreate Christ's Passion.[6] Every Sunday, Luque writes, a sermon focused on a specific mystery, and a canvas depicting it rested on an altar near the choir of the church, covered by a taffeta curtain. At the moment the priest recited a particular prayer, the curtain was drawn open revealing the image and making a strong impression on the large audience in attendance.

The powerful effect of the combination of word and spectacle comes to the fore in the description Father Luque offers of a sermon on the conversion of the Magdalene. At a given moment, a crucifix together with "a devotional image of the Magdalene that appeared very beautiful" appear, a revelation that leads to the conversion of at least one of the prostitutes brought in to attend mass.[7] All this was to the great delight of crowds inside the church and many more who climbed adjacent roofs and eaves in order to catch a glimpse of what was happening inside and hear some of the sermon through the windows.

Music and other lighting effects also joined the surprise of the *aparencia*. Describing a scene of *cantos con apariencias* (songs with special effects) on a Friday, the Sevillian priest notes that after Father Rafael Sarmiento's sermon

the Benedictus was sung and the Psalm of the Miserere in Italian falsetto style and accompanied by a wide variety of instruments such that I had never known before. The voices were supremely delightful and so appropriate to this holy devotion that it gave rise to many heartfelt tears and spiritual comfort. Moreover, at the moment when the verse *Tibi soli peccaui* [to Thee only have I sinned] was sung, an image of a Most Holy Crucifix would be revealed on the main altar by drawing two taffeta curtains slowly and authoritatively and the altar and the chapel being sufficiently illuminated by torches and candles made of white wax made everything appear like a scene from Heaven. People would naturally spend away their whole afternoon there with a delight that one can understand.[8]

Father Luque's description is thick with the sensory details of the performance, from the foreign tonality of the singing to the tactile attention to the fabric of the veiling curtains. The candles' white wax would have contributed to the marvel since the flames would have been odorless and relatively smoke-free in comparison to the glow produced by common tallow. Still, there is a slight inflection of aloofness. He notes in the first person that he had never witnessed such an assortment of musical instruments play the Miserere, but when it comes to describing the effect of the music, he moves to a passive construction that leaves unclear whether he is among those moved to tears. While he can appreciate the spectacle, he does not necessarily imagine that this holy theater was put on for his benefit. He would not actually believe that the light and sound show appeared heavenly; the *aparencias* are for those who, on a different day would have spent—or rather wasted—their afternoon at the theater.

A similar ambivalence permeated critical responses to theatrical productions of religious content. Defenders of theater often argued for its value by ascribing to it a sensory-pedagogical function: by bringing together word and image, plays represented an important and highly effective medium for making religious doctrine accessible to the public at large. An anonymous 1681 letter to King Carlos II of Spain summarizes arguments made all throughout the seventeenth century when it suggests that theater was not only a site of learning, but it was perchance even more effective than formal schooling because it harnessed doctrine to the senses. The letter reads: "It would have been very difficult for coarse ignorance to have come across these sacred matters if the shining torch of the harmonious consonance of numbers [in versification] had not illuminated the eyes and ears of those who had found themselves in the confused chaos of the horror of their helplessness."[9] Still, the letter imagines the audience to be moved through sensory impact as the hard-to-reach coarse and ignorant among the public.

Father Luque is not alone in taking his distance from the spectacle of *apariencias*. Those same playwrights who would write with a large and diverse public in mind chafed at the expectation that an audience used to multisensory experiences in church or as part of street festivals would attend the theater looking for such spectacle. The great poet and playwright Lope de Vega, author of hundreds of plays, gently mocked classicizing critics who found the *comedia nueva* lacking in artistic decorum in his *Arte nuevo de hacer comedias*, defending his decision to write for a general public instead of for the elite. Yet, even he famously decried that seeing the success of plays full of special effects was what made him turn away from neo-Aristotelian precepts.[10] The poet's goal was not to give in to the popularity of spectacle as a substitute for good poetry: in *¡Ay verdades! que en amor* (1625), a character laments that "carpentry supplies witticisms and plots."[11] Instead, Lope hoped that the changes he proposed to plot, staging, and poetry would please theatergoers enough to attend plays like his, which did not always feature the spectacles that they were used to seeing elsewhere. Once again, the hope was that judicious *logos* would save the audience from the dangerous allure of *apariencias*.

THE WONDROUS CASE OF THE *COMEDIA DE SANTOS*

Christian writers inherited a Platonic distrust of the phenomenal world. Pictured as a weak image of eternal forms, this world is already, at best, a copy of the ideal. Representations of this world—in poetry as in painting—are problematic twice over. They are not only copies of copies, but more perniciously, the pleasure they offer to the public distracts viewers from the true philosophical task of seeking out truth. This legacy, together with the particular spectacles of the early centuries of the Common Era (mime shows, gladiatorial events, and other mostly nondramatic shows), gave rise to yet another critique of theater: lasciviousness and hypocrisy. These moral flaws coincided in the theatrical practice of putting on a face. Whether this be athletes putting on oils before a match, actors donning platform shoes to seem taller, or women indulging in cosmetics, all sin when attempting to improve on a divinely given form, pridefully making themselves into something they are not. A most forceful rhetorician, Tertullian, offered lacerating critiques of public spectacles, and later critics of theater would turn to him in particular to affirm the degeneracy of actors and their craft. This critique was twofold. In addition to actors' hypocrisy of making themselves out to be

APPEARANCES ARE EVERYTHING

what they were not, Tertullian decried the misplaced empathy of the audience who—moved by plot, rhetoric, and acting—would respond positively to the representation of actions such as lying, betrayal, or murder, actions that in real life most decent people would condemn.[12]

A proper and explicit defense of theater from within Christian thought had to wait until Thomas Aquinas, who develops the idea of proper leisure from Aristotle. This form of recreation, *eutrapelia*, was conceived as a resting ground between attending to the duty owed to God, on the one hand, and to human affairs, on the other. It also represented an acknowledgment of humanity's split nature, between a spiritual part that aims for divine love (but often falls short) and the pull of the animal part that requires us to labor for sustenance. This Christian anthropology that sees human beings as fallen yet perfectible through grace transforms the idea of performance: performance ceases to be only a matter of pretense, of putting on a mask, and it lives up to its original meaning of giving form to or accomplishing what had only been potential before.

In her study of the ethics of acquired virtue, imitation, and authenticity, Jennifer Herdt does not deal with *eutrapelia* per se, but she does pick up on the importance of the "essential theatricality of virtue" in Christian ethics, which she sees primarily expressed in Aquinas's work.[13] The main concern of Herdt's *Putting on Virtue* is to trace, from Augustine to contemporary ethicists, the different answers given to the question of whether virtue acquired through habit, through playing the part, may still be considered genuine virtue and not hypocrisy. In doing so she uncovers the ways in which the relative weight of either individual will or divine grace colors the answer given by theologians and philosophers to the question. Ultimately, Herdt finds in Erasmus the most elegant and generous account of acquired virtue. In his works, according to Herdt, the difference between acting (human will and desire) and being acted upon (the work of grace) is less important than the acceptance of the "paradoxical convergence of outer and inner, ideal and real, grace and nature, other and self."[14] And at the heart of this paradox we find imitation. Herdt writes:

> For Erasmus, grace is active in our acting, in the beauty of the virtue displayed that engages and transforms our affections, allowing us to play a part that becomes our own as we play it. While imitation is an act, there is also a chastening of human agency implied in the cascade. We must be inspired by our exemplars; we cannot simply decide to love them, to find them beautiful.[15]

Erasmus's account of virtue depends on the imitation of Christ, but an imitation that is not mere cloning of sameness. Instead, the humanist defends a form of imitation that responds to circumstance and allows for the imitator to become at once more herself and a recognizable exemplar of the model imitated. Here, a parallel to Erasmus's contribution to the debates around the proper use of Latin might be helpful. Erasmus mocked the position of those who argued that the only proper Latin was Cicero's and that the humanists' task is to recuperate and reanimate only that rhetorician's vocabulary in order to be good. In contrast to this sort of necromancy, Erasmus espoused a rebirth model of imitation. The proper imitator of Cicero's Latin is one who considers the new speaker's circumstances and creates a language that is in the spirit of Cicero's eloquence but is also a marker of the speaker's own style.

It can be said, then, that Erasmus provides a theory for a performance-centered vision of virtue (i.e., we develop virtue partly by putting it on; conversely, putting on virtue transforms the self rather than merely disguise it). The task of bringing that theory to fruition is later taken on by the tradition of Jesuit school theater. In Spain as in France, the use of theater as a medium for Christian exemplarity left indelible marks, and many of the Jesuits' pupils—Lope de Vega, Calderón de la Barca, Molière, and the Corneille brothers—went on to become illustrious playwrights. Throughout Catholic Europe then, there was an intellectual and practical example of how theater could find a place in a well-governed republic by appealing to its potential exemplarity. Nevertheless, this potential often remained theoretical for detractors of theater. They would blame the medium for successfully corrupting the audience, inciting them to sinfulness, while in the same breath they denied that virtue could be communicated through an inherently corrupt medium. Such was, as I examined above, the judgment by the inquisitor who criticized Juan Pérez de Montalbán's adaptation of the life of Saint Mary of Egypt claiming that the "before" of sinfulness was more attractive and effective than the "after" of holiness.

The social context for public theaters in sixteenth-century Spain also helped to find a legitimate place for theatrical display. Public theaters in Spain had close relationships to guilds that turned profits over to charity hospitals, which made them a useful part of a city's civic infrastructure. Subsequently, theaters were less often subject to official censure than in England. And yet, moralists, sometimes the same Jesuits who had done much to popularize hagiography and theatrical practice, still spilled rivers of ink expressing concern over the negative effects of theater for this mixed public. Significantly, the Jesuit author of a best-selling compilation of saints' lives, Pedro de Ribadeneira (1527–1611), condemned theater as a false retreat from humanity's woes in his *Tratado de la tribulación*.

In describing how theater heightens the temptations present already in daily life, Ribadeneira refers to Saint John Chrysostom's critique of spectacle:

> if upon encountering a woman on the street whose dress has no particular care, the heart of he who looks on intently can be entranced and perverted, and sight is enough to grab and bind him, what shall we say about those who spend all day purposefully looking at beautiful and made-up women in plays? Where, in addition to the poisoned sight there are lascivious and impudent words, siren songs, delicate and sensual voices, eyes all made-up, countenances all neat, the entire body spruced up and smartly dressed, and a thousand other artifices meant to deceive and trap those who look.[16]

This description of theatrical seduction is representative in two respects. First, Ribadeneira, through Chrysostom, makes explicit the fear of theater's feminizing effects on the public. This gendering of the medium passes through the association of theater with feminine bodies exposed to public view, as they would have been in Spain, where actresses shared the stage with their male counterparts, unlike in England. The second feature of the Jesuit priest's critique addresses the uniqueness of theatrical seduction: the assault on the senses that the spectacular combination of visual enticements (the exposure to feminine bodies made all the more alluring for their use of cosmetics and fancy dress) with other sensory stimulation (charming voices lent to salacious lyrics). One image stands out from Ribadeneira's description: the comparison of theater and women on stage to the mythological sirens, composite creatures whose sight and voice charm, lull, and ultimately destroy the men who succumb to their charisma.

The image of the siren appears again at the end of Ribadeneira's chapter against theatrical escapism, but this time in the context of his response to those who would defend theater by appealing to Thomas Aquinas and the theory of *eutrapelia*, moderate and judicious recreation, that the Dominican philosopher developed from Aristotle. Ribadeneira does not deny the necessity for humans to engage in proper forms of entertainment, but he argues that such are not actually found in his own time. His main objection to theater, even when it deals with holy matter, as in hagiographic drama, has to do with the genre's excessive nature. Its total lack of proportion results in monstrosities on both sides of the stage:

> The very same angelic Doctor teaches us that in these [legitimate] recreational activities it is sinful to include lascivious words or ugly and ignominious actions; also sinful is to get too carried away, without a bridle, by pleasure and entertainment [. . .], and to say or do anything that is not well-appointed by the circumstance and proper to time, place and the person who is taking some leisure. And according to this doctrine, while it may be that the matter represented [on stage] may be honest and holy and represented by such people and in such a way that they will not offend mores but will serve as honest recreation; but it is true that those that are represented by disreputable men and wenches, and deal with lascivious and erotic themes are the ruin and destruction of the republic. And the interludes that are mixed in amidst sacred matter are very harmful and unworthy of Christian gravity. [. . .] Especially because, as Salvianus said, [in a play] all the senses are assaulted and contaminated. [. . .] For the wenches who act are typically beautiful, lascivious, and have sold their honesty; and [making use] of their whole body they sway and gesticulate, and with a soft and delicate voice, with dress and apparel, much like sirens, they charm and transform men into beasts.[17]

To be acceptable, theater has to adhere to the rules of decorum. First of all, its content and form must bend to the circumstance of topic, time, place, and public. One of the most common objections to hagiographic drama was precisely its tendency to mix matters sacred and profane, historical (hagiography being historical) and fantastical (false miracles and tropes borrowed from romance) to attract audiences.[18] A telling example of such a mixture is Lope de Vega's *El divino africano*, a play depicting the conversion of Saint Augustine. It features a love affair between the protagonist and demon who borrows the likeness of a woman to tempt the hesitating master rhetorician.

Hagiographic drama, then, would have been acceptable if it had fulfilled its task of putting virtuous and true matter before the eyes of restless theatergoers. However, by the early seventeenth century, the complaint had become commonplace that saints' plays fell short of their mission because they blended in profane situations and fictional characters and situations. Famously, already in 1605, Miguel de Cervantes depicts a mock literary debate between Don Quixote's village priest, Pero Pérez, and the Canon of

Toledo, in which the priest launches on a diatribe against the absurdities he sees in contemporary plays:

> And then if we turn to sacred dramas—what miracles they invent in them! What apocryphal, ill-devised incidents, attributing to one saint the miracles of another! And even in human plays they venture to intro- duce miracles without any reason or object except that they think some such miracle, or transformation as they call it, will come in well to aston- ish stupid people and draw them to the play.[19]

Ribadeneira goes a step further in his critique. The combination of spec- tacular extravagance and loose relation to the letter of traditional hagio- graphic matter runs counter to the delicate balance of recreation. Sweeping the audience into the arms of mere pleasure, theatrical plays overcome the audience's reason with an appeal to the senses, and theatergoers become victims of a theater that is personified in Ribadeneira's account as a mixture of Odyssean Sirens and Circe. The symbolic association of dangerous, magi- cal, feminine creatures with theatrical arts finds a concrete counterpart in the moralist's fear of the feminine body on stage. Traditionally associated with cosmetics, makeup, and gallant dress, actresses embodied deception and underscored theater's original sin of hypocrisy. Initially a neutral term in rhetoric, *hypocrisis* encompassed the delivery or performance of a speech, including the regulation of voice and gesture. By the early seventeenth cen- tury, however, it was associated with false appearances, specifically of some- one who pretends to be good but is actually evil. Compounding this threat, the act of make-believe is done for profit (on the part of the actress, another aspect that linked the theatrical profession to prostitution in the writing of moralists) and taken in for mere pleasure (on the part of the audience). Instead of harmless recreation, Ribadeneira and his followers came to imag- ine theater as a conduit of concupiscence—and as I shall show shortly, the lust was not only carnal but also cognitive and affective, extending to the desire for novelty (*curiositas*) underlying many stage innovations.

In conclusion, moralists' objections to theater, as well as the arguments of its defenders, appeal to a *proper* use of imitation. This propriety demands both a change of focus in the plays from earthly to divine love, from adul- terous pagan stories to edifying saints' lives *and* a way to subordinate the sensory power of appearances and spectacle to reason so that the play's exemplarity may shine through. In contrast, Juan Pérez de Montalbán's dramatization of the life of Saint Mary of Egypt offers a very different model, as he figures his protagonist as an image for a theater that will sacrifice neither the beauty of appearances nor holiness.

COMEDIA, NOT *FLOS SANCTORUM*

Pérez de Montalbán's audience would have been familiar with a general outline of the legend of Saint Mary the Egyptian. Literate and prosperous theatergoers could have encountered it in any one of the many immensely popular anthologies of saints' lives printed at the end of the sixteenth century. The *Flos Sanctorum* (1599), compiled by the same Ribadeneira who criticized theater, went through more than twenty editions and translations through the seventeenth century, while the anthology by the Dominican Alonso de Villegas (1534–1603) saw around sixty editions and translations.[20] For the more impecunious in the audience, broadsheets printed with ballads retelling the life of the Mary of Egypt or manuscript copies of translations of selections from Voragine's *Golden Legend* were easily available. As Julio Caro Baroja notes, it would be anachronistic—and difficult—to draw a clear distinction between elite and mass cultures, especially when dealing with the popular genre of saints' lives, which would have touched the lives of wealthy and poor alike through listening to church sermons, participating in feasts, or simply through the presence of relics, statues, or images depicting the life of Mary of Egypt.[21] As discussed in the previous chapter, the figure of the penitent in general and of the holy harlot in particular was immensely compelling, and it jumped from the pages of hagiography to the real world. Clergy in large cities often enrolled the figures of Mary Magdalene and Mary of Egypt in efforts to convert prostitutes, parading statutes and relics of the two saints through the streets of Madrid or Seville. In the countryside, miraculous interventions of Mary the Egyptian led to the establishment of local shrines to the saint.[22]

The overall architecture of *La gitana de Menfis* retains much of the traditional material from the legend of Mary of Egypt, but Juan Pérez de Montalbán does make some changes in order to fit the model of Lopean new theatrical conventions, including a three-act structure. The first act depicts her departure from the family home after her father has died and she refuses the two options offered to her—marriage or the convent. She falls into degeneracy, including the seduction of sailors, though in this play they take her from her native Memphis to Alexandria, Tyre, and Antioch rather than straight to Jerusalem as in the traditional legend. An angel disguised as a shepherd visits her, though she misunderstands his message and attempts to seduce him. Act 2 takes place two years later, as she is cast overboard by the ship's crew frightened by the mayhem that her lust has caused. She finds harbor with well-meaning shepherds whom she betrays to follow the rogues Anselmo and Ventura into the Holy Land. There, she attempts to follow the crowd into the Church of the Holy Sepulchre, where she hopes to oppose her superior beauty to that of the priest's preaching. Halted by invisible forces in front of the church, she takes stock of her life and, inspired by an image of the Virgin Mary, converts. A miraculous sign from Mary Magdalene assures her future path of penitence as she makes up her mind to leave behind secular pleasures for the rigors of the desert. Following her decision, a flying angel saves her from the wrath of a twice-abandoned Anselmo. The final act depicts her apotheosis and the effects that her conversion and miracles have on the characters that have followed her journey from Memphis to the Jordan desert.

While the broad strokes of the plot are recognizable, Pérez de Montalbán did not merely serve a slavish repetition of known narrative elements, thereby risking the disappointment of an audience that came to see a *comedia* and not read a *flos sanctorum*. Lope de Vega's favorite disciple, Pérez de Montalbán, was a successful playwright and author of more than fifty plays in all genres, including four *comedias de santos* and five others on religious topics ranging from biblical plays to *autos sacramentales*. He understood the conventions of the theater of his time, and his plays remained popular on stage and in printed editions well into the nineteenth century.[23] To turn hagiographic material into a successful play, Pérez de Montalbán added new characters. Keeping with theatrical convention, Mary of Egypt gets a female companion in Teodora in the first act, and in the last act a *gracioso* (comic figure), Ventura, who parodies Mary's conversion. Her normally anonymous suitors become recognizable stage types: Julio and Ricardo are baffled *galanes* (suitors), and Anselmo and Ventura are a pugnacious ruffian and a cowardly *gracioso*, respectively. The second act expands the role of unnamed shepherds into the generous but naive Gerardo and Fileno. Using stage machinery and accompanied by music, the play also punctuates each act with a wondrous entrance or exit of a divine character. Finally, the most significant change to the legend is also the play's first surprise for the audience. Shockingly, in the opening act, Zozimas appears, not as holy monk, but as Mary's suitor and executor of her father's will. This surprising turn fulfills, though in unexpected ways, the audience's anticipation of a romantic subplot.

Recasting the monk from the legend as Mary's suitor is a radical move: beyond the surprise, it allows Pérez de Montalbán to treat two important aspects of Mary's legendary character separately. On the one hand, it transforms Zozimas's plot arc into an exploration of *eros*—misguided love of another human being and its redirection toward a love of God. This shift, in turn, frees Pérez de Montalbán to explore a different form of Mary's concupiscence, one that would bind the figure of this particular holy harlot to theater. Mary becomes the personification of the "concupiscence of the eyes," or what Augustine would qualify as unwholesome curiosity to see, hear, experience, and know what is harmful to one's virtue as intellectual and spiritual transgression.[24] As we shall see, Pérez de Montalbán's greatest innovation was to recognize in Mary a model of curiosity, rather than simply of carnal love, and as such cast her as a potent metatheatrical figure through which he can make a defense of the *comedia de santos'* appeal to appearances.

ZOZIMAS, LOVE'S LABORS LOST AND GAINED

Juan Pérez de Montalbán fills in some of Mary's backstory in order to set the play into action. The opening of the play establishes that she is, in a sense, a free woman because her father, an honorable military man, has just died. Not being rich, he stipulated in his will that his daughter must either marry or enter a convent. She, unenthusiastic about both options, flees. This paternal detail stands in contrast to the medieval tradition, in which both parents are alive and where the mother plays an important role in the thirteenth-century verse *VSME*, pleading in a scene with her daughter to change her lascivious ways. The role of the parents in other seventeenth-century versions of the legend is minimal. Ribadeneira mentions them only once in passing.[25] Andrés Antonio Sánchez de Villamayor's retelling of Mary's vita, *La mujer fuerte*, recognized the interest and pathos of the family drama, and he amplifies his sources' scant reference to the parents. Their misguided love for their daughter, in their inability to deny her anything, first prefigures Mary's own unbridled love and then, in the dramatization of their grief over her decision to abandon her home in pursuit of pleasure, offers a model of how the reader should react.[26]

A central element of dramatic action in plays of the period was the exploration of paternal power, where the father figure represents social order and normativity. In this context, it makes sense that Pérez de Montalbán chose to have the father, even in absentia, launch the plot of the play. The paternal desire for a conventional ending to Mary of Egypt's story—marriage or the convent—haunts the first act of the play through the presence of a father figure: the executor of the father's will. Moreover, this detail paves the way for the first of the evening's surprises. The audience learns at the beginning of the play that this executor, who is also a suitor for Mary's affections, is none other than Zozimas, who does not turn to religious life until the end of the first act, in atonement for not being able to keep Mary on the straight-and-narrow path her father wanted for her.

The grafting of a romantic subplot to the staged adaptation of a saint's life was rather common, and it caused unease among moralists who worried that the representation of the "before" of sinfulness would prove all too convincing. For them, an audience steeped in this sensuality would be unable to receive the message of the "after" of holiness and salvation. Perhaps in response to those misgivings, playwrights adapting the lives of the holy harlots to the stage typically included at least one demon among the lovers, as to underline the ridiculous and unholy aspect of the amorous intrigue in contrast to the serious matter of the play. Elma Dassbach's study of the hagiographic drama of Lope and Calderón has outlined three main functions of the romantic plot: to show how the saint rejects secular life for their religious vocation, to humanize the saint by showing their struggle to make sacrifices, and last, to contrast the saint's life with other characters.[27] Pérez de Montalbán, however, in his depiction of Saint Mary of Egypt does something very different with the love plot.

Traditionally, Zozimas's presence in the legend offers a foil to Mary's life. Whereas his life stands for the masculine values of monastic life, spiritual community, and the gradual approach to holiness through prayer and good works, Mary's embodies the power of grace, of feminine intercession, and of solitary contemplation and penance. But his quest is always for spiritual perfection while hers is initially for perfect pleasure. By having Zozimas appear at the beginning as a suitor, Pérez de Montalbán achieves three things. First, he places his two main characters on the same plane: both are initially too preoccupied with earthly pursuits to care for their salvation. In a striking exchange with an angel disguised as a shepherd, Mary twice expresses an insouciance regarding the afterlife worthy of Don Juan. An angel tries to remind her in act 1 of the transience of youth and beauty compared to eternal torments, but she dismisses those concerns: "As long as our time here lasts, / I want to experience joy; / let death come afterwards, / let sadness and misfortunes come later."[28] Not long after this exchange, Zozimas echoes her words when he laments that his uncompromising stand to have her married or cloistered has made her flee: "I, miserable one, was the cause of losing her, / I spoke to her in anger, / but I would rather choose death / over not seeing her again" (10).[29]

Second, Pérez de Montalbán's erotization of the relationship between Zozimas and Mary shows how human love need not be antithetical to divine love. At the end of act 1, after Mary has rebuffed Zozimas's advances a second time in order to run away with some sailors, he decides to turn away from human society and seek refuge in the solitude of the desert. His choice reflects as much his rejection of the world as Mary's rejection of him. The expression of his conversion, therefore, remains at this point ambiguous. It is unclear whether his move to the desert represents an outdated chivalric desire to mourn Mary's rejection of his love (along the lines of Cardenio's madness in the Sierra Morena episodes in *Don Quixote* and of his model Amadís) or a desire to expiate his sins and lead a holy life in authentic eremitic fashion:

> And I, in the desert,
> will lead a miserable life
> [. . . . .]
> My life
> from now on will be a wonder.
> I am going to the desert. Lord,
> have mercy on me. (11)[30]

It would be easy to interpret Zozimas's decision to retire from secular life as an honest and direct turn to divine love. This would be in keeping with his role as the normative guardian and executor of Mary's deceased father's will and his more traditional function in the legend as the straight saint to Mary's more circuitous journey to holiness. However, his valediction to secular life shows a more conflicted path for him, too. The image he paints of his future self, leading a melancholy life that will be the wonder of the world, hardly fits the image of a true anchorite who rejoices in solitude because it allows for communion with God. Instead of a sharp turn toward divine love, Zozimas's conversion first follows the script of a jilted lover who must endure hardships to be worthy of love. Rather, putting on the mask of penitent, he sooner or later (or at least by act 3) comes to inhabit the role of holy man seeking to be worthy of God's love.

Third, the innovation of having Zozimas as Mary's suitor produces a more structurally balanced play. Rather than introducing a new character at the end of the story, the play opens and closes with the main couple, first in open conflict with each other and finally united in God's love.[31] Equally important, Pérez de Montalbán successfully creates in Zozimas a more complex character than what the traditional legend allows. By placing the monk initially on the side of the profane and making the audience witness his own spiritual transformation—more prosaic and gradual than Mary's and thus more accessible—the playwright offers the audience a character they can identify with, without taking away the focus from Mary of Egypt.

And it is on Mary that we will focus for the remainder of this chapter—particularly, on Mary as a figure for a new theatrical practice.

MARY OF EGYPT'S CURIOUS BEAUTY

In order to understand how Pérez de Montalbán mounts a defense of theater through the personification of spectacle in the figure of Mary of Egypt in *La gitana de Menfis*, we must begin with the title. Why a gypsy? The easy answer responds to etymology: gypsies, any Spanish dictionary will explain, were believed to come from Egypt originally, so *gitano* stems from *egiptano*. That makes sense, but it results in a strangely tautological title: "The Egyptian Girl from Memphis, Mary the Egyptian." Taking the pulse on the connotations of the word *gitano*, Covarrubias's lexicon begins to illuminate what is at stake in the repetition. Gypsies, according to Covarrubias, are above all a people characterized by their wanderings, the result of a curse for not having given hospitality to the fleeing Holy Family.[32] This detail resonates in the play, where Pérez de Montalbán places hospitality at the core of both one of Mary's gravest transgressions (allowing Anselmo to burn down the house of the shepherds who had given her and Teodora shelter) and later in the last act the miracle that signals her holiness (praying a hostess's dead brother back to life).

The itinerant life of gypsies was dubious not only because it was a punishment for failed hospitality but also because it signaled moral shiftiness, an attribute of other groups without a fixed address such as vagrants and actors. Covarrubias elaborates that gypsy men are notorious thieves, often passing a poor horse for a great steed, while women deceived others through palmistry and other fortune-telling schemes. Covarrubias does exclude one feature typically associated with the stereotype of the gypsy and attested to in a panoply of novels, plays, and interludes: their love of music and dance. Thus, in flagging Mary of Egypt as a gypsy, Pérez de Montalbán announces to his audience from the beginning that this play will be not only about misdirected love and beauty gone awry but also about restlessness and the value of entertainment. The gypsy girl from Memphis is not just a figure of lust but, more importantly, a *mujer fuerte* (strong woman) who wants to follow her own will—and what she seeks above all is the experience of novelty. Love is part of it, but more capaciously she wants to see new things, do new things, meet new people, go new places. As a figure of theater, she is distraction personified.

The epithet that most characters use to refer to Mary of Egypt is "bella," beautiful. Julio, one of the three well-wishers who has come to offer words of comfort at the death of her father, addresses her as beautiful in the first line of the play: "Our condolences, beautiful Mary, / we have come to offer" (1).[33] A few lines later, the second *galán* repeats the phrase "bella María," which is echoed by the last character who arrives in the scene, Zozimas. In risible hyperbole, Celio, another *galán* greets Mary, abusing Petrarchist tropes: "lady, on this occasion, / Love himself would come to harvest / pearls that would rain from those / eyes that are diamonds" (1).[34] For these men, Mary's beauty is a feature that must be possessed, or at least harvested. In contrast, for the Egyptian, beauty is not something to own or to give away. It is a more active matter, as she makes clear in her response to the men's condolences:

> And so the best cure
> for the greatest sorrows
> is to flaunt the beauty
> of the ornamented sideboard;
> and so, to distract
> from my misery
> I want to see gold shine
> and diamonds dazzle.
> Nearby is the silversmith's workshop
> of Memphis, of much renown. (2)[35]

Like the magpie, Mary seeks beauty in its outer appearance: whatever shines attracts—or, rather distracts—her, but, significantly, she does not necessarily aspire to own the gold or diamonds that she seeks, much to Teodora's chagrin. In a recapitulation speech that Teodora gives at the beginning of act 2, she laments that Mary seems untouched by greed or profit: although beautiful enough to benefit materially from her lust, it is not in her nature (13). Rather than an accumulation of wealth, which would weigh her down, Mary seeks the sparkle of the new.

Similarly, for all the masculine attention to Mary's beauty and her own awareness of the effects that it can have on men, Mary defines herself—when she must—with more active descriptors than the heavy-handed, tired Petrarchist tropes her suitors serve. In a speech warning Zozimas that no amount of pleading or threatening will make her renounce her freedom, she pledges to respond to pressure thus:

> I shall be fire, which pressured
> inside volcanoes, shall erupt;
> I shall be an unleashed Fury,
> triumphant laurel tree resisting the most powerful lightning ray;
> the serpent that the heel crushed,
> and the snake that bites amidst flowers;
> a comet announcing horrors,
> the thunder that makes Memphis tremble,
> the rage threatening the world,
> and the rigor to control it;
> and finally, I shall be
> a woman who bends to nothing
> and has no more rule
> than what she desires. (5)[36]

The power of this speech depends on its astounding imagery to hammer in the idea that Mary sees herself as a force of nature. The audience, hearing this litany of primal elements conjuring a natural threat to human order, would be affected by its vivid language. Intensifying this effect is the recognition that some of the images used in the speech are also common stage effects.[37] Mary's self-presentation as erupting volcano, lightning, or comet represents more than simply examples of natural fury: she becomes artifice personified. She is a spectacle waiting to happen.

The sensational imagery is awe-inspiring, and its rhetorical strength can easily draw attention away from the most puzzling metaphor in the speech: her declared intention to become "the serpent that the heel crushed, / and the snake that bites amidst flowers" (5). Moralists would have recognized the subtle allusion to the snake's punishment in Genesis 3:15—"I will put enmity between you and the woman, and between your offspring and hers; he will strike your head, and you will strike his heel"—and interpreted it as yet another example of theatrical deviousness, as sin slipping in amid the pleasures of spectacle. But there is more than one snake at play here. And if one snake is like the siren's call, using sweet words to better deceive, the other calls forth the possibility of redemption. Indeed, Genesis 3:15 refers to God's punishment of the snake after it had worked its deception in paradise; but, this passage, also known as the protoevangelium, was also traditionally interpreted as announcing the ulterior crushing of the snake by the offspring (Christ) of the woman (Virgin Mary). Iconographically, this passage served to imagine, typologically, a move from Eve to the Virgin Mary in the guise of Apocalyptic dragon slayer, crushing a snake with her heel. As such, the allusion in the play announces two important transformations that will occur in the course of *La gitana de Memphis*. At the level of plot, the image of punishment and redemption places the story of Mary of Egypt within the script of *felix culpa*, where she plays the fallen woman who becomes first a penitent hermit and ultimately a saint. At a metatheatrical level, the biblical allusion in the midst of Mary's speech highlights the fact that Pérez de Montalbán's "converted" theater remains committed to visual display, in contrast to moralists and poets who would have theater cleansed of its dependence on spectacle. A snake remains a snake, in other words, but its function has changed from agent of mendacity to marvel to be shown—a marvel that manifests God's loving plan for humanity.

The play itself articulates what this judiciously astonishing theater entails and how it functions by incorporating its alternatives. Setting in motion the primary conflict—Mary's irreverence and curiosity wreaking havoc—the first act also presents a conflict between two different but equally inadequate forms of theatricality. On the one hand, the character of Zozimas depicts the failure of pure reason, what in the play is called *sermón* and represents the value of *logos* or reasonable speech, to move or convince characters to do good. On the other hand, Anselmo and Ventura showcase bad theater, what could be called the rogue theatrics of make-believe. Their performance, closely associated with the use of cosmetics and other subterfuges, corresponds to the biggest fears of Christian moralists: a theater of bad faith that aims to deceive by dressing up a lie in order to fool the audience into taking it for truth. Between these two modes of theatricality stands Mary of Egypt, whose curious active beauty personifies a different vision of spectacle.

APPEARANCES ARE EVERYTHING

OF ROGUE THEATRICS AND SERMONS

The play associates the aesthetically and morally bad form of theater with the roguish characters Ventura, the play's *gracioso*, and Anselmo, a pimp and possibly murderer. When these characters enter, Anselmo is fuming in anger at the loss of his lover and prostitute, Julia, who left him for an ugly man. Ventura, in a misguided attempt to soothe his master, launches on a paean to artifice:

> No longer is an ugly mien or physique an affront.
> I shall tell you how
> inventive artifice improves upon it all:
> if the calves are lacking,
> two pillows can work wonders;
> if a man is but a skeleton,
> his authority can be found in a breastplate;
> if he is bald in the head,
> a blessèd wig can help him cope:
> with artifice, in the end, all can be dressed up;
> I only lack a remedy for a hunched back,
> if it is not through outlandish fabrication
> a miller's stone straightens it up. (7)[38]

This comic speech is aptly delivered in the context of prostitution, a practice that proves problematic not only on account of misguided erotics but because of its dependence on the ruses of makeup and fancy clothing, which deceive by covering moral and physical rot with superficial beauty. While the use of artifice to produce a specifically erotic effect through public display was a central concern of moralists, their apprehension extended to the very idea of disguise as an ontological sham. In his critique of theater as an activity that steals energy from Christian works, *Bienes de el honesto trabajo y daños de la ociosidad* (1614), Father Pedro de Guzmán criticizes the care actors take in creating such duplicitous spectacles and decries the appeal of costumes on stage:

> They enter the stage in rich attire, modern or ancient, representing the clever one, the old man, the young one, [. . .], the whore, the procuress,

the angry man, the lover, [. . .], the king, the emperor, the lord, the vassal, [. . .] (the stage looks like a miniature world), each one puts forth through words, actions, and costume their ventures or misadventures; their quest or purpose, and the person that each is, all done so properly that the two senses I mentioned before [sight and hearing] are enraptured, and the soul follows after them, and the spectacle has the audience entertained and hanging on the entire afternoon, and the entire day, and their entire life.[39]

As if the threat of emptiness—that any person can pick up the robes of a king and through the appropriate words and actions *play* and possibly *become* king—were not enough, the rogue theatrics that Ventura proposes flips the moralist script. It is men who turn to artifice to remake themselves rather than vain women. The prescribed remedy to this ridiculous form of theater, as we have seen, passes through a purification of imitation through *logos*, according to moralists. However, in Pérez de Montalbán's play, just as in the medieval verse vita of Saint Mary of Egypt, words and reason alone— what in the play appears as *sermón*—prove to be inefficient instruments of spiritual transformation.

The word *sermón* appears already in the second scene of *La gitana de Menfis*'s first act. Zozimas, appalled that Mary is flirting with men rather than playing the role of mourning daughter, delivers a long speech on what he believes Mary owes her dead father and himself as a favored suitor and now executor of her father's will. To this harangue, Mary responds mockingly:

> Every time, good sir,
> that a death occurs
> [. . . . .]
> there is a sermon.
> My father died, and therefore,
> today at his funeral you want
> to avoid the expense
> and you preach to us
> liberally and without charge (3).[40]

Not so subtly, Mary accuses Zozimas here of deploying nothing but cheap words.

Her immunity to speech, however, does not stop her from pronouncing a lengthy defense of her own actions where she outlines her libertine philosophy. She begins by countering Zozimas's accusation of filial frailty by pointing out that death by natural causes is just that, the natural course of things, and not something to be mourned; her father's death is merely the consequence of his having been alive (3). She goes on to paint a vivid counterfactual situation, imagining that had Claudio died in battle at the hands of the enemy, she would have turned into a warrior lady to avenge him:

> and as a strong Amazon,
> angrier than strong
> I would mount a swift horse
> and reach their rebellious
> walls and throw a challenge
> so proudly and bravely done
> that it would force them
> to enter into battle with me
> and this way
> I would either punish those who offended me
> or die nobly. (4)[41]

Mary's eloquence is evident in this passage not only in the striking images she paints of herself, slightly unhinged by sorrow and anger, on horseback and challenging her opponents at the city gate, but also in the effective staccato rhythm of the parataxis proper to epic action. She concludes that since Claudio's was not an epic death, it does not deserve epic mourning. Indeed, to claim otherwise would be, she says, comparable to Lucifer's rebellion against God's design. In the end, she concedes that while she owes some feeling to her father, importantly, the debt does not extend to the ostentation of emotion:

> To say that his death must be felt
> is well said, but think
> good sir, that it is not my pleasure
> to display displeasure on account of his death.
> If I am displeased, I know it,
> for it is not becoming of brave hearts
> to not conceal their grief
> when they suffer it. (2)[42]

Once liberated from the tyranny of keeping up appearances, of the *qué dirán* of popular gossip, which Zozimas mobilized in his speech to get her to behave properly, Mary declares her freedom to be "a woman who has no other rule or allegiance than her very desire" (5).[43]

The second time the play mentions a sermon is in the second act, this time properly applied to the preaching at the Church of the Holy Sepulchre that has attracted pilgrims from all over. Teodora is first to see the crowds around them and to wonder about their purpose and destination. Ventura explains that everyone in town is making haste to hear the patriarch's sermon about to begin. Mary, too, marvels at all the people gathered and declares her intention to use her powers of seduction to disrupt peace in the city:

> Today, you shall see that
> on my account, in this most excellent city
> there will be huge disagreements:
> Today, my beauty shall be
> enough to stir up a thousand fights and brawls,
> all of which gives me most pleasure. (17)[44]

After this declaration of war by sexual means, her companions all attempt to get Mary to attend the sermon. As with Zozimas's turn to the desert in act 1, motivated by amorous distress and religious calling, the rogues' determination to get Mary into the temple is ambiguous. Their insistence on attending the sermon might be a sign of the thaumaturgic powers of the Holy Land and a prefiguration of Mary's own dramatic future conversion. Yet, their intention is colored as much by an eagerness to hear the holy words they have all been talking about as by their fear of getting caught up once again in the trouble that they know Mary's beauty can stir. Ventura is the most vocal about their equivocation when he says to Mary that he plans to be as far away from her and her desires as possible. Anselmo, too, invites her one last time to join them, but she rejects him coldly thus: "Me, a sermon? / no such madness has been seen before. / My pleasure and desire do not extend to entering the church. / Let the learned listen to it" (17).[45] Regardless of which interpretation one chooses, the rogues' sudden eagerness to hear a *sermón* should not be attributed to fickle dramaturgy that turns out inconsistent characters, convenient mouthpieces for whatever the plot needs. Instead, their various reactions dramatize for the audience the weak power of a theater based on *sermón* alone.

REDEEMED THEATRICALITY

The poverty of words has been, in fact, a peculiar characteristic of the play. In his studies of Pérez de Montalbán's contemporary Tirso de Molina, Ignacio Arellano described Molina's oeuvre as creating "la visualidad de la palabra"—painting a picture through lavish figurative language. In contrast, Pérez de Montalbán highlights Mary of Egypt's addiction to the literal and gestural aspects of speech, in both comic and serious moments. In the opening scene of the play, she gravitates toward Julio, one of the suitors, because his name echoes that of the month of July, "ultimately, a blazing month / cannot but be an ardent man" (2).[46] She derides, as I examined earlier, clichéd words and responds by literalizing them: "if eyes were diamonds, diamonds never rain" (2).[47] Similarly, moments before her conversion, she dismisses Ventura's praise for the imminent sermon, which he describes as "precious matter" (cosa rica), by declaring that a diamond would be even more precious (17). In a serious mode, Mary operates on a literal level at the end of the first act when she reacts in horror to an angel's warning. Disguised as a shepherd, the angel prophesies that her intention to pursue the path of pure pleasure will take her to a wilderness, where she will find herself naked (10). Pre-conversion Mary imagines that she will be victimized by Anselmo and Ventura—not unlike El Cid's daughters are humiliated by the Infantes de Carrión in the fields of Corpes—and she runs away by catching a ride on a ship: "If I should ever find myself / denuded by those two rogues / who are now in town, / I would much rather become a public / sinner in Alexandria" (10).[48] Mary is frightened, not so much at the threat of sexual exposure—her naked wandering—as much as she is terrified of not doing her will; that is why becoming a public woman seems preferable.

These examples might indicate that a literal understanding is of a piece with the sinful life she leads before her conversion, that she moves exclusively in the mundane, physical world. The angel's speech, however, already hints at a complication of such an easy association. The image of a naked Mary in the wilderness may well point to an epic affront, but it also describes what comes to pass in the third act: a poorly clad, penitent Mary wanders the banks of the Jordan River. The angel's warning in the first act turns out to have been prophetic in the last act of the play. Significantly, not only her conversion but also her future holiness pass through the literal.

Stage directions indicate that after the exchange with Anselmo and

Ventura at the portal of the Church of the Holy Sepulchre, Mary remains alone on stage, having declined to enter the church, which she describes as dungeon-like, echoing her earlier disdain for both religious and marital life as carceral (17). At first, solitude suits her, as she imagines herself admired by those who will be entering the church. Soon, however, her aversion to seclusion and concentration gets the best of her, and once again she wants to get her show on the road or, more precisely, to take it inside the temple, where there are onlookers:

No one is coming, nor reaches
the famous door of the Temple
open to everyone in the world:
the occasion denies me love.
But what is this? Am I blind?
entering would be better
where I shall be able, under pretext
of listening to the Sermon, overtake
the will of others with the power
of [my] superior beauty. (18)[49]

Earlier in the first act, Mary had declared her enmity toward both containment and solitude when she declared to Zozimas that "all restraint bothers me, / all solitude offends me; / to see widely brings me great relief; / to converse much, stirs me much" (4).[50] Identifying with curiosity in her drive to see and speak of many things, Mary detests arrest, so in the soliloquy before the portal of the church she reveals her double position as object and subject of distraction. Restless because left alone, she seeks new admirers who will distract her from her solitude and whom she will, in turn, distract from their Christian duty.

Moments later, supernatural forces prevent Mary from crossing the church's threshold. In contrast to the medieval poem, in which angelic knights guarded the entrance to the church, Pérez de Montalbán makes holy resistance visible to the audience through a combination of word and gesture. Mary's soliloquy forces her to process her immobility as her feet feel tied and she is weighed down, forcing her for the first time to be alone and stand still:

What's this, angered Heavens?
The weight of my sin

APPEARANCES ARE EVERYTHING

has come to oppress me so;
yet I want to go in (Woe is me!)
I cannot lift my feet
I feel inside me a new fear,
I who never before frightened
[. . . . .]
What is this, ingrate Fortune?
Who delays my design?
Once again I want to try:
not one step can I take;
without a doubt, it must be
so that such a bad woman
shall not enter such a holy place.
I have been keen to see
a variety of things, and today I fear,
that to block me, Heaven
has wanted to shackle me. (18)[51]

Up to this point, Mary has turned a deaf ear to all admonitions she calls
sermón. What is more, she neutralizes the persuasive power of words by
refusing their figurative meaning and remaining as devoted to the literal
as she is to the here and now and her quest for novelty. In this context, one
would have expected Mary's conversion to pass through a corresponding
semantic sublimation that would take her from the literal to the allegorical.
Instead, she is saved through the literal. In other words, she converts when
the heavens "speak" in a language she understands: a language of gestures.
For example, she interprets her inability to move toward the temple literally
as the very "weight of her sin." (18).[52]

Similarly, the concupiscence of the eye, manifested in her restlessness
and desire to seek diverse sights, does not so much disappear or wane;
rather, it changes in orientation. Thus, after her self-insight, she turns her
gaze toward an image of her namesake, the mother of care and ministration,
the Virgin Mary, and requests the grace necessary to "enter / even if only
this one time, / to the celebrated Sermon / which I did not want to listen to
before" (18).[53] This statement reminds the audience that while Mary of Egypt
has achieved her original goal, entering a new place, the *purpose* driving her
intention to cross the holy threshold has changed from lust and curiosity to
Christian care. In other words, from curiosity as the wanton quest for the
new for novelty's sake, Mary's conversion results in a turn to the etymologi-

cal root of curiosity in *cura*, or care. Indeed, Mary's greatest miracle in the play gives witness to her "turn" toward care. In the last act of the play, after her years in the wilderness and her reunion with now-monk Zozimas, she successfully offers a prayer to God for the resurrection of the brother of a woman who had hosted her early in her stay in the desert.

The framing of her conversion and the scene of conversion both suggest the impotence of discourse, of *logos*, in effecting a conversion on its own. Words alone fail in the play on two accounts. First, and most importantly, without grace, even the most eloquent speech leaves its audience unmoved. Mary's companions showcase the necessity of grace in their different responses to the sermon that they are, for multiple reasons, eager to hear. Anselmo is the first to exit the church, and awed by the patriarch's eloquence, he comments on its beauty declaring that the priest "preaches elegantly" (gallardamente predica) (18). Ventura agrees and adds that it would suffice to move and convert a marble statue, while Teodora, for her part, could not hear it or, as Ventura points out to her, perhaps it was less a question of ability than of will (18). Despite their professions of its power, the sermon has no lasting effect, as Mary's return on stage reveals. Anselmo quickly forgets the beauty of the sermon and, hearing Mary declare her heart full of "mysterious words" (palabras misteriosas), he draws his sword against her in a jealous fit (19). The sermon's impact dissipates in less than a scene. Ventura, upon hearing Mary's words, dismisses them, and he mocks her sermonizing: "When the devil preaches, / it bodes great harm" (19).[54] Teodora simply cannot recognize her mistress. Their skeptical and even hostile reactions to Mary's newfound Christian love give the lie to Ventura's hyperbolic claim earlier that the patriarch's words were enough to convert even a marble statue. According to the logic of *La gitana de Menfis*, neither a spectacle of pure make-believe nor one of sublime *logos* is capable of the miracle of persuasion or conversion, first because grace must intervene but also because, as my reading of Mary's conversion shows, words require flesh to reach the human heart.

Second, the play gives multiple examples of how *logos* uncoupled from the trappings of delivery—voice, gesture, spectacle, and so on—words without body, will also fall on deaf ears. Only embodied *logos*—words and spectacle together—is able to bring about meaningful change. In the final act of the play, Mary credits the words of the sermon with her conversion, but the audience knows that it was her *physical* experience of heavenly disapproval—her inability to take a step further—together with the active intervention of two visual representations outside of the temple that made her conversion possible. The first of these instances was the image of the Virgin Mary to whom the Egyptian prays in order to be allowed to enter the church. The second mediating instance occurs when Mary turns to the Virgin again after the sermon to ask whether she should atone for her sins by joining a convent or by becoming an anchorite. A painting of the Virgin flips over to reveal her answer in the figure of a third Mary—she who charts the halfway point between the Egyptian and the Holy Virgin—the Magdalene (19).

This dramatic turn is, as far as I can tell, wholly of Pérez de Montalbán's invention; in most other renditions, the answer comes through a disembodied voice that directs Mary to the desert. The intervention of an image in this context seems to tilt the scale in favor of a purely visual mode of communicating the divine, along the lines of a divinely inspired vision. However, as Mary of Egypt immediately points out, the *apariencia*—the revelatory prop—is but a mute canvas ("tabla muda," 19) that requires, like a baroque emblem, an inscription to be fully intelligible. Mary then articulates for herself and the audience the message toward which the mute canvas can only gesture: that message is one of holy imitation, that is to say, an invitation to put on the role of penitent to truly become one. Similarly, for all of Anselmo's admiration of the sermon's beauty, his true conversion does not happen listening to words alone. Instead, it takes place late in the third act, when he mistakes Zozimas's reference to the host for Mary's communion as a treasure. Anselmo then attempts to rob the monk of the monstrance housing the Eucharist, but the "greatest treasure known to men" miraculously gives way to an image of Christ (either on the cross or as a child), who addresses the rogue directly (30).[55] Here again, the words of the *apariencia* speak in the sinner's literal-minded language, and the repetition of the word *robar* (to steal) to describe both a criminal act and a spiritual one marks the turning point of the rogue's conversion: "if you want to *steal me*, come / although it would do you twice as good / *to steal me* with your soul / than with ruthless hands" (30, emphasis added).[56] Stage machinery together with language that acknowledges the literal level is central to the conversion of its sinners.

For all her flaws, Juan Pérez de Montalbán does not represent Mary of Egypt as a liar or a makeup enthusiast. He has, instead, cleverly maintained the conventional association of femininity with spectacle—the appeal of the surface, of wanton curiosity—but separated it from outright deception. Whereas moralists often wished to cleanse theater of its vices by stripping it of its *aparato* (devices and machinery), down to its textuality as saving grace, Pérez de Montalbán does something more radical. He uses the figure of Saint Mary of Egypt to present a theater that is devoted to appearances that will not lead viewers astray; for instead of offering spectacle as a cover-up for a lack and asking the audience to take its lie as the truth, *La gitana de Menfis* aspires to present spectacle as wonder, a complex theatrical experience of caring curiosity.

EPILOGUE

In the Artist's Studio

Legends often—in their own way—tell the truth.

GEORGES DIDI-HUBERMAN, *La peinture incarnée*[1]

LEGENDARY. SAINTS' LIVES by definition are legendary. They are meant to be remembered, to be written down and read; they are literally *legendae* (matter intended to be read) in an unspecified future. Without this afterlife, saints fail in their function of being an effective intermediary between humans and God, for their exemplarity would be lost. Most versions of the life of Saint Mary of Egypt do not stop at her death but include elaborate descriptions of the care that Zozimas took in burying her with the miraculous help of a lion. Many go further and follow the good monk back to his abbey where, after having kept silent about his desert encounter with the humble penitent, he will finally propagate the story of the formidable woman who taught him the true meaning of penitence and of a holiness that, while not hidden, does not proclaim itself as holy.

Jusepe de Ribera's *Saint Mary of Egypt in Ecstasy* figures the importance of this afterlife. This narrative painting, as we saw in chapter 4, foregrounds Zozimas, who witnesses a penitent Mary rise above the ground as she prays—all while he points to a tiny scene ensconced amid the rocky landscape of the background. The meaning of the painting depends on this almost imperceptible detail. Painted in blurry brushstrokes, this scene (figure 15) depicts the luminous corpse of the saint, the upright monk praying over her, and the approaching lion. It strikes a contrast to the clarity of the bodies in the foreground. On the one hand, this patchy scene functions as a poetic envoi, a valedictory move that offers an interpretation of the rest of the canvas. It is a divine signature that comments on the larger composition, marking at once the physical end of this particular saint's life and the beginning of its future as a vita, as a crafted narrative and visual whole that becomes public and goes out into the world. On the other hand, the haziness of its execution highlights Saint Mary of Egypt's lessons about images, beauty, and holiness. By harking back to the incarnational paradox of two natures in one person, these images signify beyond their representational likeness, and their surface texture invites the viewer to engage with the image carnally as an object in the world, to find in its grain a reminder that neither beauty nor holiness are graspingly—that is to say, conceptually—obvious.

As French art historian and theoretician Georges Didi-Huberman would have it, legends tell the truth, albeit in their own language. Intriguingly, his discussion of the legend of Honoré de Balzac's *Le chef-d'œuvre inconnu* also features, in a corner, a tiny patch figuring a canvas of Saint Mary of Egypt. Balzac's novella, hailed by twentieth-century critics as nothing less than a "catechism of aesthetics" and a "fable of modern art," is the literary equivalent of a diptych, juxtaposing two sections each bearing the name of a woman associated with a painter.[2] The first panel belongs to the section titled "Gillette," nubile model and lover of the young and yet unknown French painter Nicolas Poussin (1594–1665). Goaded by a third painter, Flemish master Frans Porbus (1569–1622)—in the story a mentor of sorts to Poussin—the budding artist convinces Gillette to pose nude for the fictional Master Frenhofer so he may finally complete his masterpiece, *La belle noiseuse* (The beautiful troublemaker). The second panel in the story is "Catherine Lescault," a courtesan famous for her beauty and ostensibly the inspiration for the unfinished masterpiece into which genius painter Frenhofer has poured ten years of labor but which no one has seen. After comparing his portrait to the lovely nude body of Gillette, Frenhofer is convinced of its genius and allows the two other painters to see his "unknown masterpiece." However, facing the life-size canvas, all Porbus and Poussin can see are what the young painter describes as "colors daubed one on top of the other and contained by a mass of strange lines forming a wall of paint."[3] Distraught at the reaction of his colleagues, Frenhofer fears that he has spent his everything in creating "nothing," and he dies that night after having set fire to all his works.[4]

Balzac's philosophical tale has served as a touchstone for some of the most influential modern thinkers and practitioners about images and painting, most of whom focus on the second portrait. Retrospectively, the description of this second image seems to augur an abstract art and modernism that proposes that ideal beauty is beyond mimetic representation. Legend has it that Paul Cézanne, "striking his chest with his index finger, designated himself" as Frenhofer.[5] Pablo Picasso not only produced thirteen illustrations of the story, but he even worked out of the building he believed to be the one where Frenhofer had seen his demise. Most critics associate modernity with the experiment of the patchy canvas at the end of the novella. This is true whether they admire Frenhofer's adherence to the ideal to the point of dying (rather than live with an imperfect beauty that has been defiled by the critical gaze of others) or they celebrate the dissolution of mimetic form into the materiality of the surface.

These critics at best pay only cursory attention to the presence of Saint Mary of Egypt. Dispossessed of her own panel in the story (she appears in the "Gillette" section), the saint remains central, nonetheless, to the development of the plot and to the aesthetic discussion at the heart of the novella. Close attention to her manifestation, albeit ghostly, reveals, an alternative to Frenhofer's dark tale of mastery, idealism, and possession.

The story opens with Nicolas Poussin, all anticipation and blushing excitement, hesitating reverentially before knocking at the door of the studio of the great Porbus, painter at the court of Marie de' Medici in Paris. The "neophyte," as the narrator refers to Poussin, finally enters when he follows the lead of a strange older man, Frenhofer, who looks "as if a canvas by Rembrandt were walking."[6] Once inside, the narrative takes on the young man's perspective as he marvels at the space where creation happens. Porbus's studio is a jumble of the old (plaster bits of classical sculpture) and the forthcoming (barely started canvas whose strokes of preparatory white paint are illuminated by a skylight). The site of theorizing about beauty, it is also home to the mundane stuff (brushes, oils, pigments) that makes the painter's art possible. Amid the clutter of the studio, the newcomer's gaze fixates on a particular canvas:

> A picture, which, in that age of disorder and upheavals, had already become famous and was often visited by several of those fanatics to whom we owe the preservation of the sacred fire in evil times. This lovely canvas portrayed a *Mary of Egypt* undressing in order to pay her passage to Jerusalem. Marie de Médicis, for whom it was painted, would sell this masterpiece in the days of her destitution.[7]

This astonishing introduction to the canvas highlights two important aspects associated with image theory according to Saint Mary of Egypt. First, the canvas embodies the knotty temporality of becoming that, as

I have demonstrated in previous chapters, theologians, poets, and visual artists recognized as central to the life of the saint. While still in the artist's studio, possibly still in progress, the painting already enjoyed recognition. In spite of the "disorder and upheavals" that followed the 1610 assassination of Henry IV, the painting called for the attention of royalty (the queen, for whom it was intended) and of the fanatics (*entêtés*) who came to see it, as well as the attention of young Poussin, eager to learn, and, with him, the attention of the reader. Moreover, the painting's story of becoming is embedded in a larger story of politics and religion, which in turn affects the description of its fate as material object. The canvas, available to admiring eyes in the artist's studio, will not stay there. The story anticipates its path, from the queen mother's collection and then lost to history when Marie de' Medici loses power to her son Louis XIII and the painting is sold.

Second, this introductory description of the canvas of Saint Mary of Egypt also highlights mobility in two respects. First of all, movement is the motif of the painting. Instead of a static portrait (the genre upon which Porbus staked his fame), he has, somewhat unusually and somewhat indecorously, depicted Mary of Egypt in motion. The female figure, as Poussin describes it, is in transit: Mary negotiates her passage from Alexandria, where she exerted her extreme form of erotic generosity, to Jerusalem, where she will benefit from the Virgin's equally excessive loving generosity. Second, Porbus portrays the promiscuous protagonist in the midst of an action. She is described as "*showing* readiness to pay."[8] Porbus's canvas does not exactly depict action as a fait accompli; instead, he immortalizes the sinner-saint forever on the cusp of accomplishing something, stressing visually the participial power of becoming that sets her legend apart from other tales of conversion. Thus, Porbus's canvas depicts the deep breath of consideration that precedes an action rather than the act itself. In contrast to the sheer abandon to pleasure in the triptych dedicated to the legend of Saint Mary of Egypt painted by German expressionist Emil Nolde in 1912, the canvas in Balzac's story portrays suspense much in the same way the *VSME* suspends Mary's speech to the sailors between legitimate persuasion and illicit seduction. It falls to the neophyte artist, not yet set in his ways, to notice the expectant aspect of Porbus's painting in his rebuttal to Frenhofer's savage critique. Poussin is the only one to point out that the painting is not the portrait of one figure but is instead the representation of a relationship being negotiated between *two* figures on the canvas. While Frenhofer and Porbus debate the merits of the feminine figure and her proximity to achieving true representation of life, Poussin turns the readers' attention to the exchange between the sailor and Mary: "Those two figures, Mary and the boatman, have a delicacy of purpose quite beyond the Italian painters—I can't think of a single one who could have invented the boatman's hesitation."[9]

Poussin identifies the depiction of hesitation—of a non-accomplished act—as the painting's greatest aesthetic strength. In this, the painting of the Egyptian temptress-saint is similar to the canvas of the *Belle noiseuse*: both represent incompletion. And yet an important difference separates the two paintings. Whereas Frenhofer jealously presents his life's work as his—the master's—possession, defiled by the gaze of anyone other than her creator, Porbus's canvas of Saint Mary of Egypt is as promiscuous as the saint herself had once been. Its production required the collaboration of both artists: Porbus imagined the scene of hesitation, drafted it and gave it color, and Frenhofer picks up the brush to daub the canvas with what he imagines to be the final stroke. As Hubert Damisch suggests, Frenhofer gives visibility to the quivering skin of the female figure and its perfection, obscuring what went underneath.[10] Frenhofer's efforts to "master" and fully realize the potential of the canvas, no matter how successful in giving Mary of Egypt the *je ne sais quoi* that separates mere copying of nature from true artistic creation, do not end Mary's temporality or promiscuity. Immediately after Frenhofer has "completed" Mary, Poussin gives the saint yet another afterlife in a drawing of the saint that he completes on the spot, inspired by Porbus's painting. His elders see the drawing, a copy of Porbus's work, and recognize in him a peer. Signing his name to the drawing, Poussin adds himself symbolically to the list of lovers of Mary's figure.

Beyond the frame of the short story as Balzac published it, the canvas's dissolution is even greater. In the first version of the story, Balzac included a description of its fate two centuries after it had left the hands of its intended owner, Marie de' Medici. This future includes, significantly, the profanation of the Egyptian saint's image:

> When we invaded Germany (1806), an artillery captain saved her from an impending end by hiding her in his trunk [. . .]. His soldiers had already painted a mustache on the saint protectress of penitent girls; and, drunk and sacrilegious, they were going to use the poor saint as target practice [. . .]. Today, this magnificent canvas hangs in the castle of the Grenadière.[11]

In contrast to *La belle noiseuse*, which barely admits the regard of others, Porbus's *Marie egyptienne* survives even the assault of drunken soldiers, whose act of vandalism upon the beauty of Alexandria is quite in keeping with the representations of Saint Mary of Egypt in penitence, where the masculine touch erases neither the femininity nor the holiness of the penitent figure. To the sacralization of the work of art, Mary of Egypt responds with the joyful profanation assured by the promiscuity of grace, which looks for beauty and holiness in the unexpected.

The idea for this book began with a pair of shoes. More precisely, it began with the seeming incongruence of a delicately, lovingly described object of luxury in the middle of a medieval poem that was ostensibly about sainthood and asceticism. These shoes wear the paradox animating the sort of beauty that Mary of Egypt makes visible, which I have tried to track and share with the reader throughout the preceding chapters. This beauty is not about to be sacrificed. It does not simply equal goodness. It is resolutely present in shoes crafted in leather and silk as a testament to our nature as creatures: dependent, fragile, exposed to the elements. But as Julia R. Lupton reminds the reader with philological elegance, the creature is a "fashioned thing but with the sense of continued or potential process, action or emergence built into the future thrust of its active verbal form."[12] In other words, the very same creaturely fragility underlined by the shoes is also the site of human ingenuity giving rise to artifice. More than anything else, though, these shoes are objects of beauty to be used as much as enjoyed, and above all the pleasure they offer and represent is meant to be shared. These shoes will not be fetishized; they will not be removed from circulation in order to be privately admired and adored. Instead, the shoes are to be shared and enjoyed through language. They are legendary but not sacred.

Balzac's story ends with a barely visible foot, the fragmented body of an idealized woman on which Frenhofer has lavished time, love, and effort. But this time, the foot is not made public. Within Balzac's text, the foot is barely visible beneath layers of paint (and the words to describe the different coverings):

> in one corner of the canvas, the tip of a bare foot emerging from this chaos of colors, shapes, and vague shadings, a kind of incoherent mist; but a delightful foot, a living foot![13]

A glance at this miraculously alive foot is possible only after a sacrifice. Frenhofer allows Poussin and Porbus into the hallowed high chamber of the *Belle noiseuse* because Poussin convinced Gillette to offer herself nude to serve as comparison to the painting in order to satisfy the doubts of the old master. The foot, the narrator asserts, is alive, but it cannot be described. Moreover, the idealized beauty it represents is meant to belong exclusively to the artist. If and when it is subject to a public gaze, it is not a beauty that creates community by calling out to the viewers to partake and participate in it. Instead, this absolute beauty is tyrannical. Frenhofer cries, directing the sight and reception of his work, as if only one way were possible: "you must have faith, faith in art [. . .]. Look there [. . .] Look at the light on the breast and you'll see [. . .]. Come closer, you'll see better how it's done."[14] He requires a blind faith—or rather, a faith that creates the visions upon which it depends. There is no question: this painting belongs exclusively to its master. Its achievement requires the sacrifice of love and the beloved, and it is an example of the solipsism assumed of modern art. Adding to the story of Gillette and Catherine Lescault, that of Mary of Egypt begins to hint at a different modernity, one that dwells in paradox, emerges through profanation, and makes room for an abandon to the vicissitudes of public engagement and response.

ACKNOWLEDGMENTS

IN A PROJECT CENTERED ON GRACE, it is not only proper but also a joy to acknowledge the unmerited favors and benefits I have received while working on it. Without the graciousness of generous colleagues, students, friends, and family, it would have been impossible for me to complete this project.

I wrote most of this book at Indiana University, where the Departments of Religious Studies and Comparative Literature welcomed me and have created a true intellectual home. I have benefited greatly at every stage from conversations with the most wonderful interlocutors and friends: Anke Birkenmaier, Michel Chaouli, Jason Fickel, David Fisher, Shannon Gayk, Ilana Gershon, David Hertz, Perry Hodges, Roman Ivanovitch, Giles Knox, Herbert Marks, Hélène Merlin Kajman, Douglas Moore, Anita Park, Diane Reilly, Bret Rothstein, Massimo Scalabrini, Rob Schneider, Jeremy Schott, Aaron Stalnaker, Johannes Türk, and Estela Vieira. At critical moments, the incisive comments of friends and colleagues who read chapters saved me from confusion: Heather Blair, M. Cooper Harriss, Patricia Clare Ingham, Patrick Michelson, Eyal Peretz, and Winni Sullivan. Constance M. Furey has been a tireless champion of this project. She read—and imparted grace to— far more versions of the manuscript than I can count. I am grateful beyond words for her wisdom and friendship.

Generous institutional support from Indiana University made the completion of this book possible. It is a pleasure to acknowledge time made available for me to concentrate on research through a pre-tenure, one-semester leave as well as a semester away from teaching thanks to a fellowship from the College of Arts and Humanities Institute. Nicola Pohl and Paul Gutjahr of the College of Arts and Sciences together with the Departments of Religious Studies and Comparative Literature also provided me much-needed material support at the final stages of the book.

I presented a version of what would become the introduction of the book at the University of Wisconsin–Madison, where I was a residential Solmsen Fellow at the Institute for Research in the Humanities. I learned the true meaning of hospitality while at Madison, and I am deeply appreciative to colleagues who made my stay there both *dulce et utile*: Mercedes Alcalá Galán, Elizabeth Bearden, Sarah Crover, Guillermina de Ferrari, Max and Ann Harris, Michael Harrison, David Hildner, Steven Hutchinson, Paul-Alexis Mellet, Steven Nadler, Keren Omry, and Mario Ortiz-Robles. I am also grateful for the invitation to present material from the project at Princeton University. I thank those present for their deep engagement with my work, especially Marina S. Brownlee, Christina H. Lee, Nicole Legnani, Perla Masi, and Sophia Nuñez.

At key moments of the process, Jeremy Biles, Dalia Judovitz, Natalia C. Pérez, and Rebecca Rainof read large chunks of the manuscript and saved me from infelicities of style in addition to providing substantive comments central to its improvement. I thank them for their kindness, friendship, and sharp pens. Copyeditor Clare Counihan helped tame my sentences. All remaining flaws are my own.

Gracias to my teachers. For their wit, wisdom, and exemplarity I am grateful to Luis Avilés, Marina S. Brownlee, Julia Reinhard Lupton, Jane O. Newman, John H. Smith, Francisco Prado Vilar, and the much-missed Ronald E. Surtz. Although never formally my teacher, I learned much about academia, medievalism, and the delights of nunsploitation from Michael R. Solomon.

And I owe thanks to my students, whose insights into visual and textual manifestations of religion continue to inspire me: Justin Brown, Matthew Graham, Maidah Khalid, Mihee Kim-Kort, Abby Kulisz, Nicolò Sassi, Taylor Thomas, and especially Josie Wenig, whose work as my research assistant proved invaluable. Thanks are due also to Desi Anderson, Rachel K. Carpenter, and Megan Vinson, sharp and curious undergraduates whose pointed questions helped me see things from unexpected yet rewarding angles. Víctor Sierra Matute stands in a category of his own, as someone who keeps reminding me not to lose track of the poetic.

I owe thanks of the highest order to Kyle Wagner at the University of Chicago Press and to series editors Kathryn Lofton and John Lardas Modern for their discernment, insightful suggestions, encouragement, and support throughout. I have been extremely privileged to work with them. I am especially thankful to the anonymous readers for the Press who provided crucial feedback for the revision of the manuscript. I also want to thank Kristin

Rawlings for her assistance at the production stage, Mark Reschke for his meticulous copyediting, June Sawyers for the index, and Alex Teschmacher of Indiana University for his help with some of the illustrations central to this book.

Finally, to my family in Los Angeles and Norway, many thanks for their endless support, love, and shared laughter. To Hall Bjørnstad: Thank you for believing in me when I could no longer. You are my best friend, my best reader, the hope in my harp.

This book contains material from a previously published article: in chapter 3, from "Idolatrous and Confessional Visions in *Vida de Santa María Egipciaca*," in *Reading and Writing Subjects in Medieval and Golden Age Spain: Essays in Honor of Ronald E. Surtz*, ed. Christina H. Lee and José Luis Gastañaga, 29–49 (Newark, DE: Juan de la Cuesta, 2016).

NOTES

IN A CHAPEL

1. The text on the plaque reads "this saint was depicted on the deck of a boat, her skirt hitched up to her knees and facing the boatman, [the image] had these words underneath: *How the saint offered her body to the boatman in exchange for her passage*" (cette Sainte était peinte sur le pont d'un bateau, troussée jusqu'aux genoux devant le Batelier, avec ces mots au-dessous: *Comment la Sainte offrit son corps au Batelier pour son passage*). The plaque quotes from Jacques-Antoine Dulaure, *Nouvelle description des curiosités de Paris* (Paris: Lejay, 1785), 142–43.

2. The moral judgment of the image as "indecent" is indicated by the plaque, but it is not found in Dulaure. Instead, the historian specifies that it was a local priest who asked that this windowpane be removed.

3. Émile Mâle, *Religious Art from the Twelfth to the Eighteenth Century* (New York: Noonday Press, 1958), 171. (Cette beauté qui s'évanouissait peu à peu loin de regards des hommes, comme un encens qui brûle pour Dieu seul dans la solitude.) Émile Mâle, *L'art religieux de la fin du XVIe siècle, du XVIIe siècle et du XVIIIe siècle: Étude sur l'iconographie après le Concile de Trente, Italie-France-Espagne-Flandres* (Paris: Librairie Armand Colin, 1951), 69.

4. On the origins of the legend of Saint Mary of Egypt, see Maria Kouli's introduction to the translation of the legend in *Holy Women of Byzantium: Ten Saints' Lives in English Translation*, ed. Alice-Mary Talbot (Cambridge: Dumbarton Oaks, 1996), 65–69.

5. Bernard Flusin, "Palestinian Hagiography (Fourth-Eighth Centuries)," in *The Ashgate Companion to Byzantine Hagiography*, ed. Stephanos Efthymiadis, vol. 1 (Burlington, VT: Ashgate, 2011), 212.

6. "Si Dieu n'existait pas, il faudrait l'inventer." Voltaire, "Épître à l'auteur du livre des *Trois imposteurs*," *Œuvres complètes de Voltaire*, ed. Louis Moland (Paris: Garnier, 1877–85), 10:402.

7. "Life of Saint Mary of Egypt," trans. Maria Kouli, in *Holy Women of Byzantium: Ten Saints' Lives in English Translation*, ed. Alice-Mary Talbot (Cambridge: Dumbarton Oaks, 1996), 81.

8. The legend of Mary of Egypt has two main branches. The older, Eastern branch follows the narrative organization of the seventh-century vita attributed to Sophronius. It begins with the story of Zozimas, whose quest for spiritual perfection leads him to the desert where he finds a penitent Mary who will tell him about her sinfulness, conversion, and penitence, retrospectively and in the first person. The Western branch developed in twelfth-century France, and it tells in a third-person narrative the story Mary's life chronologically, including her encounters with Zozimas.

9. For more on the importance of these two iconic female figures, see Marina Warner, *Alone of All Her Sex* (New York: Alfred A. Knopf, 1976); Margaret Miles, *A Complex Delight: Secularization of the Breast* (Berkeley: University of California Press, 2008); and Emma Maggie Solberg, *Virgin Whore* (Ithaca, NY: Cornell University Press, 2018).

10. *Nisibene Hymns* 27, 8, in William A. Jurgens, *The Faith of the Early Fathers* (Collegeville, MN: Liturgical Press, 1970), 1:313.

11. https://www.papalencyclicals.net/Pius09/p9ineff.htm, accessed March 27, 2022.

12. John Henry Newman, "The Glories of Mary for the Sake of Her Son," in *Discourses for Mixed Congregations* (London: Longmans, Green and Co., 1906), 358, http://www.newmanreader.org/works/discourses/discourse17.html, accessed Mar. 27, 2022. The idea of beauty as a guide to the divine is central to medieval Christian aesthetics from the mystical writings of Pseudo-Dionysius to Augustine, for whom the beauty of the world functions as a sign that leads the intellect toward meditating on the Creator as the source of a superior, spiritual beauty. See Edgar de Bruyne, *The Aesthetics of the Middle Ages*, trans. Eileen B. Hennessy (New York: Frederick Ungar Publishing, 1969); Richard Viladesau's *Theological Aesthetics* (New York: Oxford University Press, 1999) also examines beauty as a pathway to God in medieval and contemporary theology.

13. See Ruth Karras, "Holy Harlots: Prostitute Saints in Medieval Legend," *Journal of the History of Sexuality* 1, no. 1 (1990): 17–28, for a succinct account of the construction of the medieval Magdalene tradition in Western Christianity. For a general study of the legend's wide cultural influence, see Susan Haskins, *Mary Magdalene: Myth and Metaphor* (New York: Harcourt Brace, 1994).

14. Mary Magdalene is mentioned explicitly in all four canonical Gospels at least once, yet none of these direct references mention of any sexual impurity. However, after Pope Gregory I's sermon on Luke's Gospel (ca. 591), tradition assimilated Magdalene, the follower of Jesus, with the anonymous sinful woman who washed and anointed Christ's feet at a Pharisee's house and with the woman from whom seven demons were cast, where "sinfulness" was interpreted as synonymous with sexual impropriety.

15. Pope Gregory I, *Homily 33*, in *Forty Gospel Homilies*, trans. David Hurst (Kalamazoo, MI: Cistercian Publications, 1990), 269–70.

16. Pope Gregory I, *Homily 33*, 270. On the association of the Magdalene with vanity, see María Helena Sánchez Ortega, *Pecadoras en verano, arrepentidas de invierno* (Madrid: Alianza, 1995).

17. Grace Jantzen, "Beauty for Ashes: Notes on the Displacement of Beauty," *Literature & Theology* 16, no. 4 (2002): 433–38.

18. The figure circulated anonymously as a postcard in Germany in 1888 before it was tweaked and published in 1915 by cartoonist W. E. Hill as *My Wife and Mother-in-Law*.

NOTES TO "IN A CHAPEL"

19. David Morgan, "Introduction: The Matter of Belief," in *Religion and Material Culture: The Matter of Belief*, ed. David Morgan (New York: Routledge, 2010), 8.

20. This distinction is central to the project of the founding editors of the journal *Material Religion*. Birgit Meyer, David Morgan, Crispin Paine, and S. Brent Plate, "The Origin and Mission of Material Religion," *Religion* 40, no. 3 (2010): 209.

21. Colleen McDannell, *Material Christianity: Religion and Popular Culture in America* (New Haven, CT: Yale University Press, 1995); David Morgan, *Visual Piety: A History and Theory of Popular Religious Images* (Berkeley: University of California Press, 1998); Charles Hirschkind, *The Ethical Soundscape: Cassette Sermons and Islamic Counterpublics* (Berkeley: University of California Press, 2006).

22. Morgan, *Visual Piety*, 24–33; McDannell, *Material Christianity*, 163–67.

23. Birgit Meyer and Jojada Verrips, "Aesthetics," in *Key Words in Religion, Media and Culture*, ed. David Morgan (New York: Routledge, 2008), 21. See also S. Brent Plate, *Walter Benjamin, Religion, and Aesthetics: Rethinking Religion through the Arts* (New York: Routledge, 2005). He offers an elegant study of religion and aesthetics through the experience of material objects.

24. Birgit Meyer, *Religious Sensations: Why Media, Aesthetics and Power Matter in the Study of Contemporary Religion*, Professorial Inaugural Address (Amsterdam: Faculty of Social Sciences, Free University, 2006), 9. Meyer uses the term "transcendental" to distinguish the human experience of awe from traditional notions such as Rudolf Otto's concept of the numinous that presume a separate and inaccessible realm of radical alterity. It is important for Meyer that the transcendental name the experience of a limit that remains grounded in human experience.

25. Notable exceptions include Ann W. Astell, *Eating Beauty: The Eucharist and the Spiritual Arts of the Middle Ages* (Ithaca, NY: Cornell University Press, 2006), and Mary Carruthers, *The Experience of Beauty in the Middle Ages* (Oxford: Oxford University Press, 2013), as well as other work done under the auspices of theological aesthetics.

26. Carolyn Walker Bynum, *Holy Feast, Holy Fast: The Religious Significance of Food to Medieval Women* (Berkeley: University of California Press, 1987).

27. Amy Hollywood, *Sensible Ecstasy: Mysticism, Sexual Difference, and the Demands of History* (Chicago: University of Chicago Press, 2002), 5, 16.

28. Hollywood, 18.

29. Laurie Cassidy and Maureen H. O'Connell, "Introduction," in *She Who Imagines: Feminist Theological Aesthetics* (Collegeville, MN: Liturgical Press, 2012), ix–xviii. Beauty, in this collection of essays, expands beyond its metonymic association with female bodies to include considerations of ethics, social justice, and artistic production. See also Grace Jantzen's recuperation of beauty as an important philosophical and theological category dependent on the notion of natality, that is to say, the recognition that all humans are embodied creatures always already embedded in relational and deeply corporeal networks in *Foundations of Violence* (New York: Routledge, 2004), 1.

30. Krista Hughes, "Beauty Incarnate: A Claim for Postmodern Feminist Theology," *Revista Anglo Saxonica* 6 (2013): 107, 121.

31. Hughes, 121.

32. For a specifically medieval view of how interpretations of the incarnation inflected En-

glish poetics, see Maria Cervone, *Poetics of the Incarnation: Middle English Writing and the Leap of Love* (Philadelphia: University of Pennsylvania Press, 2012). In *Philology of the Flesh* (Chicago: University of Chicago, 2017), John Hamilton extends the doctrine of the incarnation to poetic expression more widely. That the Word became flesh is for Hamilton a grounding metaphor for what he calls a "philology of the flesh." This love (*philos*) of words (*logos*) in their carnal materiality implies that semantic content cannot be instrumentalized and separated from the materiality of form. A philology of the flesh attends, then, to the sometimes tense, sometimes harmonious relationships of the body and the spirit of literary expression.

33. Hamilton, *Philology*, 47. In distinguishing philology of the flesh (invested in the idea that meaning is only present through and as language) from a philology of the body (devoted to extracting meaning from words), Hamilton borrows from Mayra Rivera the distinction between flesh and body, where the former designates becoming, what is "formless and impermanent, crossing the boundaries between the individual body and the world" in contrast to the set confines of the body. In Mayra Rivera, *Poetics of the Flesh* (Durham, NC: Duke University Press, 2015), 2.

34. The 1737 *Diccionario de Autoridades* defines the word "promiscuous" (*promiscuo*) as both an "indiscriminate or confused mixture" and as "that which has two meanings, or can be used one way or another, being both equivalent" (mezclado confusa o indiferentemente; lo que tiene dos sentidos, o se puede usar igualmente, de un modo o de otro, por ser equivalentes). In *Nuevo tesoro lexicográfico de la lengua española*, https://apps.rae.es/ntlle/SrvltGUIMenuNtlle?cmd=Lema&sec=1.0.0.0.0, accessed March 27, 2022.

35. Marjorie Garber, "Good to Think With," *Loaded Words* (New York: Fordham University Press, 2012), 96.

36. Claude Lévi-Strauss, *Le totémisme aujourd'hui* (Paris: Presses Universitaires de France, 1962), 128.

37. The window has been dated to 1205–15, and the sequence of images depicting the life of Mary the Egyptian (bay 142) is crowned by a full-length portrait of the saint, dressed in blue. For a study of this image in relation to thirteenth-century iconography and literary representations of the legend, see Daniela Mariani, "La chevelure de sainte Marie l'Égyptienne d'après Rutebeuf: Contraste des sources et de la tradition iconographique," *Perspectives médiévales* 38 (2017), http://journals.openedition.org/peme/12698, accessed March 27, 2022.

38. The cathedral at Bourges features a stained-glass window cycle of the life of Saint Mary of Egypt that includes six panels detailing her life of pleasure before conversion in Jerusalem, though it should be noted that they are reconstructions dating from the nineteenth century (in Sylvain Clement and A. Guitard, *Vitraux de Bourges* [Bourges: Imprimerie Tardy-Pigelet, 1900], 37–42). One of these panels depicts the seduction of the mariners in a manner reminiscent of the description of the Jussienne chapel's window. On the other side of the Pyrenees, we find a magnificent fourteenth-century fresco in the monastery of San Salvador de Oña in Burgos that begins with the episode of the seduction aboard the ship. The saint's life is also depicted on windows in the cathedrals of Chartres and Auxerre, and it is carved onto the four faces of a stone capital

NOTES TO "IN A CHAPEL" 175

now in the Musée des Augustins in Toulouse, but all of these sequences focus on her conversion and subsequent penitence.

39. The entry under the Egyptian's name in Jacobus de Voragine's influential thirteenth-century collection of saints' lives, *The Golden Legend*, trans. William Granger Ryan (Princeton, NJ: Princeton University Press, 1993), begins thus "Mary the Egyptian, who is called the Sinner, led a most austere life" (227–29). Similarly, the Roman Martyrology lists under April 2 "the death in Palestine of Mary of Egypt, called the sinner." *The Roman Martyrologe, according to the reformed calendar faithfully translated out of Latin into English, by G.K. of the Society of Iesus* (Saint-Omer: Imprinted with licence [*sic*] at the English College Press, 1627), 200, Early English Books Online, http://name.umdl.umich.edu/A07132.0001.001, accessed July 28, 2022.

40. Jean-Luc Marion, *Believing in Order to See: On the Rationality of Revelation and the Irrationality of Some Believers*, trans. Christina M. Gschwandtner (New York: Fordham, 2017). Marion's project in this collection of essays is primarily to question the opposition of faith (believing) to reason (seeing). In the last chapter, "The Invisible Saint," he argues that holiness is grounded in a fundamental invisibility that prevents it from becoming the object of appropriation. However, whereas Marion's ultimate goal is to extend reason's reach into the invisibility of faith, my aim is to explore how holiness, while "invisible by right," becomes recognizable, albeit incompletely, not only through revelation or divine vision, but also in the here and now of the experience of narrative and visual representations.

41. *Oxford English Dictionary*, s.v. "concept," https://www-oed-com, accessed March 27, 2022. I use brackets around ellipses here and elsewhere to mark that the omissions are my own and not part of the original quotation.

42. Roland Barthes, *S/Z*, trans. Richard Miller (New York: Hill and Wang, 1974), 33. (La beauté (contrairement à la laideur) ne peut vraiment s'expliquer: elle se dit, s'affirme, se répète en chaque partie du corps mais ne se décrit pas. Tel un dieu (aussi vide que lui), elle ne peut que dire: *je suis celle qui suis*.) Roland Barthes, *S/Z*, in *Œuvres completes III* (Paris: Seuil, 2002), 145.

43. Barthes, *S/Z*, trans. Richard Miller, 33–34. (Tout prédicat direct lui est refusé; les seuls prédicats possibles sont ou la tautologie (*un visage d'un ovale parfait*) ou la comparaison (*belle comme une madone de Raphaël, comme un rêve de pierre*, etc.); de la sorte, de la beauté est renvoyée à l'infini des codes: *belle comme Vénus*? Mais Vénus? Belle comme quoi?) Barthes, *S/Z*, in *Œuvres*, 146. The invisibility Barthes has in mind carries a theological charge as he understands beauty to be as unavailable to human vision as a mysterious god, but it also has a more pernicious social manifestation. In today's vernacular culture, where beauty—and feminine beauty in particular—adheres to a very constricted ideal, often racially marked, bodies that do not conform to it are condemned to social invisibility. Paul C. Taylor has spelled out some of the philosophical implications of the racialized underpinnings of what he calls somatic aesthetics in *Black Is Beautiful: A Philosophy of Black Aesthetics* (Hoboken, NJ: Wiley, 2016), 106–52.

44. "The prudish priests thought they were performing a 'pious act' by 'expurgating' the windows whose subjects seemed to them inconvenient or scabrous" (Les curés pudibonds croient faire "œuvre pie" en "expurgeant" les vitraux dont les sujets leur

paraissent inconvenants ou scabreux). In Louis Réau, *Les monuments détruits de l'art français: Histoire du vandalisme* (Paris: Hachette, 1959), 128.

45. Dulaure, *Nouvelle description*, 143.

46. Pierre Laubriet, *Un catéchisme aesthétique: Le chef d'œuvre inconnu de Balzac* (Paris: Didier, 1961), 161–80.

47. Réau, *Les monuments*, 128.

48. E. Ernesto Delgado, "Penitencia y eucaristía en la conformación de la vertiente occidental de la leyenda de santa María Egipcíaca: Un paradigma de negociación cultural en la baja edad media," *Revista de poética medieval* 10 (2003): 25–55.

49. For an overview of the literary and visual expectations of the representation of old women, see Erin J. Campbell, *Old Women and Art in the Early Modern Italian Domestic Interior* (Farnham: Ashgate, 2015).

50. Occasionally, the iconography of Mary Magdalene borrows from the Egyptian the abundance of hair covering a naked body. See Daniela Mariani, "La chevelure de sainte Marie l'Égyptienne d'après Rutebeuf," https://journals.openedition.org/peme /12698#bodyftn36, accessed March 27, 2022. On Agnes and other saints who sprout hair as a defense against sexual violence, see Carlos Vega, *El transformismo religioso: La abnegación sexual de la mujer en la España medieval* (Madrid: Editorial Pliegos, 2008), especially chap. 3 (133–200).

51. Mary's enduring sexual allure even during her time in the desert has long been recognized. However, whereas it was initially interpreted as a symptom of Christian misogyny, of the impossibility of imagining a feminine form of holiness, scholars have recuperated more recently the saint's agency in old age and even death. Virginia Burrus, for example, reads three of the lives of the holy harlots, including that of Saint Mary of Egypt, as examples of Jean Baudrillard's intuition that one seduces God with faith and acts of sacrifice. On the particular case of the Egyptian, she writes, "her promiscuous mobility meets its consummate end in the dissolution of a nakedly yearning body, mingled with the innumerable grains of sand in a desert as vast and open as her desire." *The Sex Lives of Saints: An Erotics of Ancient Hagiography* (Philadelphia: University of Pennsylvania Press, 2004), 155. Similarly, Cary Howie has studied in detail the erotics of Mary of Egypt's last gesture, closing herself to the world in death, as an example of how "the sexed body, the body as both genitally specific and potentially sexual makes an essential contribution to the saint's emergence" ("As the Saint Turns: Hagiography at the Threshold of the Visible," *Exemplaria* 17, no. 2 [2005]: 318).

52. Charlotte Higgins "Master of Gore: The Violent, Shocking Genius of Jusepe de Ribera," *Guardian*, September 19, 2018, https://www.theguardian.com/artanddesign/2018/sep /19/jusepe-de-ribera-art-of-violence-master-of-gore-dulwich, accessed March 27, 2022.

53. Campbell, *Old Women*, 52.

54. See Burrus, *Sex Lives*, 155.

55. Eve Kosofsky Sedgwick, "Introduction," in *Tendencies* (Durham, NC: Duke University Press, 1993), viii. On how Mary of Egypt, interpreted as a trans-masculine saint, troubles central axes of identity such as gender and race, see Roland Betancourt, "Introduction," in *Byzantine Intersectionality: Sexuality, Gender, and Race in the Middle Ages*

NOTES TO CHAPTER ONE

(Princeton, NJ: Princeton University Press, 2020), 1–14. On the queering of space in the French legend of Mary of Egypt, see Cary Howie, "As the Saint Turns," 317–46.

56. Sedgwick, "Introduction," in *Tendencies*, viii.

57. Sedgwick, *Tendencies*, 9.

58. David Marno, *Death Be Not Proud: The Art of Holy Attention* (Chicago: University of Chicago Press, 2016), 34.

59. Melissa Sanchez, for example, understands grace's promiscuity, the gratuitous forgiveness offered by God to his faithless people, as the basis for a secular, queer sexual ethics and poetics. In *Queer Faith: Reading Promiscuity and Race in the Secular Love Tradition* (New York: New York University Press, 2019), 99–111. More generally, Ita MacCarthy argues for the "chameleon" nature of the concept of grace in the Italian Renaissance, and she tracks its influence in discourses ranging from the religious to the political and aesthetic. In *The Grace of the Italian Renaissance* (Princeton, NJ: Princeton University Press, 2020), 19–24.

60. *Life of Saint Mary of Egypt*, trans. Maria Kouli, 81.

61. Sebastián de Covarrubias Orozco, *Tesoro de la lengua castellana o española: Biblioteca áurea hispánica, 21*, ed. Ignacio Arellano and Rafael Zafra (Madrid: Iberoamericana; Frankfurt am Main: Vervuert, 2006), s.v. "gracia." On the connection between grace (a natural gift or talent) and *sprezzatura* (the nonchalant expression of work that mimics grace as to become graceful), see David Marno, *Death Be Not Proud*, 16–19; and Maria Teresa Ricci, "La grâce et la sprezzatura chez Castiglione," *Bibliothèque d'Humanisme et Renaissance* 65, no. 2 (2003): 233–48.

62. Marcel Hénaff, "Grâce, œuvre d'art et espace publique," *La Beauté* 1, September 14, 2011, http://www.mouvement-transitions.fr/index.php/intensites/la-beaute/sommaire-des -articles-deja-publies/519-grace-uvre-dart-et-espace-public, accessed March 13, 2022. (Cette grâce [. . .] tient à l'énergie de la conviction du locuteur, au rythme de son dire, à la clarté de son discours, mais aussi à cette certitude si profonde que la communauté de pensée passe par un partage des sentiments, par une joie sensible sans laquelle les discours restent abstraits et indifférents à la réponse des destinataires.)

CHAPTER ONE

1. Jean-Luc Marion, "The Invisible Saint," in *Believing in Order to See: On the Rationality of Revelation and the Irrationality of Some Believers*, trans. Christina M. Gschwandtner (New York: Fordham University Press, 2017), 144. The translator notes that in French the word *saint* encompasses both the specificity of a saint and the abstraction of the holy.

2. Margaret Miles, *Vision as Insight: Visual Understanding in Western Christianity and Secular Culture* (Boston: Beacon Press, 1985).

3. Eusebius of Caesarea, *The Life of the Blessed Emperor Constantine*, in vol. 1, *Nicene and Post-Nicene Fathers*, 2nd ser., ed. Philip Schaff and Henry Wace (Grand Rapids, MI:

Wm. B. Eerdmans, 1955; Internet Medieval Sourcebook, 1997), book 3, chap. 27, http://www.fordham.edu/halsall/basis/vita-constantine.html, accessed March 27, 2022.

4. Arthur D. Nock, *Conversion: The Old and the New in Religion from Alexander the Great to Augustine of Hippo* (Oxford: Oxford University Press, 1961), 134 (emphasis added).

5. The turn of phrase "book of the illiterate" conveys the general idea found in two passages in letters written by Pope Gregory the Great against the destruction of images by Serenus of Marseilles at the end of the sixth century. On the meaning of Gregory's statement in its time, see Lawrence G. Duggan, "Was Art Really the 'Book of the Illiterate'?," *Word and Image* 5, no. 3 (1989): 227–51, and Peter Brown, "Images as a Substitute for Writing," in *East and West: Modes of Communication: Proceedings of the First Plenary Conference at Merida* (Boston: Brill, 1999), 15–34. On the influence and different interpretations of Gregory's statements in the later Middle Ages, see Celia Chazelle, "Pictures, Books and the Illiterate: Pope Gregory I's Letters to Serenus of Marseilles," *Word and Image* 6, no. 2 (1990): 138–53, and Michael Camille, "Seeing and Reading: Some Visual Implications of Medieval Literacy and Illiteracy," *Art History* 8, no. 1 (1985): 26–49.

6. W. J. T. Mitchell, *Picture Theory: Essays on Visual and Verbal Representation* (Chicago: Chicago University Press, 1994), 49.

7. On the history of theory as a disembodied practice that privileges sight at a distance, see David Morgan, *The Embodied Eye: Religious Visual Culture and the Social Life of Feeling* (Berkeley: University of California Press, 2012), 7–16.

8. S. Brent Plate, "Material Religion: An Introduction," *Key Terms in Material Religion*, ed. S. Brent Plate (New York: Bloomsbury, 2015), 4.

9. This chapter focuses on the visibility of holiness. Chapter 4 will concentrate on what the legend of Mary of Egypt has to say about the visibility of beauty.

10. David Morgan, *The Thing about Religion: An Introduction to the Material Study of Religions* (Chapel Hill: University of North Carolina Press, 2021), 88.

11. Linear perspective and its illusionistic effects were, of course, not an invention of the Renaissance. As a representational technique, it was already known to antiquity (Plato, expectedly, distrusted it as a perversion of perception), but the full implications for painting (foreshortening, anamorphosis, quadratura, etc.) were not fully explored in theory and practice until the fifteenth century.

12. Jay David Bolter and Richard Grusin, *Remediation* (Cambridge, MA: MIT Press, 2000), 11.

13. Birgit Meyer, "Medium," in *Key Terms in Material Religion*, ed. S. Brent Plate (New York: Bloomsbury, 2015), 142.

14. Leonardo da Vinci, *Leonardo da Vinci's Paragone: A Critical Interpretation with a New Edition of the Text in Codex Urbinas*, trans. by Claire J. Farago (Leiden: E. J. Brill, 1992), 355.

15. Leonardo da Vinci, 179–81. (Perché la poesia / pon le sue cose nella immaginatione de lettere e la pittura / le dà realmente fori de l'occhio, dal qual occhio ricceve / le similitudini non altrimente che s'elle fussino natturali, / e poesia le dà sanza essa similitudine.)

16. Claire J. Farago, "On Leonardo da Vinci's Defense of Painting against Poetry and Music and the Grounding of Aesthetic Experience," *Italian Culture* 9, no. 1 (1991): 155.

NOTES TO CHAPTER ONE

17. Leonardo da Vinci, *Leonardo da Vinci's Paragone*, 210–11. (Ma io non / voglio da questi tali altro che uno bono pittore che figuri / 'l furore d'una battaglia, et ch'el poeta ne scrivi / un'altra, e che sieno messi in pubblico de compagnia. / Vedrai dove più si fermeranno li veditori, dove più consideraranno, dove si dara più laude, et quale / sattisfara meglio. Certo la pittura, di gran longa più / uttile et bella, più piaccera. Pone in scritto il nome / d'Iddio in un locho, et ponni la sua figura a riscontro, / vedrai quale si più reverita. [. . .] // Tolgassi un poeta che descriva le bellezze d'una donna / al suo inamorato, et tolgassi un pittore che la figuri, / vedrassi dove la natura volgera più il giudicatore / inamorato.)

18. Leonardo da Vinci, *Leonardo da Vinci's Paragone*, 200–1. (il pittore ti supera, perché la tua penna sia consumata / inanzi che tu descriva a pieno quel che imediate il pittore / rappressenta con la sua scientia. // Et la tua lingua sara impedita dalla sete, et il corpo / dal sonno e fame, prima che tu con parole dimostri quelo che / in un istante il pittore ti dimostra.)

19. Francisco Pacheco, *El arte de la pintura*, ed. Bonaventura Bassegoda i Hugas (Madrid: Cátedra, 1990), book 1, chap. 11, 248.

20. Pacheco, *El arte de la pintura*, 248–54. (La parte no sólo propia, pero más principal a que se encamina la pintura, es a mover el ánimo de quien la mira [. . .]. Que si el orador por saber, con la facultad del decir, volver los ajenos afectos a esta, o aquella parte, merece eterna alabaza, ¿quién duda que la pintura cristiana, acompañada de la belleza y consideración espiritual, tanto más eficaz y noblemente podrá conseguir este efecto respeto de la muchedumbre, que universalmente es indocta? y el fin a que ella mira es más sublime y glorioso dixo el poeta lírico en esta sentencia *Segnius irritant animum demissa per aures, / quam quae sunt oculis subiecta fidelibus*. Que yo volví desta suerte: "Las cosas percebidas / de los oídos, mueven lentamente; / pero siendo ofrecidas / a los fieles ojos, luego siente / más poderoso efeto / para moverse, el ánimo quieto.")

21. Horace, *Ars Poetica*, in *Horace: Satires, Epistles, Ars Poetica*, trans. H. Rushton Farclough, Loeb Classical Library (Cambridge, MA: Harvard University Press, 1926), 179–82.

22. On the double meaning of *fidelidad* as artistic and religious faithfulness, see Felipe Pereda, *Imágenes de la Discordia: Política y poética de la imagen sagrada en la España del cuatrocientos* (Madrid: Marcial Pons Historia, 2013), 237–39.

23. Tomás Tamayo de Vargas, "Ars Poetica," in Jesús Alemán Illán, "Una traducción inedita del 'Ars Poetica' de Horacio por Tomás Tamayo de Vargas," *Criticón* 70 (1997): 133; Francisco de Cascales, "Arte Poética," in José Luis Pérez Pastor, "La traducción del licenciado Francisco de Cascales del *Ars poetica* de Horacio," *Criticón* 86 (2002): 34.

24. Canons and Decrees of the Sacred and Oecumenical Council of Trent, "The Twenty-Fifth Session," ed. and trans. J. Waterworth (London: Dolman, 1848), 235, Hanover Historical Texts Project, https://history.hanover.edu/texts/trent.html, accessed March 20, 2022.

25. Seventh Ecumenical Council, *The Second Council of Nicaea, 787, in Which the Worship of Images Was Established, with Copious Notes from the "Caroline Books,"* trans. John Mendham (London: William Edward Painter, 1850), 132. The original text in Greek can be found in *Patrologiae Graecae*, vol. 46, col. 472.

NOTES TO CHAPTER ONE

26. Pacheco, *El arte de la pintura*, 257. (Vi, dice, muchas veces la imagen de la inscripción, y no pude pasar sin lágrimas: por poner la pintura ante los ojos tan eficazmente la historia.)

27. Seventh Ecumenical Council, 132.

28. Seventh Ecumenical Council, 137.

29. Pacheco, *El arte de la pintura*, 257.

30. Pacheco, 257–58. (De Santa María se lee [. . .] que viendo un día numeroso pueblo entrar en el templo y que ella por oculta fuerza era detenida, acordándose de la libertad de las costumbres, alzó los ojos a una imagen en la Santa Cruz, y a otra de la gloriosa Virgen, y le pareció que de ellas salían dardos agudos, que le traspasaban el corazón, y dixo estas sentidas palabras, "Embistióme un horror y arrebatamiento del ánimo, y comencé a temblar toda y perturbarme." Y siguióse luego aquella conversión e inusitada penitencia suya.)

31. Pacheco, 258 (emphasis added). (*Apenas pisó* de la primera / puerta el umbral, *cuando ocupó sus ojos* / la imagen [. . .] de el grande Polemón, que *al mesmo punto* / [. . .] su culpa acusar pudo.)

32. Seventh Ecumenical Council, 142.

33. Seventh Ecumenical Council, 213.

34. Seventh Ecumenical Council, 214.

35. Seventh Ecumenical Council, 252.

36. Thomas F. X. Noble warns judiciously that while the incarnation is mentioned at Nicaea, it would be a mistake to imagine it as a fully developed Christological defense of images, which according to him was not articulated as such except by John of Damascus, and while the council makes use of John's sermons, it does not follow the subtle distinctions that characterize the original. In *Images, Iconoclasm, and the Carolingians* (Philadelphia: University of Pennsylvania Press, 2009).

37. Thomas Pfau, "Rethinking the Image: With Some Reflections on G. M. Hopkins," *Yearbook of Comparative Literature* 57 (2011): 126.

38. Seventh Ecumenical Council, 214.

39. Martin Jay's classic *Downcast Eyes: The Denigration of Vision in Twentieth-Century French Thought* (Berkeley: University of California Press, 1993) has analyzed the simultaneous fear and fetishizing of images. On the denigration of the embodied eye and its effects on the study of religion, see David Morgan, *The Embodied Eye*, 3–28. For a more recent assessment of the argument, including explicit consideration of the visual in a Christian context, see Pfau, "Rethinking." From a Protestant perspective, see James Simpson, *Under the Hammer: Iconoclasm in the Anglo-American Tradition* (Oxford: Oxford University Press, 2010). On the association of Spanish painting in particular with the representation of "true life" and the skepticism toward the devotion such visual representations elicited, see Felipe Pereda, "True Painting and the Challenge of Hypocrisy," in *After Conversion: Iberia and the Emergence of Modernity*, ed. Mercedes García Arenal (Leiden: Brill, 2016): 358–94.

40. "Life of Saint Mary of Egypt," trans. Maria Kouli, in *Holy Women of Byzantium: Ten Saints' Lives in English Translation*, ed. Alice-Mary Talbot (Cambridge: Dumbarton Oaks, 1996), 76.

NOTES TO CHAPTER ONE

41. The Greek and Latin legends of Saint Mary of Egypt do describe in detail the penitent running away from the monk Zozimas when they spy each other in the desert, but this is not to be interpreted as the concealment of holiness but rather as a statement on her newly developed sense of modesty and shame at her nakedness. Cary Howie reads the medieval French legend in terms of multiple instances of turning rather than hiding or revealing, which seems more appropriate and arguably also applicable to the other versions of the Egyptian's story (in "As the Saint Turns: Hagiography at the Threshold of the Visible," *Exemplaria* 17, no 2 [2005]: 317–46).

42. Jean-Luc Marion, "The Invisible Saint," 144.

43. Marion has written about this biblical episode to account for the faith in revelation and the creation of concepts in "They Recognized Him and He Became Invisible to Them," in *Believing in Order to See: On the Rationality of Revelation and the Irrationality of Some Believers*, trans. Christina M. Gschwandtner (New York: Fordham, 2017), 136–43. He argues that contrary to common opinion, faith does not compensate for a lack of evidence or experience of the divine. Instead, faith aids the understanding of an experience, like that of seeing the resurrected Christ, that otherwise overwhelms us because we have no ready-made concept within which to contain it. Shane Mackinlay criticizes Marion for ascribing to faith a role only at the end of revelation, which he argues leads Marion to misread the episode. He proposes instead that faith *makes* revelation possible and that can only happen when the disciples are open to seeing that there is more than meets the eye. In Mackinlay's account, then, the disciples are initially blind to the real identity of their companion, not because they are overwhelmed and lacking in concepts (as in Marion's interpretation), but because they are too certain about what they see and understand, leaving little room for faith to act as conduit to revelation. In "Eyes Wide Shut: A Response to Jean-Luc Marion's Account of the Journey to Emmaus," *Modern Theology* 20, no. 3 (2004): 447–56.

44. The qualifier denoting inversion was first used by Ingvar Bergström in *Dutch Still-Life Painting in the Seventeenth Century*, trans. Christina Hedström and Gerald Taylor (New York: T. Yoseloff, 1956). More recently, Victor Stoichita proposed the term "split painting," primarily as a way to recognize the status of these objects as "self-aware" images, but also to avoid anachronism since still life was a nascent genre at the time. In *The Self-Aware Image: An Insight into Early Modern Meta-Painting*, trans. Anne-Marie Glasheen (London: Harvey Miller, 2015): 3. All while acknowledging the anachronism, I retain "inverted still life" because of what the locution tells us about the place and function of religion in these images.

45. Natasha Trethewey, "Kitchen Maid with Supper at Emmaus, or The Mulata," in *Thrall* (Boston: Houghton Mifflin, 2012), 27.

46. Tanya J. Tiffany, *Diego Velázquez's Early Paintings and the Culture of Seventeenth-Century Seville* (University Park: Pennsylvania State University Press, 2012), 43.

47. In other words, some of the perplexity that the modern reader encounters in the narrative of the Egyptian's conversion is due to anachronistic expectations of the conversion experience. William James is the touchstone for this modern, psychological understanding of religious conversion focused on the individual's transformation. He defines conversion as "the process, gradual or sudden, by which a self hitherto divided, and

consciously wrong inferior and unhappy, becomes unified and consciously right superior and happy, in consequence of its firmer hold upon religious realities." In *Varieties of Religious Experience* (New York: New American Library, 1958), 157. Arthur D. Nock's definition of conversion owes much to James, though it is more grounded in historical analysis. For Nock, conversion entails "deliberate turning from indifference or from an earlier form of piety to another, a turning which implies a consciousness that a great change is involved, that the old was wrong and the new is right." In *Conversion*, 7. Both of these works remain powerful accounts of conversion, although their Protestant bias has been noted by Lewis R. Rambo and Charles Farhadian, in *The Oxford Handbook of Religious Conversion* (Oxford: Oxford University Press, 2014), and the modernist expectations of unity criticized by Laura S. Nasrallah, "The Rhetoric of Conversion and the Construction of Experience: The Case of Justin Martyr," *Studia Patristica* 40 (2006): 467–74.

48. Jean-Luc Marion, "The Invisible Saint," 146.

49. Julia Kristeva, *Étrangers à nous-mêmes* (Paris: Fayard, 1998).

50. The importance of the choreographic metaphor to a scene of conversion or transformation is spelled out in detail in chapter 4.

51. The Filangieri canvas is the last of three surviving portraits made of Mary of Egypt that follow this particular composition (the earlier paintings may be found at the Muzeul de Arta in Bucharest, Romania, and in the Convent of San Giuseppe dei Cappuccini in Bologna, Italy). This particular composition is not the only representation of the saint that Ribera made. At least three other compositional motifs exist; chapter 4 discusses these in detail.

52. Sebastián de Covarrubias Orozco, *Tesoro de la lengua castellana o española: Biblioteca áurea hispánica, 21*, ed. Ignacio Arellano and Rafael Zafra (Madrid: Iberoamericana; Frankfurt am Main: Vervuert, 2006), s.v. "retrato." (La figura contrahecha, de alguna persona principal y de cuenta, cuya efigie y semejanza es justo quede por memoria a los siglos venideros.)

53. Harry Berger, *Fictions of the Pose: Rembrandt against the Italian Renaissance* (Stanford, CA: Stanford University Press, 2000).

54. Alice Spawls, "Portraits Put to Use—And Misuse," *New York Review of Books*, February 23, 2017, 51.

55. Victor I. Stoichita, *Visionary Experience in the Golden Age of Spanish Art* (London: Reaktion Books, 1995), 172.

56. Louis Réau, *L'iconographie de l'art chrétien* (Paris: Presses Universitaires de France, 1952–58), vol. 3.2, 886–88.

57. Denise Maria Pagano, "Saint Mary of Egypt (Musée Favre, Montpellier)," in *Jusepe de Ribera, 1591–1652*, ed. Alfonso E. Pérez Sánchez and Nicola Spinosa (New York: Metropolitan Museum of Art, 1992), 158; Craig Felton with William Jordan, "Saint Mary of Egypt," in *Jusepe de Ribera, lo Spagnoletto, 1591–1652*, ed. Craig Felton and William B. Jordan (Fort Worth, TX: Kimbell Art Museum, 1982), 232.

58. Stoichita, *Visionary Experience*, 172.

59. William B. Jordan and Peter Cherry, *Spanish Still Life from Velázquez to Goya* (London: National Gallery Publications, distributed by Yale University Press, 1995), 22–23.

CHAPTER TWO

1. Théophile Gautier, *Ouvrages: Voyage en Espagne, nouvelle édition* (Paris: G. Chapentier, 1878), 239. (Nous autres catholiques un peu superficiels, nous avons besoin du pittoresque pour arriver au sentiment religieux.)

2. Ryan Giles, *Laughter of the Saints: Parodies of Holiness in Late Medieval and Renaissance Spain* (Toronto: Toronto University Press, 2009); Dorothy S. Severin, *Religious Parody and the Spanish Sentimental Romance* (Newark, DE: Juan de la Cuesta, 2005).

3. Mary Carruthers, *The Experience of Beauty in the Middle Ages* (Oxford: Oxford University Press, 2014), 135–64; Jill Ross, *Figuring the Feminine: The Rhetoric of Female Embodiment in Medieval Hispanic Literature* (Toronto: University of Toronto Press, 2008); Catherine Brown, *Contrary Things: Exegesis, Dialectic, and the Poetics of Didacticism* (Stanford, CA: Stanford University Press, 1998).

4. Barbara Newman, *Medieval Crossover: Reading the Secular against the Sacred* (Notre Dame, IN: University of Notre Dame Press, 2013).

5. Augustine, *On Christian Doctrine*, trans. D. W. Robertson (Indianapolis: Bobbs-Merrill, 1958), 14.

6. Jill Ross, *Figuring the Feminine*, 16–49. John Hamilton, in *Philology of the Flesh*, traces a different philosophical genealogy for the distrust of the flesh by making a distinction between wayward flesh and the instrumentalization of corporeal imagery that presumes consolidation and integrity (a corpus).

7. Margaret Ferguson, "St. Augustine's Region of Unlikeness: The Crossing of Exile and Language," *Georgia Review* 29, no. 4 (1975): 861.

8. "The Life of Saint Mary the Egyptian," trans. Hugh Feiss, in *Saint Mary of Egypt: Three Medieval Lives in Verse* (Kalamazoo, MI: Cistercian Publications, 2005), 127. Feiss translates from *Vida de Santa María Egipciaca, Estudios, vocabulario, edición de los textos*, vol 2, edited by Manuel Alvar (Madrid: Consejo Superior de Investigaciones Científicas, 1972). Hereafter abbreviated *VSME*. All subsequent quotations from the English translation will be cited parenthetically by page number while the corresponding Spanish passages will refer to Alvar's *VSME* by line number. I occasionally make changes to Feiss's translation to bring out specific aspects present in the Spanish.

> (Iuro vos por Dios verdadero,
> non he conmigo más de un dinero.
> Fevos aquí el mió tresoro,
> todo mi argente e todo mi oro.
> Si en la nave me quisiéredes meter,
> servir vos é de volonter. [Lines 345–48])

9. "Yo, dieze, he buen cuerpo; / est' le daré a gran baldón" (lines 310–11).

10. "Semejádesme buenos omnes" (line 336).

11. Joan Corominas, *Diccionario crítico etimológico castellano e hispánico* (Madrid: Editorial Gredos, 1980–91), 3:335.

12. The Spanish word *he* and its medieval spelling *fe* are not, as some philologists had con-

184   NOTES TO CHAPTER TWO

jectured previously, an imperative form of *haber* (to possess, to hold or to take place). Instead, as Ramón Menéndez Pidal showed, its etymology harks back to the classical Arabic *hā*, an adverb whose function is to call for the attention of an interlocutor. See María Moliner, *Diccionario de uso del español* (Madrid: Editorial Gredos, 1966–67), 23.

13. Oit, varones, huna *razón*
en que non ha si verdat non.
Escuchat de coraçón,
sí ayades de Dios perdón.

Toda es fecha de verdat
non a y ren de falsedat.
[. . . . .]

Si escucharedes esta palabra,
más vos valdrá que huna *fabla*. (Lines 1–6, 15–16; emphasis added)

14. In contrast to today's usage, medieval "honesty" is linked to propriety and not always necessarily to sincerity or truth-telling. On the multiple meanings of *honestus*, spanning the aesthetic (linked to decorum, what is most fitting or reasonable in a specific context) and the ethical, see Carruthers, *Experience of Beauty*, 112–25.

15. For a review of the different nuances of *fabla*, particularly in its intersection with literary fiction in a specifically medieval Castilian context, see Barry Taylor, "La Fabliella de Don Juan Manuel," *Revista de poética medieval* 4 (2000): 187–200. On the adaptation of classical rhetoric by medieval Iberian writers, see Jesús Montoya Martínez, "Retórica medieval ¿Continuidad o ruptura?," In *Retórica medieval ¿Continuidad o ruptura? Actas del simposio internacional, Granada, enero de 1995*, ed. Antonio Rubio Flores, 79–101 (Granada: ADHARA), 1996.

16. Ramón Menéndez Pidal, *Poesía juglaresca y juglares: Aspectos de la historia literaria y cultural de España* (Madrid: Publicaciones de la Revista de Filología Española, 1924), 348–49. (El cantor de vidas de santos proclama su arte como más digno que el de los demás juglares, incluso los de gesta; los asuntos piadosos que trata le permiten despreciar las mentiras del rey Artus [. . .] y dejar a un lado las historias de Ogier y de Roldán. [. . .] El cantor de vidas santas funda su superioridad en el provecho moral que procura a sus oyentes.)

17. "Si escucharedes esta palabra / mas vos valdrá que huna fabla" (lines 15–16).

18. Menéndez Pidal's distinction of medieval narrative poetry based on content and intention (religious matter and didactic intent, on the one hand, and fictional stories whose aim is to entertain, on the other) has been challenged by more recent scholarship. Michèle Schiavone de Cruz-Sáenz, "La *Vida de Santa María Egipciaca*: Texto juglaresco u obra de clerecía," in *La juglaresca: Actas del I Congreso Internacional sobre la Juglaresca*, ed. Manuel Criado de Val (Madrid: EDI, 1986): 275–81, concludes that *VSME* represents the most erudite and highly respected aspects of minstrel and clerical poetry. Similarly, Carina Zubillaga, in the most recent edition of the poem in its manuscript context argues that for the fourteenth-century compiler the distinction between the two forms of poetry is not as sharp as present-day scholars imagine them to be. Carina

NOTES TO CHAPTER TWO

Zubillaga, *Poesía narrativa clerical en su contexto manuscrito: Estudio y edición del ms. Esc. K-III-4* (Buenos Aires: SECRIT, 2014), xix.

19. "Escuchat de coraçón, / sí ayades de Dios perdón" (lines 3–4).

20. Todos aquellos que a Dios amarán
estas palabras escucharán;
[. . . . .]
bien se que de voluntat la oirán
aquellos que a Dios amarán;
essos que a Dios amarán,
grant gualardón end' reçibirán. (Lines 7–14)

21. *La Vie de Sainte Marie l'Egyptienne, ms. B* in *The Life of Saint Mary of Egypt: An Edition and Study of the Medieval French and Spanish Verse Redactions*, ed. Michèle Schiavone de Cruz-Sáenz (Barcelona: Puvil Editor, 1979), 117.

22. Aldo Ruffinatto, "Hacia una teoría semiológica del relato hagiográfico," *Berceo* 94–95 (1978): 108–9.

23. Ruffinatto, 109.

24. Recent scholarship has worked hard to trace alternate ways of understanding the relationship between a learned, often ecclesiastic didactic tradition (*mester de clerecía*) and a more popular so-called profane vein (*mester de juglaría*), and more generally between didacticism and pleasure. The categorical distinction between the two *mesteres* had, until the 1980s, organized the study of the vernacular literary production of thirteenth- and fourteenth-century Spain. This model has undergone radical revisions especially thanks to the work of Isabel Uría Maqua (who focuses on matters of poetic form), Julian Weiss (who attends to matters of ideology and transmission), and Carina Zubillaga (who places poetry in its manuscript context). On the pleasures of didacticism and the didactics of pleasure, see also Catherine Brown's *Contrary Things*, which recuperates for criticism the medieval force of contradiction as an interpretative strategy that maintains a commitment to both edification and delight.

25. Lynn Rice Cortina, "The Aesthetics of Morality: Two Portraits of Mary of Egypt in the *Vida de Santa María Egipciaca*," *Hispanic Journal* (1980): 41–45.

26. De huna duenya que auedes oida,
quier' vos comptar toda su vida:
de santa María Egipçiana,
que fue huna duenya muy loçana
<et de su cuerpo muy loçana>
quando era mançeba e ninya.
Beltad le dio Nuestro Sennyor
porque fue fermosa pecador.
Mas la merçet del Criador
después le fizo grant amor. (Lines 17–26)

27. William Caxton, trans., *Golden Legend*, compiled by Jacobus de Voragine (1483), in *Temple Classics*, ed. F. S. Ellis (1900), *Internet Medieval Sourcebook*, ed. Paul Halsall, https://sourcebooks.fordham.edu/basis/goldenlegend/GoldenLegend-Volume7.asp

#Katherine, n.p., accessed July 28, 2022. Caxton, who was working from a French edition of *The Golden Legend*, includes the significant episode of Catherine's conversion to Christianity and her spiritual betrothal to Christ, which is missing from other versions of the legend.

28. Caxton.

29. Caxton.

30. Sarah Salih, *Versions of Virginity in Late Medieval England* (Cambridge: Boydell & Brewer, 2001); Claire Waters, "Dangerous Beauty, Beautiful Speech: Gendered Eloquence in Medieval Preaching," *Essays in Medieval Studies* 14 (1997).

31. Porque era tanto bella e genta,
mucho fiaba en su juventa;
tanto amaba fer sus plaçeres,
que non ha cura d'otros aberes
mas despender e desbaldir,
que nol membraba de morir. (Lines 89–94)

32. "Tanto fue plena de luxuria" (line 88).

33. Andrew Beresford, "'Ençendida del ardor de la luxuria': Prostitution and Promiscuity in the Legend of Saint Mary of Egypt," in *"Quien hubiese tal ventura": Medieval Hispanic Studies in Honour of Alan Deyermond*, ed. Andrew M. Beresford (London: Department of Hispanic Studies, Queen Mary & Westfield College, 1997), 49; Beresford, "'Oit, varones, huna razón': Sobre la función del prólogo en la *Vida de Santa María Egipciaca*," *Acta Poética* 20 (1999): 259.

34. I am grateful to Ronald E. Surtz for pointing out that the description "fermosa pecador" might also be applied to the poem itself being a thing of beauty, since poetry, being the meaningful and ornamental arrangement of words, is by definition "formed," and in the sense of *formositas*, always beautiful. Moreover, *formositas* is a type of beauty considered by medical treatises to be a cause of love-sickness (*amor hereos*) when the psychological or humoral conditions are right. In the *Viaticum*, Constantine the African writes that "sometimes the cause of eros is also the contemplation of beauty. For if the soul gazes at a form similar to itself it goes mad in order to satisfy its will" (Aliquando etiam eros causa pulchra est formositas considerata. Quam si in sibi consimili forma conspiciat, quasi insanit anima in ea ad voluntatem explendam). In Mary Frances Wack, "The *Liber de heros morbo* of Johannes Afflacius and Its Implications for Medieval Love Conventions," *Speculum* 62, no. 2 (1987): 327–28.

35. Ferguson, "St. Augustine's Region of Unlikeness," 846.

36. Ross, *Figuring the Feminine*, 28–34; Claire Waters, *Angels and Earthly Creatures: Preaching, Performance, and Gender in the Later Middle Ages* (Philadelphia: University of Pennsylvania Press, 2004), 73–95.

37. Chapter 4 addresses this preoccupation in detail.

38. Michael Camille, *The Gothic Idol: Ideology and Image-Making in Medieval Art* (Cambridge: Cambridge University Press, 1999), 35–50.

39. Tertullian, "On the Apparel of Women," in *Ante-Nicene Fathers*, vol. 4, trans. Rev. S. Thelwall, The Tertullian Project, ed. Roger Pearse, updated January 26, 2018, http://www.tertullian.org/anf/anf04/anf04-06.htm, chap 5, accessed July 28, 2022.

NOTES TO CHAPTER TWO

40. Augustine, *On Christian Doctrine*, 12.
41. Rita Copeland, "Rhetoric and Religious Community," in *Sacred and Secular in Medieval and Early Modern Cultures: New Essays*, ed. Lawrence Besserman (New York: Palgrave Macmillan, 2006), 138.
42. Ross, *Figuring the Feminine*, 3–49.
43. Howard Bloch, "Medieval Misogyny," *Representations* 20 (1987): 1–24; Bloch, *Medieval Misogyny and the Invention of Western Romantic Love* (Chicago: Chicago University Press, 1991), 37–63.
44. Ferguson, "St. Augustine's Region of Unlikeness," 861.
45. Joseph Anthony Mazzeo, "St. Augustine's Rhetoric of Silence," *Journal of the History of Ideas* 23, no. 2 (1962): 187.
46. Mazzeo, 196.
47. Rowan Williams, "Language, Reality and Desire in Augustine's *De Doctrina*," *Journal of Literature and Theology* 3 (1989): 144.
48. Williams, 148.
49. Williams, 142.
50. Jean Leclercq, *The Love of Learning and the Desire for God: A Study of Monastic Culture*, trans. Catharine Misrahi (New York: Fordham University Press, 1961), 257.
51. James J. Murphy, "Saint Augustine and the Debate about a *Christian Rhetoric*," *Quarterly Journal of Speech* 46, no. 4 (1960): 409.
52. Murphy, 409.
53. Mary Carruthers, *Experience of Beauty in the Middle Ages* (Oxford: Oxford University Press, 2014), 15.
54. *Poema de mio Cid*, ed. Ian Michael (Madrid: Editorial Castalia, 1987), 76, line 7.
55. Charles Fraker, *Celestina: Genre and Rhetoric* (London: Támesis Books, 1990), 41.
56. For the text of the relevant sections of the decree and a discussion of thirteenth-century attitudes toward the various types of *ioculatores*, see Helen F. Rubel, "Chabham's *Penitential* and Its Influence in the Thirteenth Century," *PMLA* 40, no. 2 (1925): 225–39.
57. J. C. Musgrave, "Tarsania and Juglaría in the *Libro de Apolonio*," in *Medieval Studies Presented to Rita Hamilton*, ed. Alan D. Deyermond (London: Támesis, 1976), 131; Jesús Montoya Martínez, "Juglar," in *Medieval Iberia: An Encyclopedia*, ed. E. Michael Gerli (New York: Routledge, 2003), 455.
58. Helen F. Rubel, "Chabham's *Penitential* and Its Influence in the Thirteenth Century," *PMLA* 40, no. 2 (1925): 232–33.
59. Mary Jane Kelley, "Ascendant Eloquence: Language and Sanctity in the Works of Gónzalo de Berceo," *Speculum* 79, no. 1 (2004): 66.
60. Nicolette Zeeman, "The Idol of the Text," in *Images, Idolatry, and Iconoclasm in Late Medieval England: Textuality and the Visual Image*, ed. Jeremy Dimmick, James Simpson, and Nicolette Zeeman (Oxford: Oxford University Press, 2002), 44.
61. On the different registers of "sweetness" as a rhetorical feature and an ethical position, see Mary Carruthers, *Experience of Beauty*, 80–108.
62. Brigitte Cazelles, *The Lady as Saint: A Collection of French Hagiographic Romances of the Thirteenth Century* (Philadelphia: University of Pennsylvania Press, 1991), 22 (emphasis added).

NOTES TO CHAPTER TWO

63. Kelley, "Ascendant Eloquence," 77.

64. Harriet Goldberg, "Moslem and Spanish Christian Literary Portraiture," *Hispanic Review* 45, no. 3 (1977): 326.

65. Julian Weiss, *The "Mester de Clerecía": Intellectuals and Ideologies in Thirteenth-Century Castile* (Woodbridge: Támesis, 2006), 78.

66. Emily C. Francomano, "'Lady, You Are Quite a Chatterbox': The Legend of St. Katherine of Alexandria, Wives' Words, and Women's Wisdom in MS Escorial h-I-13," in *St. Katherine of Alexandria: Texts and Contexts in Medieval Europe*, ed. Jacqueline Jenkins and Katherine Lewis (Turnhout: Brepols, 2003): 131–52, and Larissa J. Taylor, "Apostle to the Apostles: The Complexity of Medieval Preaching about Mary Magdalene," in *Mary Magdalene in Medieval Culture: Conflicted Roles*, ed. Peter Loewen and Robin Waugh (London: Routledge, 2014), 33–50. On the issue of gendered eloquence in the Magdalene and Catherine legends in Latin and in English, see Waters, *Angels and Earthly Creatures*, 96–120.

67. *Santa María Madalena*, in *Antología castellana de relatos medievales (Ms. Esc. h-I-13)*, ed. Carina Zubillaga (Buenos Aires: SECRIT, 2008), 8. (E en la mañana, llegó la mala gente de la villa por fazer sacrifiçio a los ídolos; e quando ellos llegaron, levantárase ya la Magdalena. Ella era muy fermosa e de buen donaire, e muy sesuda, e de muy buena palabra e muy arreziada; e començó de pedricar las palabras de la vida e de la salut; asy que todos se maravillaron de la su beldat e de las sus sesudas palabras, de cómo las mostrava sesudamente.) In their earlier edition of this hagiographical account of the life of Mary Magdalen, John K. Walsh and Billy Bussell Thompson note that a later manuscript (Escorial k-II-12) avoids the repetition of the word *sesuda* (prudent) in the last sentence "*sesudas* palabras, de como las mostrava *sesudamente*" by changing the final adverb to *sabrosamente*, pleasurably. *Vida de Santa María Magdalena*, in *The Myth of the Magdalen in Early Spanish Literature, with an edition of the Vida de Santa María Magdalena in Ms. H-1-13 of the Escorial Library*, Coll. Pliegos hispánicos 2 (New York: L. Clemente, 1986), 28.

68. "Vida de Santa María Magdalena," 28. (E non devedes maravillar si la boca de la Magdalena bien fablava e sesudamente, ca ella avía besado los pies de Jesu Cristo.)

69. See Waters, *Angels and Earthly Creatures*, 103; Karen Winstead, *Virgin Martyrs: Legends of Sainthood on Late Medieval England* (Ithaca, NY: Cornell University Press, 1997): 101.

70. *Del enperador Costantino (De Santa Catalina)*, in *Antología castellana de relatos medievales (Ms. Esc. h-I-13)*, ed. Carina Zubillaga (Buenos Aires: SECRIT, 2008), 59. (Callose e escuchola bien; e fue maravillado de su beldat e de su paresçer, e del afincamiento de sus palabras.)

71. *Del enperador* (emphasis added). (Señor, sé conmigo e mete en mi boca *buena* palabra, *sesuda e fermosa*, asy que aquellos que aquí son por abaxar el tu santo nonbre non ayan fuerça contra mí e ayan sus sesos menguados, e sean vençidos por la virtud de tu palabra o sean convertidos e den Gloria al tu santo nonbre.)

72. *Del enperador*, 78. (Tollet vuestros vanos duelos que fazedes de mi beldat que non val' nada.)

73. Tertullian, "On Idolatry," *Ante-Nicene Fathers*, vol. 3, trans. Rev. S. Thelwall, The Tertullian Project, ed. Roger Pearse, updated January 26, 2018, https://www.tertullian.org/anf/anf03/anf03-07.htm, accessed July 28, 2022.

NOTES TO CHAPTER THREE

74. Caxton, *Golden Legend*. This commentary is also missing from Ryan's English translation of *The Golden Legend*, so I quote from William Caxton's translation with modifications in brackets to be closer to the Spanish. (Cinco cosas especialmente dignas de admiración caracterizaron a esta santa: su sabiduría, su elocuencia, su fortaleza, su purísima castidad y los muchos privilegios con que Dios quiso honrarla [. . .] . Hay cinco cosas que hacen sumamente difícil la perseverancia en la guarda de la castidad, a saber: la abundancia de riquezas [. . .], determinadas ocasiones, aptas de suyo para arrastrar a las personas que en ellas se encuentran hacia el pecado de la lascivia; la edad juvenil, en la que la presión de la lujuria es más fuerte; la libertad, poco amiga de frenos; y la belleza, que por sí es provocativa.) Jacobus [Santiago] de Voragine, *Leyenda Dorada*, trans. José Manuel Macías (Madrid: Alianza Editorial, 2006–8), 2:773–74.

75. Waters, *Angels and Earthly Creatures*, 103.

CHAPTER THREE

1. Jean-Louis Chrétien, *The Call and the Response*, trans. Anne A. Davenport (New York: Fordham University Press, 2004), 35.

2. Book of Tobit 12:7, in "Life of Saint Mary of Egypt," trans. Maria Kouli, 70.

3. "Life of Saint Mary of Egypt," trans. Maria Kouli, 70.

4. "Pora más fer su voluntat" (line 133).

5. En beber e en comer e follía
   cuidaba noche e día.
   Cuando se lleva de yantar,
   con ellos va deportar.
   Tanto quiere jugar e reir,
   que nol miembra que ha de morir. (Lines 165–70)

6. Los mancebos de la çibdat
   tanto les plaze de la beltat,
   que cada día la van veyer
   que non se pueden d'ella toller.
   Tantas hi van de conpanyas
   que los juegos tornan a sanyas;
   ante las puertas, en las entradas,
   dábanse [los mancebos] grandes espadadas:
   la sangre que d'ellos sallía
   por medio de la cal corría. (Lines 171–80)

7. Robert Holcot, *Commentary on the Book of Wisdom*, quoted in Camille, *Gothic Idol*, 298.

8. Camille, *Gothic Idol*, 298–302.

9. "A la cativa cuando lo vedié, / nulla piedat no le prendié" (lines 181–82).

10. Peter L. Podol, "The Stylized Portrait of Women in Spanish Literature," *Hispanófila* 71 (1981): 1–21.

11. De la beltat de su figura,

como dize la escriptura,
ante que siga adelante,
direvos de su semblante. (Lines 205–8; emphasis added)

12. Alastair J. Minnis and Ian Johnson, "Introduction," in *The Cambridge History of Literary Criticism*, vol. 2, *The Middle Ages*, ed. Alastair J. Minnis and Ian Johnson (Cambridge: Cambridge University Press, 2008), 1–12.

13. Alan Deyermond, "Thirteenth-Century Expansion: I.7 Vida de Santa María Egipciaca," in *Literary History of Spain* (New York: Barnes & Noble. 1971), 70–71.

14. John Maier, "Sainthood, Heroism, and Sexuality in the *Estoria de Santa Maria Egipçiaca*," *Revista Canadiense de Estudios Hispanicos* 8, no. 3 (Spring 1984): 428.

15. Lynn Rice Cortina, "The Aesthetics of Morality: Two Portraits of Mary of Egypt in the *Vida de Santa María Egipciaca*," *Hispanic Journal* (1980): 42.

16. Cortina, 43.

17. Cortina, 43–45.

18. Minnis and Johnson, "Introduction," 4–5.

19. On the scholarly temptation to explain away strangeness through allegory, see Sahar Amer and Noah D. Guynn, "Preface," in "Re-Reading Allegory: Essays in Memory of Daniel Poiron," ed. Sahar Amer and Noah D. Guynn, *Yale French Studies* 95 (1999): 1.

20. El peyor día de la semana
non vistie panyo de lana;
assaz prendie oro e argento
bien se vistie a su talento.
Brial de xamit se vistié,
manto erminyo cobrié.
Nunqua calçaba otras çapatas
sino de cordobán entretalladas,
pintadas con oro e con plata,
cuerdas de seda con que las ata. (Lines 235–44)

21. *La Vie de Sainte Marie l'Egyptienne, ms. B* in *The Life of Saint Mary of Egypt: An Edition and Study of the Medieval French and Spanish Verse Redactions*, ed. Michèle Schiavone de Cruz-Sáenz (Barcelona: Puvil Editor, 1979), 119.

(Ele recivoit grans presenz
S'en achatoit chier garnimenz;
Bons dras avoit et avenanz,
Por miez plaissir a ses amanz. [Lines 185–88])

22. "Ystoria de Santa Pelagia," in *The Legends of the Holy Harlots: Thaïs and Pelagia in Medieval Spanish Literature*, ed. Andrew M. Beresford (Woodbridge: Támesis, 2007), 137.

23. Patricia Grieve, "Paradise Regained in *Vida de Santa María Egipciaca*: Harlots, the Fall of Nations and Hagiographic Currency," in *Translatio Studii: Essays by His Students in Honor of Karl D. Uitti for His Sixty-Fifth Birthday*, ed. Renate Blumenfeld-Kosinski et al. (Amsterdam: Rodopi, 2000), 141.

24. De su beltat dexemos estar,
que non vos lo podría contar.

NOTES TO CHAPTER THREE

Contar vos e de los sus vestimentes
e de los sus guarnimentes. (Lines 231–34)

25. Alice Colby, *The Portrait in Twelfth-Century French Literature* (Geneva: Droz, 1965).

26. Camille, *The Gothic Idol*, 330.

27. Grieve, "Paradise Regained," 141, 152.

28. "'¡Qué domatge / desta fembra de paratge!' / De todas cosas semeja sabida, / ¿cómo passa tan mala vida?" (lines 255–58).

29. Michael Solomon, "Catarsis sexual: *La Vida de Santa María Egipcíaca* y el texto higiénico," in *Erotismo en las letras hispánicas: Aspectos, modos y fronteras*, ed. Luce López-Baralt and Francisco Márquez Villanueva (Mexico City: Centro de Estudios Lingüísticos y Literarios: Colegio de México, 1995), 437.

30. "Todos la hi van corteyar / por el su cuerpo *acabar*" (lines 159–60; emphasis added).

31. "Grant maravilla puede omne aber, / que una fembra tant' puede fer" (lines 393–94).

32. Admiration rather than lust also characterizes the response that Bishop Nonnus has upon seeing the entrance into the city of beautiful Pelagia, another holy harlot. Rather than reprimand her for her ostentatious vanity, Nonnus is in awe of the care she has taken to be pleasing to men, and he bids his fellow clergymen to follow her in the desire to please, turning their whole attention to God.

33. Jill Ross, *Figuring*, 126–44.

34. Toda se mudó d'otra figura,
qua non ha panyos nin vestidura.
Perdió las carnes e la color,
que eran blancas como la flor;
los sus cabellos, que eran rubios,
tornáronse blancos e suzios.
Las sus orejas, que eran albas,
mucho eran negras e pegadas. (lines 720–27)

35. Podol, "The Stylized Portrait of Women in Spanish Literature," 14–15.

36. E. Ernesto Delgado, "Penitencia y Eucaristía en la conformación de la vertiente occidental de la leyenda de Santa María Egipcíaca: Un paradigma de negociación cultural en la Baja Edad Media," *Revista de poética medieval* 10 (2003): 40.

37. Connie Scarborough, "Seeing and Believing: The Gaze in the *Vida de Santa María Egipçiaca*," *La Corónica* 42 (2013): 309.

38. Simon Gaunt, *Gender and Genre in Medieval French Literature* (Cambridge: Cambridge University Press, 1995), 219, quoted in Julian Weiss, *Mester De Clerecía: Intellectuals and Ideologies in Thirteenth-Century Castile* (Woodbridge: Támesis, 2006), 86.

39. Weiss, *Mester*, 87.

40. On the use of specific rhetorical devices in both portraits, see Kassier, "Rhetorical Devices of the Spanish 'Vida de Santa María Egipciaca,'" and Swanberg, "The Singing Bird."

41. Patricia Cox Miller, "Is There a Harlot in This Text? Hagiography and the Grotesque," *Journal of Medieval and Early Modern Studies* 33, no. 3 (2003): 426.

42. Miller follows Lynda Coon's interpretation of the figure of Mary of Egypt in *Sacred Fictions: Holy Women and Hagiography in Late Antiquity* (Philadelphia: University of

Pennsylvania Press, 1997), as shaped by both masculine and feminine allusions and influences. Yet, whereas for Coon what matters is the masculinization of Mary's body as she approaches holiness, Miller highlights the co-presence of genders as the "realization of a contradiction" (426). A different version of the grotesque as encompassing a beauty on the horizon will be discussed in the following chapter.

43. El diablo la quiso tentar
e todo lo quisiera remembrar
lo que ella solía amar:
los grandes comeres e los buenos lechos
do solie fer los sus deletos.
Mas tanto fue bien aventurada,
que de todo fue olvidada,
Assí que en toda su vida
non le miembra de tal enemiga. (Lines 781–89)

44. Importantly, while Mary is allowed to forget her sinful past, the poet stresses the penitent's remembrance of her personal covenant with the Virgin Mary: "Many days and many nights she traveled. / She found many rough ways [. . .] / But she never forgot night and day / To call upon Holy Mary. / Constantly she remembered what she had said / And what she had proposed to her / When she had entrusted herself to her / Before the image of her Lord" (137–38). (Tanto anda noches e días / e tanto falló ásperas vías; [. . .] / mas no olvidó noche e día / de rogar a santa María. / Toda hora l' miembra lo quel' dixiera / e lo que con ella pusiera: / cóm' la metiera por fiador / ante la imagen del su Senyor [lines 702–11].)

45. Hildebert of Lavardin, "The Life of Saint Mary of Egypt," trans. Ronald Pepin, in *Saint Mary of Egypt: Three Medieval Lives in Verse* (Kalamazoo, MI: Cistercian Publications, 2005), 103.

46. "No es de llorar el su pecado / del cuerpo que assí anda lazrado" (lines 778–79).

47. "Comién pan de ordio, que non d'al, / por çierto non echaban sal" (lines 818–19; 141).

48. "Ni yazién en lechos ni en camenyas" (line 807).

49. "Cuand' huna espina le firía, / de sus pecados uno perdía; / e mucho era gozosa / porque sufrié tan dura cosa" (lines 752–55).

50. "Por alimpiarse de sus pecados" (line 808).

51. "Por amor de Dios lo fazién" (line 817).

52. Duncan Robertson, "Twelfth-Century Literary Experience: The Life of St. Mary the Egyptian," *Pacific Coast Philology* 22, no. 1/2 (1987): 73; Delgado, "Penitencia," 44–46; Julian Weiss, "Mester De Clerecía," 87.

53. "Aquí comiença a pensar / e de coraçon a llorar" (lines 456–57).

54. "Un nombre abemos yo e ti, / mas mucho eres tú luenye de mí: / Tu María e yo María, / mas non tenemos amas huna vía" (lines 533–36).

55. "Tú ameste siempre castidat, / e yo luxuria e malveztad. [. . .] / Tú eres duenya mucho omildosa / e yo só pobre e ergullosa, / e de mi cuerpo luxuriosa" (lines 537–43).

56. On the less than chaste medieval representations of the Virgin Mary, see Emma Maggie Solberg, *Virgin Whore* (Ithaca, NY: Cornell University Press, 2018).

NOTES TO CHAPTER FOUR

57. Catherine E. Winiarski, "Adultery, Idolatry, and the Subject of Monotheism," *Religion and Literature* 38, no. 3 (2006): 52.

58. "Nuestro Senyor amó a tí, / e pues Él amó a ti / duenya, abe mercé de mí [. . .] / en ti preso carn' el Rey del çielo" (lines 544–49).

59. "En buena forma fue tajada / nin era gorda nin muy delgada, / nin era luenga nin era corta, / mas de mesura bona" (lines 227–30).

60. "La imagen era bien figurada, / en la mesura era tajada" (lines 475–77).

61. "Vió unas letras escritas en tierra: / mucho eran claras e bien tajadas, / que en çielo fueron formadas" (lines 1368–70).

62. Lloyd August Kasten and Florian J. Cody, *Tentative Dictionary of Medieval Spanish* (New York: Hispanic Seminary of Medieval Studies, 2001), s.v. adj. "tajado."

63. "Ay duenya, dulçe madre, / que en el tu vientre tóviste al tu padre" (lines 483–84).

64. "Creyo bien en mi creyençia / que Dios fue en tu nascençia: / en ti priso humanidat, / tú non perdiste virginidat. / Grant maravilla fue del padre / que de su fija fizo su madre" (lines 524–28).

65. "E fue maravillosa cosa / que de la espina salló la rosa; / et de las rosa fruto salló / por que todo el mundo salvo" (lines 529–32).

66. Robertson, "Poem and Spirit," 318.

CHAPTER FOUR

1. Arthur Danto, *The Abuse of Beauty: Aesthetics and the Concept of Art* (Chicago: Open Court, 2003), 89.

2. Alexander Nehamas, *Only a Promise of Happiness: The Place of Beauty in a World of Art* (Princeton, NJ: Princeton University Press, 2007), 29–30. Nehamas contrasts the easy beauty of the quotation with twentieth-century aesthetics.

3. Stendhal, *On Love*, trans. Philip Sidney Woolf and Cecil N. Sidney Woolf (New York: Brentano's 1916), 55. Stendhal, *De l'amour* (Paris: Garnier-Flammarion, 1965), 64. (La beauté détrônée par l'amour.)

4. Stendhal, *On Love*, 55; *De l'amour*, 64. (Mille sentiments en présence de cette marque de petite-vérole, que ses sentiments sont pour la plupart délicieux, sont tous du plus haut intérêt.)

5. Stendhal, *De l'amour*, 64. (Je le vois aimer la laide au bout de huit jours qu'il emploie à effacer sa laideur par ses souvenirs.) My translation, in order to maintain the ambiguity present in the French use of the present tense of the verb "voir." It is unclear whether Stendhal witnessed what he describes or he is imagining a likely scenario. A colloquial English rendition of this option would be along the lines of "I can easily see him . . ."

6. "La beauté n'est que la *promesse* du bonheur. Le bonheur d'un Grec était différent du bonheur d'un Français de 1822. Voyez les yeux de la Vénus de Médici et comparez-les aux yeux de la Madeleine de Pordenone (chez M. de Sommariva)." (Emphasis added.)

7. Stendhal, *Mémoires d'un touriste*, in *Œuvres completes*, vol. 17, ed. Louis Royer (Geneva:

NOTES TO CHAPTER FOUR

Slatkine Reprints, 1986), 188. (Horrible vieille, d'autant plus horrible que l'on voit qu'elle a été belle.) In Rome, at the Borghese gallery, he saw another image of Saint Mary of Egypt by Ribera, but his opinion remained the same. See Jean Habert, "Italian Baroque Paintings: Marseilles," *Burlington Magazine* 131, no. 1030 (1989): 59.

8. Kathy Eden, *Hermeneutics and the Rhetorical Tradition: Chapters in the Ancient Legacy* (New Haven, CT: Yale University Press, 1997).

9. Leonardo da Vinci, *Trattato de la pittura*, in *The Fabrication of Leonardo da Vinci's Trattato della pittura*, vol. 2, trans. Janis Bell and Claire J. Farago (Leiden: E. J. Brill, 2018), 646. (Le vecchie si devono figurar ardite, e pronte, con rabbiosi movimenti, a guisa di furie infernali, et i movimenti devono parer più pronti nelle braccia et testa, che nelle gambe.)

10. Canons and Decrees of the Sacred and Oecumenical Council of Trent, "The Twenty-Fifth Session," ed. and trans. J. Waterworth (London: Dolman, 1848), 235, Hanover Historical Texts Project, https://history.hanover.edu/texts/trent.html, accessed July 20, 2021.

11. Alfonso Rodríguez G. de Ceballos, "Image and Counter-Reformation in Spain and Spanish America," in *Sacred Spain: Art and Belief in the Spanish World*, ed. Ronda Kasl (New Haven, CT: Yale University Press for the Indianapolis Museum of Art, 2009), 25.

12. Quoted in Rodríguez G. de Ceballos, "Image," 27.

13. Bernardino de Villegas, *La esposa de Christo instruída con la vida de Santa Lutgarda virgen* (Murcia: Juan Fernández de Fuentes, 1635), 430–37. For a more detailed account of the development of the concept of decorum's insistence on moral and didactic aspects, see Palma Martínez-Burgos García, "El decoro: La invención de un concepto y su proyección artística," in *Revista de la Facultad de Geografía e Historia* 2 (1988) and *Idolos e imágenes: La controversia del arte religioso en el siglo XVI español* (Valladolid: Secretariado de Publicaciones, Universidad de Valladolid, 1990), 270–80.

14. Martínez-Burgos García, *Idolos*, 272.

15. Quoted in Erwin Panofsky, "Erasmus and the Visual Arts," *Journal of the Warburg and Courtauld Institutes* 32 (1969): 208.

16. Quoted in Panofsky, 208.

17. Quoted in Panofsky, 213–14.

18. Quoted in Panofsky, 213.

19. Villegas, *La esposa*, 431. (¡Qué cosa mas indecente que una imagen de Nuestra Señora con saya entera, ropa, copete, valona, arandela, gargantilla, y cosas semejantes; y que unas vírgenes vestidas tan profanamente con tantos dijes y galas que no traen más las damas más bizarras del mundo! Que a veces duda un hombre, si adora a santa Lucía, o a santa Catalina, o si apartará los ojos por no ver la profanidad de los trajes, porque en sus vestidos y adornos no parecen santas del cielo, sino damas del mundo, y a no estar santa Catalina con su espada en la mano, y santa Lucía con sus ojos en el plato, por lo que toca a su vestido y traje galán con que las visten, nadie dijera que eran santas ni vírgenes honestísimas, como lo fueron.)

20. Alain Saint-Saëns, *Art and Faith in Tridentine Spain (1545–1690)* (New York: Peter Lang, 1995), 32.

NOTES TO CHAPTER FOUR

21. Palma Martínez-Burgos García, "Ut picture natura: La imagen plástica del santo ermitaño en la literatura espiritual del siglo XVI," *Norba-Arte* 10 (1989): 19.

22. A. A. Parker, "Bandits and Saints in the Spanish Drama of the Golden Age," in *Critical Studies of Calderón's Comedias*, ed. J. E. Varey (Farnborough: Gregg International, 1973), 151–68.

23. See Javier Portús ("Indecencia," 68–69) on the cultural resonance of tropes of penitence and conversion in early modern Spain.

24. Martínez-Burgos García ("Ut pictura natura," 19, 23–24) has studied how saints such as Peter, Dominic, and Francis acquired penitential selves in literature and visual arts in the course of the seventeenth century.

25. See Palma Martínez-Burgos García, "La meditación de la muerte en los penitentes de la pintura española del Siglo de Oro: Ascetas, melancólicos y místicos," *Espacio, tiempo y forma* 12 (1999): 152–72.

26. Ana García Sanz and Juan Martínez Cuesta, "La serie iconográfica de ermitaños del monasterio de las Descalzas Reales," *Cuadernos de arte e iconografía* 47, no. 74 (1991): 291.

27. The Sadeler prints were gathered under different names in multiple volumes. The royal convent in Madrid owned at least three of these volumes (*Solitudo sive vitae patrum eremicolarum, Solitudo, sive vitae foeminarum*, and *Sylvae sacrae*). It is possible that the anonymous painter had been familiar with other collections since his hermit saints do not always follow those owned by the convent directly, although the figures clearly belong to the "family."

28. On Borromeo's commission in relationship to pictorial and spiritual trends that favored the imagination, see García Sanz and Martínez Cuesta, "La serie." On Borromeo's pursuit of meditational landscapes in real life and in art, see Christine Göttler, "The Temptation of the Senses at the Sacro Monte di Varallo," in *Religion and the Senses in Early Modern Europe*, ed. Wietse de Boer and Christine Göttler (Leiden: Brill, 2012), 440–43.

29. The identification of these two figures has been in question since they do not have titles, but Elizabeth Carroll Consavari ("Tintoretto," in *Mary Magdalene, Iconographic Studies from the Middle Ages to the Baroque* [Leiden: Brill, 2012], 135–60) makes a persuasive argument that their pairing makes sense in light of the Marian cycle depicted in the rest of the room as well as in the saints' associations with healing and charity, consistent with the works undertaken by the confraternity of San Rocco, especially the care of those afflicted with syphilis.

30. Javier Portús Pérez, *Ribera* (Barcelona: Polígrafa, 2011), 40.

31. This series was likely painted in 1641, and there is some debate among scholars about their whereabouts before 1658. For an overview of Ribera's commissions in Italy and Spain, see Alonso E. Pérez Sánchez, "Ribera and Spain: His Spanish Patrons in Italy and Spain; The Influence of his Work on Spanish Artists," in *Jusepe de Ribera, 1591–1652*, ed. Alfonso E. Pérez Sánchez and Nicola Spinosa (New York: Metropolitan Museum of Art, 1992), 35–49.

32. *Guía de la Pintura Barroca Española* (Madrid: Museo Nacional del Prado, 2001), 70.

33. David Hugh Farmer, "Bartholomew," in *Oxford Dictionary of Saints* (Oxford: Oxford University Press, 1992), 39.

34. Cited in Alison Weber, "Locating Holiness in Early Modern Spain: Convents, Caves, and Houses," in *Structures and Subjectivities: Attending to Early Modern Women*, ed. Joan Hartman and Adele Seeff (Cranbury, NJ: Associated University Presses, 2007), 58–59.

35. Alison Weber and others have warned against the temptation to read the normative ambitions of enclosure as descriptive of what happened in practice. She offers, for example, a nuanced analysis of how three women negotiated authorities and sociocultural expectations in order to pursue their own visions of holiness that muddled the norms: the nun (Ana de San Agustín), the hermitess (Catalina de Cardona), and the *beata*, a religious woman loosely affiliated with a community of other religious women who perform charitable works (Águeda de la Cruz). In "Locating Holiness in Early Modern Spain: Convents, Caves, and Houses," in *Structures and Subjectivities: Attending to Early Modern Women*, ed. Joan Hartman and Adele Seeff (Cranbury, NJ: Associated University Presses, 2007), 50–74.

36. Alain Saint-Saëns, "A Case of Gendered Rejection: The Hermitess in Golden Age Spain," in *Spanish Women in the Golden Age: Images and Realities*, ed. Magdalena S. Sánchez and Alain Saint-Saëns (Westport, CT: Greenwood Press, 1996), 58.

37. For a helpful account of how the trope of the "female man of God" took form in early Christianity and shaped later gendered understandings of holiness, see Margaret Miles, *Carnal Knowing: Female Nakedness and Religious Meaning in the Christian West* (Boston: Beacon Press, 1989).

38. Quoted in Adelaida Cortijo Ocaña and Antonio Cortijo Ocaña, "*Vida de la madre Catalina de Cardona por fray Juan de la Miseria*: Un texto hagiográfico desconocido del siglo XVI (Bancroft Library, UCB, Fernán Nuñez Collection, vol. 143)," *Dicenda* 21 (2003): 31.

39. Cortijo Ocaña, "Vida," 31. (Como oveja con su boca misma / por tierra pacía y comía yerbas, / las que ella conocía ser buenas de / comer.)

40. Quoted in Weber, "Locating Holiness," 60.

41. Weber, 60.

42. Saint-Saëns, "Gendered Rejection," 56.

43. Saint-Saëns, 57.

44. Gabriele Paleotti, *Discourse on Sacred and Profane Images*, trans. William McCuaig (Los Angeles: Getty Research Institute, 2012), 274.

45. Patricia Cox Miller, "Is There a Harlot in This Text? Hagiography and the Grotesque," *Journal of Medieval and Early Modern Studies* 33, no. 3 (2003): 423. On the narrative trope of "becoming male" used by hagiographers in late antiquity as a strategy to render legible the holiness of female bodies in display, see Miles, *Carnal Knowing*.

46. Miller, "Is There a Harlot," 425.

47. George Santayana, *The Sense of Beauty*, in *The Works of George Santayana*, vol. 2, ed. William G. Holzberger and Herman J. Saatkamp Jr. (Cambridge, MA: MIT Press, 1986), 159.

48. Santayana, *The Sense of Beauty*, 159.

NOTES TO CHAPTER FOUR

49. Gabriele Finaldi and María Cruz de Carlos Varona write about the political and religious significance of the saints in Madrid and Naples in their respective essays for *Jusepe de Ribera's Mary Magdalene in a New Context*, ed. Gabriele Finaldi (Dallas: Meadows Museum, Southern Methodist University, 2011).

50. With very few notable exceptions, after the sixteenth century most representations of the apostle to the apostles in Catholic Europe and its colonies depict her as sweet, graceful, and young. The best known of these exceptions, the poignant sculpture of a penitent Mary Magdalene by Florentine artist Donatello, dates back to the fifteenth century. Salvatore Lo Re has written about the few images that feature a pained, penitent Magdalene in Florence that could give background to understanding Titian's representation of the repentant sinner (in "'Fresca e rugiadosa in quella penitenza': La Maddalena, Tiziano e Baccio Valori," *Intersezioni* 1 [1998], 33–46).

Later examples of a less than lovely Magdalene are few, and they include *Mary Magdalene in the Desert* by the seventeenth-century Flemish painter Livio Mehus and his Spanish contemporary Pedro de Orrente's *Penitent Magdalene* (both reproduced in *María Magdalena: Éxtasis y arrepentimiento*, ed. Odile Delenda [Distrito Federal, Mexico: CONACULTA, Instituto Nacional de Bellas Artes, 2001], 132–33, 204–5). Significantly, when writing about the Mehus painting, Odile Delenda acknowledged that the saint's age and visible signs of wasting away are, in fact, more typical of representations of Mary of Egypt (in *María Magdalena*, 204).

51. Italian original and English translation quoted in Haskins, *Mary Magdalene*, 245. (Anche mi ricordo hora che dicendoli che era da piacer troppo, come fresca e rugiadosa in quella penitenza. Conosciuto che io voleo dire che devese con scarna del digiuno, mi ripose ghignando, avvertisce [?], che l'è ritratta pel primo dì che rientra, innanzi che cominciasse a digiunare, per rappresentar la pittura penitente sì, ma piacevole quanto poteva. E per certo era tale.)

52. Heather Sexton Graham, "Renaissance Flesh and Women's Devotion: Titian's *Penitent Magdalen*," *Comitatus: A Journal of Medieval and Renaissance Studies* 39 (2008): 137.

53. Giorgio Vasari, *The Lives of the Artists*, trans. Julia Conaway Bondanella and Peter Bondanella (Oxford: Oxford University Press, 1998), 504. (Con i capelli che le cascano sopra le spalle, intorno alla gola e sopra il petto; mentre ella, alzando la testa con gli occhi fissi al cielo, mostra compunzione nel rossore degli occhi, e nelle lacrime dogliezza de' peccati.) Vasari, *Le vite de' più eccellenti pittori, scultori ed architettori, con nuove annotazioni e commenti di Gaetano Milanesi*, vol. 7 (Florence: Sansoni Editore, 1878–81), 454.

54. Steven Stowell, "Art and Compunction: Francesco Bocchi's Mystical Experience of Art," in *The Spiritual Language of Art: Medieval Christian Themes in Writings on Art of the Italian Renaissance* (Leiden: Brill, 2004), 25–31.

55. Vasari *Lives*, 504. (Onde muove questa pittura, chiunque la guarda, estremamente; e, che è più, ancorchè sia bellissima, non muove a lascivia ma a commiserazione; Vasari *Le vite*, 454.)

56. *Copia de los pareceres y censuras de los reverendísimos padres y señores catedráticos de las insignes Universidades de Salamanca y Alcalá y de otras personas doctas sobre el abuso de figuras y pinturas lascivas y deshonestas; en que se muestra que es pecado*

198   NOTES TO CHAPTER FOUR

mortal pintarlas, esculpirlas y tenerlas patentes donde sean vistas (Madrid: Viuda de Alonso Martín, 1632), in Francisco Calvo Serraller, *Teoría de la Pintura del Siglo de Oro* (Madrid: Cátedra, 1991), 237–58.

57. *Copia de los pareceres*, 244. See also Martínez-Burgos, "Decoro," 96–97. (La pérdida sería ninguna, antes grande ganancia en transformarse una Venus en Santa María Magdalena, y una Diana en Santa María Egipcíaca, y otras Santas, o como mejor se pudieren acomodar.)

58. Javier Portús, "Indecencia, mortificación y modos de ver en la pintura del Siglo de Oro," *Espacio, Tiempo y Forma* 8 (1995): 55–88.

59. Quoted in Benito Navarrete Prieto, "La Magdalena en la pintura española del Siglo de Oro," in *María Magdalena: Éxtasis y arrepentimiento*, ed. Odile Delenda (Museo Nacional de San Carlos de México, 2001), 62.

60. Pacheco, *Arte de la pintura*, 657.

61. Pacheco, 658. (Que es muy puesto en razón que se pinte muy hermosa y de mucho menos edad que tenía; por cuanto la virginidad conserva la belleza y frescura exterior, como se ve en muchas religiosas ancianas.)

62. Katherine L. Jansen "Like a Virgin: The Meaning of the Magdalen for Female Penitents of Later Medieval Italy," *Memoirs of the American Academy in Rome* 45 (2000): 131–52.

63. Quoted in Jansen, 141.

64. Marjorie Malvern, *Venus in Sackcloth: The Magdalen's Origins and Metamorphoses* (Carbondale: Southern Illinois University Press, 1975).

65. Marina Warner, *Alone of All Her Sex: The Myth and the Cult of the Virgin Mary* (New York: Knopf, 1976), 237.

66. Margaret Miles, *A Complex Delight: The Secularization of the Breast, 1350–1750* (Berkeley: University of California Press, 2008), 76.

67. Historians, from Susan Haskins (*Mary Magdalen*) to Heather Graham ("Renaissance Flesh"), have identified Florentine neo-Platonism (and its view that beauty served as stepping-stone to goodness) as the lubricant for the conceptual loop tying holiness and beauty. Concretely, when it came to the saint that embodied human and divine love, it means that the surface beauty of both the painting as art and of the saint as subject is supposed to lead male and female viewers *elsewhere* to engage in meditation or experience commiseration.

68. Filippo Baldinucci, *Vocabolario toscano dell'arte del disegno* (Florence: Santi Franchi, 1681), 64, Bibliothèque Nationale de France, https://gallica.bnf.fr/ark:/12148/bpt6k9762 233v/, accessed July 28, 2022.

69. Craig Felton, "The Paintings of Ribera," in *Jusepe de Ribera, lo Spagnoletto, 1591–1652*, ed. Craig Felton and William B. Jordan (Fort Worth, TX: Kimbell Art Museum, 1982), 58.

70. The study of the representation of old age (male and female) in the early modern period is a relatively recent academic development. In a Spanish context, Joseph Snow's article focuses on the medieval erasure of the positive image of the wise crone in literary portraiture in order to leave only the Virgin and Mother as models. Snow's work sets the stage for later scholarship, which not surprisingly focuses on the complex figure of Celestina, in whom scholars recognize the tropes of women as naturally promiscuous

NOTES TO CHAPTER FOUR

and as physically decayed (Encarnación Juárez-Almendros). On Italian models and the gerontophobia that informed medical, philosophical, and artistic attitudes toward the male and female aging body, see Philip Sohm. Erin J. Campbell's work turns to didactic treatises on female virtue, especially by Christian humanist reformers such as Juan Luis Vives and Gabriele Paleotti, to explore how the masculinized matron offers an alternative to the negative vision of the old woman.

71. Quoted in Miles, *A Complex Delight*, 139.

72. Quoted in Miles, 139. (Erunt tamen membra feminea non adcommodata usui veteri sed decori novo, quo non alliciatur aspicientis concupiscentia quae nulla erit, sed Dei laude-tur sapientia atque clementia qui et quod non erat fecit et liberavit a corruptione quod fecit.) Augustine, *City of God*, vol. 7, *Books 21–22*, trans. William M. Green, Loeb Classical Library no. 417 (Cambridge, MA: Harvard University Press, 1972), book 22, 17, 280–81.

73. Carlos Alberto Vega, *El transformismo religioso: La abnegacion sexual de la mujer en la España medieval* (Madrid: Pliegos, 2008).

74. Quoted in Campbell, "Prophets, Saints, and Matriarchs: Portraits of Old Women in Early Modern Italy," *Renaissance Quarterly* 63, no. 3 (2010), 814.

75. Campbell, 820–21.

76. Campbell, 840 (emphasis added).

77. https://www.museodelprado.es/en/the-collection/art-work/saint-mary-of-egypt/1a0b50dc-1aa5-4e02-844b-6da30547b218, accessed March 24, 2022.

78. The close association of landscape and eremitical saints is a cultural development that Martínez-Burgos has traced in Spain to the popularity of spiritual treatises (i.e., San Juan de la Cruz's *La subida del Monte Carmelo*, Alfonso de Orozco's *Vergel de oración*, San Pedro de Alcántara's *Vergel spiritual del alma religiosa*, etc.) that propose natural sites as real and symbolic aids to meditation ("Ut pictura," 16–19).

79. Pilar Pedraza, "El anciano y la vieja: Carne de Dios, carne del Diablo," in *El desnudo en el Museo del Prado*, ed. Rafael Argullol (Madrid: Galaxia Gutenberg, 1998), 195. (Se vuelve sospechosa, es bruja, celestina, su cuerpo no solo se supone feo sino horroroso.)

80. For a study of the poetic functions of the ugliness of the old woman in late Renaissance and baroque Italian poetry, see Patrizia Bettella, *The Ugly Woman: Transgressive Aesthetic Models in Italian Poetry from the Middle Ages to the Baroque* (Toronto: University of Toronto Press, 2005). On the baroque invective against old women, especially in the poetry of Francisco Quevedo, see Jaime Hernández Vargas, "Dos viejas celestinas y hechiceras en la lírica quevediana: Fisonomía y retratos sociales como instrumentos punitivos," *La Perinola* 19 (2015), 161–80.

81. Augustine, *City*, 280–81. (Non est autem vitium sexus femineus, sed natura.)

82. Nicola Spinosa, "José de Ribera, un español en Nápoles entre la realidad, la naturaleza y el color," in *Jusepe de Ribera, el Españoleto*, ed. Nicola Spinosa and Alfonso E. Pérez Sánchez (Barcelona: Lunwerg Editores, 2003), 62–63. (Representada como una anciana entumecida, herida, desgreñada y doliente, una figura que sólo podía encontrarse en los barrios bajos y en los callejones oscuros de la Nápoles virreinal y española.)

83. María Cruz de Carlos Varona, "Saints and Sinners in Madrid and Naples: Saint Mary Magdalene as a Model of Conversion and Penance," in *Jusepe de Ribera's Mary Mag-*

dalene in a New Context, ed. Gabriele Finaldi (Dallas: Meadows Museum, Southern Methodist University, 2011), 81.

84. Compare the descriptions quoted by art historians of the Montpellier Saint Mary of Egypt to that of a companion portrait of the ascetic Saint Onophrious (1642, Museum of Fine Arts Boston): "Here [Ribera] rendered the hermit Saint Onophrius—unkempt, wearing a loincloth of leaves—with great realism: dirty fingernails, hollowed cheeks, flesh sagging from his emaciated frame. The monochromatic palette reinforces the subject's asceticism and piety" (http://www.mfa.org/collections/object/saint-onophrius -32565, accessed July 28, 2022). Both holy figures have the same faraway gaze, only one is deemed sickly and cadaverous. Martha Levine Dunkelman has also studied the tendency of viewers to interpret artistic images of female asceticism as illustrations of suffering and fragility rather than strength and endurance. In "Donatello's *Mary Magdalen*: A Model of Courage and Survival," *Women's Art Journal* 26, no. 2 (2005): 10–13.

85. Philip L. Sohm, *The Artist Grows Old: The Aging of Art and Artists in Italy, 1500–1800* (New Haven, CT: Yale University Press, 2007), 358.

86. Juvenal, "Satire X," in *Juvenal and Persius*, ed. and trans. Susanna Morton Braund, Loeb Classics Latin no. 91 (Cambridge, MA: Harvard University Press, 2004), 383.

87. Eve Kosofsky Sedgwick, "Paranoid Reading and Reparative Reading, or You Are So Paranoid, You Probably Think This Essay Is about You," in *Touching Feeling: Affect, Pedagogy, Performativity* (Durham, NC: Duke University Press, 2003), 123–52.

88. In this Ribera's representations of Mary of Egypt differ significantly from the Byzantine tradition that depicts her body in a more clearly masculinized way. Roland Betancourt has recently argued that this tradition depicts the saint as a transmasculine figure. See Roland Betancourt, *Byzantine Intersectionality: Sexuality, Gender, and Race in the Middle Ages* (Princeton, NJ: Princeton University Press, 2021), 5–14.

89. Vega, *El transformismo religioso*, 35.

90. Calves and feet were notoriously eroticized body parts in the early modern period. To get a sense of Ribera's daring depiction of Mary here, it is enough to remember that while decorum allows for holy breasts to be shown (maternally when belonging to the Virgin, ambiguously eroticized when the Magdalene's, and heroically when shown on Agnes's tray after her martyrdom), one rarely sees the bare calves of holy women.

91. Julian Carter, "Embracing Transition, or Dancing in the Folds of Time," in *The Transgender Studies Reader 2*, ed. Susan Stryker and Aren Z. Aizura (New York and London: Routledge, 2013), 130–43.

92. Krista Hughes, "Beauty Incarnate: A Claim for Postmodern Feminist Theology," *Revista Anglo Saxonica* 6 (2013): 121.

CHAPTER FIVE

1. "El Poeta mire cómo dispone las cosas, que aunque sea menester hacer violencia a la historia, aunque la comedia sea de S. Alejo, o S. Bruno, ha de hacer lugar al galanteo, y a los amores profanos, y si no le dirán que es *Flos Sanctorum*, y no comedia." Ignacio

NOTES TO CHAPTER FIVE

Camargo, *Discurso teológico sobre los teatros y comedias de este siglo* (Lisbon: Miguel Manescal, 1690), 68.

2. Inquisitor's report, Archivo Histórico Nacional, Inquisición, Madrid, leg. 4421, quoted in María Helena Sánchez Ortega, *Pecadoras de verano, arrepentidas en invierno: El camino de la conversion femenina* (Madrid: Alianza, 1995), 299. (Pinta en voca de la ramera y de sus cortejos los atractivos todos del vicio del modo más irritante y aun, valiéndose de Zósimas, quiere el autor ponerle un corretivo lo hace con tal debilidad y que no sirve de remedio.) For a study of the reception of early modern plays representing female penitent sinners, see Natalia Fernández Rodríguez, "Veneno mortal para la juventud: Público y censura ante las pecadoras penitentes de la comedia nueva," *Bulletin of Hispanic Studies* 88, no. 8 (2011): 911–30.

3. Sebastián de Covarrubias Orozco, *Tesoro de la lengua castellana o española: Biblioteca áurea hispánica, 21,* ed. Ignacio Arellano and Rafael Zafra (Madrid: Iberoamericana; Frankfurt am Main: Vervuert, 2006), s.v. "aparencia." [(*Aparencia* lo que a la vista tiene un buen parecer y puede engañar en lo intrínseco y sustancial. *Razones aparentes* las que de repente mueven, pero consideradas no tienen eficacia ni son concluyentes. *Aparencias*, son ciertas representaciones mudas, que corrida una cortina, se muestran al pueblo, y luego se vuelven a cubrir.)

4. Hugo A. Rennert, *The Spanish Stage in the Time of Lope de Vega* (New York: Hispanic Society of America, 1909), 98–99.

5. Emilio Orozco Díaz, "Sobre la teatralización del templo y la función religiosa en el barroco: El predicador y el comediante," *Cuadernos para investigación de la literatura hispánica* 2–3 (1980).

6. Francisco de Luque, *Copia de una carta, que el Licenciado, Francisco de Luque, Clerigo de Seuilla escriuió á la Congregacion de Clerigos y Sacerdotes de la misma ciudad, estando en la villa de Madrid, en las casas del Cauallero de Gracia, en veynte dias del mes de Mayo, de 1601,* in José Simón Díaz, ed. *Relaciones breves de actos públicos celebrados en Madrid de 1541 a 1650* (Madrid: Instituto de Estudios Madrileños, 1982), 47. See also José María Díez Borque, "Algunas notas sobre géneros y espacios teatrales del Siglo de Oro," in *El redescubrimiento de los clásicos: Actas de las XV jornadas de teatro clásico, Almagro, julio 1992,* ed. Felipe B. Pedraza Jiménez (Almagro, Ciudad Real, Spain: Universidad de Castilla-La Mancha, Festival de Almagro, 1993), 129–30.

7. Francisco de Luque, *Copia* 47. (Una devota imagen de la Madalena que pareció muy bien.)

8. Luque, 47. (Se cantaba en el coro el Cantico de Benedictus, y el Psalmo de Misere [*sic*], en música Italiana de falsetes con tanta variedad de instrumentos cual nunca yo tenia noticia. Las voces eran regaladísimas y tan a propósito de esta santa devoción que ocasionaba a muchas lagrimas de sentimiento y consuelo espiritual, y más juntándose a esto, que al tiempo del verso: *Tibi soli peccaui* se descubría la venerable imagen de un Santísimo Crucifijo que está en el altar mayor, corriendo dos cortinas de tafetán con pausa y autoridad y estando el altar y capilla bastantemente adornados de antorchas y cera blanca, que todo parecía una representación del cielo, en que ordinariamente gastaban toda la tarde con el gusto que se puede entender.)

9. Quoted in Emilio Cotarelo y Mori, *Bibliografía de las controversias sobre la licitud*

del teatro en España (Edición Facsímil) (Granada: Universidad de Granada, 1997), 42 (emphasis added). (Estas representables sagradas noticias difícil fuera que las hallara la ruda ignorancia si la resplandeciente antorcha de la armoniosa consonancia de los números no hubiera iluminado los ojos y los oídos de quantos se hallaban en el confuso caos del horror de la incapacidad.)

10. Lope de Vega, *Lo fingido verdadero*, in *Comedias* (Barcelona: Editorial Iberia, 1955), 1; lines 33–41.

11. Lope de Vega, *¡Ay verdades! que en Amor*, quoted in Hugo Rennert, *The Spanish Stage in the Time of Lope de Vega* (New York: Hispanic Society of America, 1909), 98. (La carpintería / suple concetos y trazas.)

12. Tertullian, "De spectaculis," trans. T. R. Glover, in *Apology; De Spectaculis*, Loeb Classical Library no. 250 (New York: Putnam's Sons, 1931), 277–78.

13. Jennifer Herdt, *Putting on Virtue: The Legacy of the Splendid Vices* (Chicago: University of Chicago Press, 2008), 119.

14. Herdt, 119.

15. Herdt, 119.

16. Pedro de Ribadeneira, *Tratado de las tribulaciones, repartido en dos libros* (Valencia: Imprenta de Ildefonso Mompie, 1831), 95. (Si vemos que una mujer que se topa acaso en la calle sin ninguna curiosidad de vestido, muchas veces roba y pervierte el corazón del que la mira con atención, y que sola su vista basta para prenderle y encadenarle, ¿qué diremos de los que están todo el día muy de propósito mirando a las mujeres hermosas y compuestas en las representaciones? Adonde, demás de la vista ponzoñosa, hay palabras lascivas y torpes, canciones de sirenas, voces suaves y muelles, los ojos pintados, afeitados los rostros, todo el cuerpo galano y compuesto, y otros mil lazos para engañar y prender á los que miran.)

17. Ribadeneira, 103–5. (El mismo Angélico Doctor nos enseña, que es pecado el usar en estas recreaciones y entretenimientos de palabras lascivas, o de hechos torpes y feos, y el dejarse llevar demasiado y sin rienda del gusto y entretenimiento [...] y el hacer o decir cosa que no sea muy circunstanciada y muy conveniente al lugar y al tiempo, y á la persona que se recrea. Y conforme á esta doctrina, puesto caso que pueda ser que las cosas que se representan sean tan honestas y santas, y representadas por tales personas, y de tal modo que no dañen a las costumbres sino que sirvan de honesta recreación [...]; pero cierto que las que se representan por hombres y mujercillas infames, y de cosas lascivas y amorosas, son la ruina y destruccion de la república. Y los entremeses que se mezclan entre las cosas sagradas son muy perjudiciales é indignos de la gravedad cristiana [...]. Especialmente que en las representaciones, como dijo Salviano, todos los sentidos son combatidos y contaminados. [...] Pues las mujercillas que representan comunmente son hermosas, lascivas, y que han vendido su honestidad, y con los meneos y gestos de todo el cuerpo, y con la voz blanda y suave, con el vestido y gala, a manera de sirenas, encantan y transforman los hombres en bestias.)

18. On the historical aspect of hagiographic drama, see Noelia Cirnigliaro, "Versiones de la historia, versiones de la leyenda: Sobre la comedia hagiográfica de Lope de Vega," *Filología* 33, no. 1–2 (2000): 187–206.

19. Miguel de Cervantes, *The History of Don Quixote*, trans. John Ormsby, Project Guten-

NOTES TO CHAPTER FIVE

berg. (Pues ¿qué, si venimos a las comedias divinas? ¡Qué de Milagros falsos se fingen en ellas, qué de cosas apócrifas y mal entendidas, atribuyendo a un santo los Milagros de otro! Y aun en las humanas se atreven a hacer Milagros sin más respeto ni consideración que parecerles que allí estará bien el tal milagro y apariencia [...] para que gente ignorante se admire y venga a la comedia.) *Don Quijote de la Mancha*, ed. Francisco Rico (Barcelona: Crítica, 2001), 1:48, 554.

20. While both Ribadeneira and Villegas declared Paul the Deacon's Latin text of Mary of Egypt's life an important source, the many reprints and editions of these much-appreciated works created variation across editions, both with regards to which saints' lives appeared and to the saints' individual narrative details. It is no surprise, then, that the Villegas collection printed in Alcalá de Henares in 1609 did not contain a reference to Mary of Egypt, while the 1588 Madrid edition frames her legend with an allegory from the Apocalypse about a battle between a dragon and a woman who is given wings to flee to safety in the quiet of the desert.

21. Julio Caro Baroja, "Religión, historia y literatura," in *Ensayo sobre literatura de cordel*, *Fundamentos 109* (Madrid: Ediciones Istmo, 1990), 393–96.

22. On the public use of Mary Magdalene and Mary of Egypt in Sevillian religious festivals, see Mary Elizabeth Perry, *Gender and Disorder in Early Modern Seville* (Princeton, NJ: Princeton University Press, 1990), 47–52. On the miraculous interventions attributed to Mary of Egypt in the sixteenth century, including the "apparition" of images, which led to the establishment of shrines in the Spanish countryside, see William A. Christian, *Local Religion in Sixteenth-Century Spain* (Princeton, NJ: Princeton University Press, 1981), 75–76.

23. On the performance of Pérez de Montalbán's *Gitana de Menfis* in Valladolid and Valencia in the eighteenth century and the presence of the play in bookseller catalogs in the nineteenth (though sometimes with altered titles such as *La gitanilla de Menfis* or *La pecadora penitente*), see Francisco Sánchez-Castañer, "Alusiones teatrales en *La Pícara Justina*," *Revista de Filología Española* 25 (1941): 234–35.

24. P. G. Walsh, "The Rights and Wrongs of Curiosity (Plutarch to Augustine)," *Greece & Rome* 35, no. 1 (1988): 73–74.

25. Pedro de Ribadeneira, "La vida de Santa María Egipciaca, 2 de Abril," in *Segunda parte del Flos sanctorum, o libro de las vidas de los santos* (Madrid: Luis Sánchez, 1616), 186.

26. Andrés Antonio Sánchez de Villamayor, *La mujer fuerte, asombro de los desiertos, penitente y admirable Santa María Egipciaca* (Madrid: Francisco Sanz, 1685), 5–10.

27. Elma Dassbach, *La comedia hagiográfica del Siglo de Oro español: Lope de Vega, Tirso de Molina y Calderón de la Barca* (New York: Ibérica, 1997), 131–35.

28. Juan Pérez de Montalbán, *La gitana de Menfis santa María Egypciaca [Madrid: Antonio Sánz, 1756]. Comedia 159 de la Segunda parte de las comedias del doctor Juan Pérez de Montalván, microform, recogidas por C.H. Ternaux*, Spanish drama of the Golden Age, reel 41, n.p., 1833, 10. Further passages from the play will be from this text and cited parenthetically by page number. (Este tiempo que durare / quiero tener alegría, / y después venga la muerte, / vengan penas, y desdichas.)

29. "Yo triste fui la causa de perderla: / hablela con enojo, / mas ya la muerte escojo, / primero que no verla."

30. Y yo en el desierto hare
    vida triste
    [. . . . . . .]
    Ya mi vida
    será desde hoy prodigiosa:
    al desierto voy: Señor,
    ten de mí misericordia.

31. This happy ending *a lo divino* (turning to the divine) has made scholars such as Sánchez Ortega read Pérez de Montalbán's play as a sort of "taming of the shrew" (297–303), where the plot focuses on thwarting of Mary's pre-conversion, proto-feminist declaration of independence by the play's end. Although it is true that in the last third of the play Mary's role is less prominent, I would contend that she remains throughout, including at the end, an example of self-possession, turned now to godly ends rather than earthly ones. What is more, at no time does she endure anything like the humiliation of a typical shrew.

32. Covarrubias, *Tesoro*, s.v. "gitano."

33. "El pésame, María bella, / os damos los tres."

34. "Señora, en esta ocasión / que porque Amor a cogerlas / llegase, lloviesen perlas / ojos, que diamantes son."

35. Y así, el remedio major
    para la mayor tristeza
    es ostentar la belleza
    del dorado aparador;
    y así, para divertir
    mi dolor, y mi pesar,
    oro quiero ver brillar,
    y diamantes relucir.
    Cerca está la platería
    de Menfis tan celebrada.

36. Seré fuego, que oprimido
    entre volcanes, reviente;
    seré furia desatada,
    laurel a rayo más fuerte,
    Víbora del pie pisada;
    Áspid que entre flores muerde;
    Cometa, que anuncie horrores;
    trueno, de quien Menfis tiemble;
    furor, que el mundo amenace;
    y rigor, que le sujete;
    y finalmente, seré
    una mujer, que no tiene
    más imperio, y sujeción
    de aquello mismo que quiere.

    I thank Natalia Pérez for her help in translating this passage.

NOTES TO CHAPTER FIVE

37. Theatrical representations of thunder, lightning, and celestial bodies such as the sun, stars, or comets go back to antiquity and were certainly used in medieval cycles. There is also evidence of more elaborate stage effects such as volcanoes erupting in courtly spectacles such as the performance of Pedro Calderón de la Barca's *El mayor encanto, amor* (1635) on the pool of El Buen Retiro, and of the use of mechanical animals, including a snake in his *Hado y divisa de Leonido y Marfisa* (1680).

38. Ya el mal rostro, ni el talle no es afrenta.
   Yo diré de qué modo
   ya la invención lo perfecciona todo:
   si hay falta en pantorrillas
   luego hacen dos colchones maravillas;
   si un hombre es esqueleto,
   luego le presta autoridad un peto;
   si es calvo de mollera,
   luego encaja la santa cabellera:
   con artificio, al fin, todo se adoba;
   solo no hallo remedio a la corcova,
   sino es que con ingenio peregrino
   la enderece una rueda de molino.

39. Pedro de Guzmán, *Bienes de el honesto trabajo y daños de la ociosidad, en ocho discursos* (Madrid: Iaques Vervliet, 1614), quoted in Emilio Cotarelo y Mori, *Bibliografía de las controversias sobre la licitud del teatro en España (Edición Facsímil)* (Granada: Universidad de Granada, 1997), 350. (Salen al teatro con ricos trajes antiguos o modernos, representando al vivo, el viejo, el mozo, [. . .], la ramera, la tercera, el airado, el enamorado, [. . .], el rey, el emperador, el señor, el vasallo, [. . .] (parece el teatro un mundo abreviado), significando cada uno con palabras acciones y traje, su ventura o desventura, su propósito o intento, o la persona que es con tanta propiedad que arrebata estos dos sentidos que digo [vista y oído], y tras ellos el alma, y los tiene entretenidos y suspensos toda una tarde y todo un día y toda la vida.)

40. Siempre, señor Caballero,
   que alguna muerte sucede
   [. . . . .]
   hay un Sermón en su muerte.
   Mi padre murió, y así
   hoy en sus exequias quiere,
   por evitar tantos gastos,
   predicarnos libremente.

41. Y como fuerte Amazona,
   más enojada, que fuerte,
   subir en veloz caballo,
   y llegar a sus rebeldes
   murallas, y echar un reto
   airosa, y gallardamente,
   con que obligarles pudiera

206   NOTES TO CHAPTER FIVE

> a batalla, y desta suerte,
> o castigara ofensores,
> o muriera noblemente.

42. Decir que su muerte sienta,
    está bien dicho; mas piense
    vuessarced, que no es mi gusto
    mostrar disgusto en su muerte.
    Si le tengo, yo lo sé;
    que no es de pechos valientes
    no ocultar la pesadumbre
    al tiempo que la padecen.

43. "Una mujer, que no tiene / más imperio y sujeción / de aquello mismo que quiere."

44. Hoy has de ver, que por mí,
    en ciudad tan excelente,
    ay inmensas disensiones:
    hoy mi hermosura ha de ser
    suficiente a revolver
    mil pendencias y cuestiones
    que es de lo que yo más gusto.

45. "¿Sermón yo? / Locura igual no se vio; / mi gusto a entrar no se aplica, / óigale quien le estudió."

46. "Al fin, ardiente mes, / no puede dejar de ser / caluroso."

47. "Si son diamantes los ojos, nunca llueven los diamantes."

48. "Si me he de ver algún día / desnuda por estos dos, / que están ahora en la villa, / más quiero ser pecadora / pública en la Alejandría."

49. Ninguno pasa, ni llega
    del Templo a la insigne puerta,
    para todo el mundo abierta:
    amor el lance me niega:
    pero, ¿qué es esto? ¿estoy ciega?
    entrar adentro es mejor,
    donde podré, con color
    de oír el Sermón, prender
    voluntades con poder
    de hermosura superior.

50. "Toda reclusión me enfada, / toda soledad me ofende; / ver mucho, me alivia mucho; / mucho hablar, mucho me mueve."

51. ¿Qué es aquesto, Cielo airado?
    El peso de mi pecado
    me llega a oprimir así;
    mas quiero entrar (¡ay de mí!)
    los pies levantar no puedo,
    y en mí siento un nuevo miedo

NOTES TO THE EPILOGUE

aunque yo nunca temí
[. . . . .]
¿Qué es esto fortuna ingrata?
¿Quién mis intentos dilata?
Otra vez quiero probar:
ni un paso yo puedo dar;
sin duda debe de ser,
porque tan mala mujer
no entre en tan santo lugar.
Yo he sido amiga de ver
varias cosas, y hoy recelo,
que por atajarme, el Cielo
grillos me quiere poner.

52. "El peso de mi pecado."
53. "Entrar, / siquiera en esta ocasión, / al celebrado Sermón / que antes no quise escuchar."
54. "Quando el diablo nos predica, / algun gran daño barrunta."
55. "Tesoro, que los hombres / no le conocen mayor."
56. "Si quieres *robarme*, llega: / mas mejor te fuera al doble / el *robarme* con el alma, / no con manos de rigores." The 1756 edition of *Gitana* from which I quote describes the performance of this miracle in the stage directions thus: "Zozimas places the wafer box at the foot of a tree, where an image of Christ on the Cross or as a Child appears" (Ha puesto Zózimas el Hostiario al pie de un árbol, donde se descubre una imagen de un Santo Cristo, o de un Niño) (30). An imprint of the play from 1740 (Burgos: Imprenta de la Santa Iglesia) is a little more explicit, suggesting that the tree trunk opens up to reveal the sacred image. In both cases, the vision of an image (most likely, a statue) hiding and revealing itself in a landscape would have resonated with legends of statues appearing in particular places as a sign of the saint's desire to be worshipped at that site.

EPILOGUE

1. Georges Didi-Huberman, *La peinture incarnée* (Paris: Minuit, 1985), 8. (Souvent les légendes disent—à leur manière—le vrai.)
2. Pierre Laubriet, *Un Catéchisme esthétique: Le chef-d'œuvre inconnu de Balzac* (Paris: Didier, 1961); Dore Ashton, *A Fable of Modern Art* (Berkeley: University of California Press, 1991). Both works are dedicated to Balzac's short story.
3. Honoré de Balzac, "The Unknown Masterpiece," in *The Unknown Masterpiece and Other Stories*, trans. Richard Howard (New York: New York Review, 2001), 40. (Des couleurs confusément amassées et contenues par une multitude des lignes bizarres qui forment une muraille de peinture.) Honoré de Balzac, "Le chef d'œuvre inconnu," in *Études philosophiques, Le chef-d'œuvre inconnu, La Comédie humaine*, vol. 10, ed. P.-G. Castex (Paris: Gallimard, Collection Bibliothèque de la Pléiade, 1979), 436.

208   NOTES TO THE EPILOGUE

4. Balzac, "The Unknown Masterpiece," 43; Balzac, "Le chef d'œuvre inconnu," 438.

5. Quoted in Ashton, *A Fable of Modern Art*, 9.

6. Balzac, "The Unknown Masterpiece," 9. (Vous eussiez dit une toile de Rembrandt marchant silencieusement.) Balzac, "Le chef d'œuvre inconnu," 415.

7. Balzac, "The Unknown Masterpiece," 10–11. (Un tableau qui, par ce temps de trouble et de révolutions, était déjà devenu célèbre, et que visitaient quelques-uns de ces entêtés auxquels on doit la conservation du feu sacré pendant les jours mauvais. Cette belle page représentait une *Marie égyptienne* se disposant à payer le passage du bateau. Ce chef d'œuvre, destiné à Marie de Médicis, fut vendu par elle aux jours de sa misère.) Balzac, "Le chef d'œuvre inconnu," 416.

8. Balzac, "The Unknown Masterpiece," 11 (emphasis added). (*Se disposant* à payer.) Balzac, "Le chef d'œuvre inconnu," 416.

9. Balzac, "The Unknown Masterpiece," 16. (Ces deux figures, celle de la sainte et celle du batelier, ont une finesse d'intention ignorée des peintres italiens, je n'en sais pas un seul qui eût inventé l'indécision du batelier.) Balzac, "Le chef d'œuvre inconnu," 420.

10. Hubert Damisch, "The Underneaths of Painting," *Word and Image* 1, no. 2 (1985): 197–98.

11. Quoted in Balzac, "Le chef d'œuvre inconnu," 1412 (Lors de notre invasion en Allemagne (1806), un capitaine d'artillerie la sauva d'une destruction imminente, en la mettant dans son porte-manteau [. . .]. Ses soldats avaient déjà fait des moustaches à la sainte protectrice des filles repenties, et allaient, ivres et sacrilèges, tirer à la cible sur la pauvre sainte [. . .]. Aujourd'hui cette magnifique toile est au château de la Grenadière.)

12. Julia R. Lupton, *Citizen-Saints: Shakespeare and Political Theology* (Chicago: Chicago University Press, 2014), 161.

13. Balzac, "The Unknown Masterpiece," 40–41. (Dans un coin de la toile le bout d'un pied nu qui sortait de ce chaos de couleurs, de tons, de nuances indécises, espèce de brouillard sans forme; mais un pied délicieux, un pied vivant!) Balzac, "Le chef d'œuvre inconnu," 436.

14. Balzac, "The Unknown Masterpiece," 41–42. (Il faut de la foi, de la foi dans l'art [. . .]. Tenez [. . .]. Regarde la lumière du sein, et vois [. . .]. Approchez et vous verrez mieux ce travail]. Balzac, "Le chef d'œuvre inconnu," 436–37.)

BIBLIOGRAPHY

PRIMARY SOURCES

Augustine. *City of God.* Vol. 7, *Books 21–22.* Translated by William M. Green. Loeb Classical Library no. 417. Cambridge, MA: Harvard University Press, 1972.

Augustine. *On Christian Doctrine.* Translated by D. W. Robertson. Indianapolis: Bobbs-Merrill, 1958.

Baldinucci, Filippo. *Vocabolario toscano dell'arte del disegno.* Florence: Santi Franchi, 1681. Bibliothèque Nationale de France. Accessed July 28, 2022. https://gallica.bnf.fr/ark: /12148/bpt6k9762233v/.

Balzac, Honoré de. *Le chef d'œuvre inconnu.* In *Études philosophiques, Le chef-d'œuvre inconnu, La Comédie humaine,* vol. 10, edited by P.-G. Castex, 413–38. Paris: Gallimard, Collection Bibliothèque de la Pléiade, 1979.

Balzac, Honoré de. *The Unknown Masterpiece and Other Stories.* Translated by Richard Howard. New York: New York Review, 2001.

Camargo, Ignacio. *Discurso teológico sobre los teatros y comedias de este siglo.* Lisboa: Miguel Manescal, 1690.

Canons and Decrees of the Sacred and Oecumenical Council of Trent. Edited and translated by J. Waterworth. "The Twenty-Fifth Session," 232–89. London: Dolman, 1848. Hanover Historical Texts Project. Accessed May 23, 2021. http://history.hanover.edu /texts/trent/ct25.html.

Cascales, Francisco. "Arte poética." In "La traducción del licenciado Francisco de Cascales del *Ars poetica* de Horacio," edited by José Luis Pérez Pastor. *Criticón* 86 (2002): 21–39.

Caxton, William, trans. *Golden Legend,* compiled by Jacobus de Voragine. 1st English ed., 1483. From *Temple Classics,* edited by F. S. Ellis (1900). Medieval Sourcebook, edited by Paul Halsall. Accessed March 15, 2022. http://www.fordham.edu/halsall/basis /goldenlegend/GoldenLegend-Volume7.htm.

Cervantes, Miguel de. *Don Quijote de la Mancha.* Edited by Francisco Rico. Barcelona: Crítica, 2001.

Cervantes, Miguel de. *The History of Don Quixote*. Translated by John Ormsby. Project Gutenberg. Accessed July 25, 2021. http://www.gutenberg.org/files/5921/5921.txt.

Covarrubias Orozco, Sebastián de. *Tesoro de la lengua castellana o española: Biblioteca áurea hispánica, 21*. Edited by Ignacio Arellano and Rafael Zafra. Madrid: Iberoamericana; Frankfurt am Main: Vervuert, 2006.

Cruz-Sáenz, Michèle Schiavone, ed. "Edition of Ms. B (Medieval French)." In *The Life of Saint Mary of Egypt: An Edition and Study of the Medieval French and Spanish Verse Redactions*, 117–83. Barcelona: Puvill, 1979.

Del Enperador Costantino (De Santa Catalina). In *Antología castellana de relatos medievales (Ms. Esc. h-I-13)*, edited by Carina Zubillaga, 57–79. Buenos Aires: SECRIT, 2008.

De Santa María Madalena. In *Antología castellana de relatos medievales (Ms. Esc. h-I-13)*, edited by Carina Zubillaga, 7–16. Buenos Aires: SECRIT, 2008.

Diccionario de Autoridades (1737). Nuevo tesoro lexicográfico de la lengua española. Accessed July 28, 2022. https://apps.rae.es/ntlle/SrvltGUISalirNtlle.

Eusebius of Caesarea. *The Life of the Blessed Emperor Constantine*. In vol. 1, *Nicene and Post-Nicene Fathers*, 2nd ser., edited by Philip Schaff and Henry Wace. Grand Rapids, MI: Wm. B. Eerdmans, 1955. Medieval Sourcebook. Accessed March 27, 2022. http://www.fordham.edu/halsall/basis/vita-constantine.html.

Gautier, Théophile. *Ouvrages: Voyage en Espagne, nouvelle edition*. Paris: G. Charpentier, 1878.

Gregory of Nyssa. "On the Divinity of the Son and the Holy Spirit." In *Patrologiae Graecae*, vol. 46, *Gregory of Nyssa*, edited by Jean Paul Migne. Accessed May 23, 2022. http://phoenix.reltech.org/cgi-bin/Ebind2html/Migne/Gk046?seq=554.

Gregory the Great. *Forty Gospel Homilies*. Translated by David Hurst. Kalamazoo, MI: Cistercian Publications, 1990.

Gregory the Great. "Selected Epistles of Gregory the Great." In *A Select Library of the Nicene and Post-Nicene Fathers of the Christian Church*, 2nd ser., vol. 13, *Gregory the Great (II), Ephraim Syrus, Aphrahat*, edited by Philip Schaff and Henry Wace. Grand Rapids, MI: Christian Classics Ethereal Library. Accessed May 23, 2022. http://www.ccel.org/ccel/schaff/npnf213.ii.vii.iii.html.

Guzmán, Pedro de. *Bienes de el honesto trabajo y daños de la ociosidad, en ocho discursos*. Madrid: Iaques Vervliet, 1614. In Emilio Cotarelo y Mori, *Bibliografía de las controversias sobre la licitud del teatro en España (Edición Facsímil)*, 347–51. Granada: Universidad de Granada, 1997.

Hildebert of Lavardin. "The Life of Saint Mary of Egypt." Translated by Ronald Pepin. In *Saint Mary of Egypt: Three Medieval Lives in Verse*, 71–114. Kalamazoo, MI: Cistercian Publications, 2005.

Horace. *Ars Poetica*. In *Horace: Satires, Epistles, Ars Poetica*, translated by H. Rushton Farclough. Loeb Classical Library. Cambridge, MA: Harvard University Press, 1926.

Jacobus de Voragine. *The Golden Legend: Readings on the Saints*. 2 vols. Translated by William Granger Ryan. Princeton, NJ: Princeton University Press, 1993.

Jacobus de Voragine. *Leyenda Dorada*. Translated by José Manuel Macías. Madrid: Alianza Editorial, 2006–8.

BIBLIOGRAPHY

Juvenal. "Satire X." In *Juvenal and Persius*, edited and translated by Susanna Morton Braund. Loeb Classics Latin no. 91. Cambridge, MA: Harvard University Press, 2004.

Leonardo da Vinci. *Leonardo da Vinci's Paragone: A Critical Interpretation with a New Edition of the Text in Codex Urbinas*. Translated by Claire J. Farago. Leiden: E. J. Brill, 1992.

Leonardo da Vinci. *Trattato de la pittura*. In *The Fabrication of Leonardo da Vinci's Trattato della pittura*, vol. 2. Translated by Janis Bell and Claire J. Farago. Leiden: E. J. Brill, 2018.

Libro de Apolonio. Edited by Carmen Monedero. Madrid: Castalia, 1987.

Life of Saint Mary of Egypt. Translated by Maria Kouli. In *Holy Women of Byzantium: Ten Saints' Lives in English Translation*, edited by Alice-Mary Talbot, 65–93. Cambridge: Dumbarton Oaks, 1996.

"The Life of Saint Mary the Egyptian" (English translation of *VSME*). Translated by Hugh Feiss. In *Saint Mary of Egypt: Three Medieval Lives in Verse*, 115–59. Kalamazoo, MI: Cistercian Publications, 2005.

Luque, Francisco de. *Copia de una carta, que el Licenciado, Francisco de Luque, Clerigo de Seuilla escriuió á la Congregacion de Clerigos y Sacerdotes de la misma ciudad, estando en la villa de Madrid, en las casas del Cauallero de Gracia, en veynte dias del mes de Mayo, de 1601*. In *Relaciones breves de actos públicos celebrados en Madrid de 1541 a 1650*, edited by José Simón Díaz, 46–48. Madrid: Instituto de Estudios Madrileños, 1982.

The New Oxford Annotated Bible. 3rd ed. Edited by Michael D. Coogan. Oxford: Oxford University Press, 2001.

Nisibene Hymns 27, 8. In *The Faith of the Early Fathers*, vol. 1, edited by William A. Jurgens, 313. Collegeville, MN: Liturgical Press, 1970.

Pacheco, Francisco. *El arte de la pintura*. Edited by Bonaventura Bassegoda i Hugas. Madrid: Cátedra, 1990.

Paleotti, Gabriele. *Discourse on Sacred and Profane Images*. Translated by William McCuaig. Los Angeles: Getty Research Institute, 2012.

Paul, Deacon of the Holy Church of Naples. *Life of St. Mary of Egypt*. Translated by Benedicta Ward. In *Harlots of the Desert: A Study of Repentance in Early Monastic Sources*, 35–56. Cistercian Studies Series no. 106. Kalamazoo, MI: Cistercian Publications by Liturgical Press, 1987.

Pérez de Montalbán, Juan. *Comedia famosa, la gitana de Menfis, Santa María Egypciaca*. Burgos: Imprenta de la Santa Iglesia, 1740. Digitized by Repositorio de la Universidad de Oviedo, Spain, coll. Pliegos del teatro. Accessed December 10, 2021. http://hdl .handle.net/10651/2347.

Pérez de Montalbán, Juan. *La gitana de Menfis Santa María Egypciaca*. Madrid: Antonio Sánz, 1756. In *Comedia 159 de la Segunda parte de las comedias del doctor Juan Pérez de Montalván, microform, recogidas por C. H. Ternaux*. Spanish drama of the Golden Age, reel 41. n.p., 1833.

Poema de mío Cid. Edited by Ian Michael. Madrid: Editorial Castalia, 1987.

Ribadeneira, Pedro. "La vida de Santa María Egipciaca, 2 de Abril." In *Segunda parte* del *Flos sanctorum, o libro de las vidas de los santos. En la qual se contienen las vidas de muchos Santos de todos estados, que comunmente llaman Extrauagantes*, 185–90. Madrid: Luis Sánchez, 1616.

Ribadeneira, Pedro. *Tratado de la tribulación, repartido en dos libros.* Valencia: Imprenta de Ildefonso Mompie, 1831.

The Roman Martyrologe, according to the reformed calendar faithfully translated out of Latin into English, by G.K. of the Society of Iesus. Saint-Omer: Imprinted with licence [sic] at the English College Press, 1627. Early English Books Online. Accessed July 29, 2022. http://name.umdl.umich.edu/A07132.0001.001.

Sánchez de Villamayor, Andrés Antonio. *La mujer fuerte, asombro de los desiertos, penitente y admirable santa María Egipciaca.* Madrid: Francisco Sanz, 1685.

Seventh Ecumenical Council. *The Second Council of Nicaea, 787, in Which the Worship of Images Was Established, with Copious Notes from the "Caroline Books."* Translated by John Mendham. London: William Edward Painter, 1850.

Stendhal. *De l'amour.* Paris: Garnier-Flammarion, 1965.

Stendhal. *Mémoires d'un touriste.* In *Œuvres completes*, vol. 17, edited by Louis Royer. Geneva: Slatkine Reprints, 1986.

Stendhal. *On Love.* Translated by Philip Sidney Woolf and Cecil N. Sidney Woolf. New York: Brentano's, 1916.

Tamayo de Vargas, Tomás. "Ars Poetica." In "Una traducción inédita del '*Ars Poetica*' de Horacio por Tomás Tamayo de Vargas," edited by Jesús Alemán Illán. *Criticón* 70 (1997): 117–48.

Tertullian. "De Spectaculis." Translated by T. R. Glover. In *Apology; De Spectaculis*, 230–301. Loeb Classical Library no. 250. New York: G. P. Putnam's Sons, 1931.

Tertullian. "On Idolatry." In *Ante-Nicene Fathers*, vol 3., translated by Rev. S. Thelwall. Accessed July 28, 2022. https://www.tertullian.org/anf/anf03/anf03-07.htm.

Tertullian. "On the Apparel of Women." In *Ante-Nicene Fathers*, vol 4., translated by Rev. S. Thelwall. Accessed July 28, 2022. https://www.tertullian.org/anf/anf04/anf04-06.htm.

Tragicomedia de Calisto y Melibea. Edited by P. E. Russell. Madrid: Castalia, 1991.

Trethewey, Natasha. *Thrall.* Boston: Houghton Mifflin, 2012.

Vasari, Giorgio. *Lives of the Artists.* Translated by Julia Conaway Bondanella and Peter Bondanella. Oxford Classics. Oxford: Oxford University Press, 1998.

Vasari, Giorgio. *Le vite de' più eccellenti pittori, scultori ed architettori, con nuove annotazioni e commenti di Gaetano Milanesi.* Vol. 7. Florence: Sansoni Editore, 1878–81.

Vega, Lope de. *Lo fingido verdadero.* In *Comedias*, 1:191–288. Barcelona: Editorial Iberia, 1955.

Vida de la madre Catalina de Cardona por fray Juan de la Miseria. In "*Vida de la madre Catalina de Cardona por fray Juan de la Miseria*: Un texto hagiográfico desconocido del siglo XVI (Bancroft Library, UCB, Fernán Nuñez Collection, vol. 143)," edited by Adelaida Cortijo Ocaña and Antonio Cortijo Ocaña. *Dicenda* 21 (2003): 21–34.

La Vida de Santa María Egipçiaca: A Fourteenth-Century Translation of a Work by Paul the Deacon. Edited by John K. Walsh and Billy Bussell Thompson. Exeter: University of Exeter, 1977.

BIBLIOGRAPHY

Vida de Santa María Egipciaca: Estudios, vocabulario, edición de los textos. Vol 2. Edited
by Manuel Alvar. Madrid: Consejo Superior de Investigaciones Científicas, 1972.
"Vida de Santa María Magdalena." In *The Myth of the Magdalen in Early Spanish Lit-
erature, with an Edition of the Vida de Santa María Magdalena in Ms. h-1-13 of the
Escorial Library,* edited by John K. Walsh and Billy Bussell Thompson. Coll. Pliegos
hispánicos 2. New York: L. Clemente, 1986.
Villegas, Alonso de. *Flos sanctorum, historia general de la vida, y hechos de Jesu-Christo,
Dios, y Señor nuestro; y de los santos, de que reza y haze fiesta la Iglesia Catholica.*
Barcelona: Isidro Aguasvivas, 1794.
Villegas, Bernardino de. *La esposa de Christo instruída con la vida de Santa Lutgarda
virgen.* Murcia: Juan Fernández de Fuentes, 1635.
Voltaire. "Epître à l'auteur du livre des *Trois imposteurs.*" In *Œuvres complètes de Voltaire,*
vol. 10, edited by Louis Moland. Paris: Garnier, 1877–85.
"Ystoria de Santa Pelagia." In *The Legends of the Holy Harlots: Thaïs and Pelagia in
Medieval Spanish Literature,* edited by Andrew M. Beresford, 137–38. Woodbridge:
Támesis, 2007.

SECONDARY SOURCES

Amer, Sahar, and Noah D. Guynn. "Preface." *Yale French Studies* 95 (1999): 1–10.
Arellano, Ignacio. "Valores visuales de la palabra en el espacio escénico del siglo de oro."
Revista Canadiense de Estudios Hispánicos 19 (1995): 411–43.
Ashton, Dore. *A Fable of Modern Art.* Berkeley: University of California Press, 1991.
Astell, Ann W. *Eating Beauty: The Eucharist and the Spiritual Arts of the Middle Ages.*
Ithaca, NY: Cornell University Press, 2006.
Bailey, Matthew. *The Poetics of Speech in the Medieval Spanish Epic.* Toronto: University of
Toronto Press, 2010.
Barthes, Roland. *S/Z.* Translated by Richard Miller. New York: Hill and Wang, 1974.
Barthes, Roland. *S/Z.* In *Œuvres complètes III,* edited by Éric Marty. Paris: Seuil, 2002.
Beresford, Andrew M. "'Ençendida del ardor de la luxuria': Prostitution and Promiscuity
in the Legend of Saint Mary of Egypt." In *"Quien hubiese tal ventura": Medieval His-
panic Studies in Honour of Alan Deyermond,* edited by Andrew M. Beresford, 45–56.
London: Department of Hispanic Studies, Queen Mary & Westfield College, 1997.
Beresford, Andrew M. "'Oit varones, huna razón': Sobre la función del prólogo en la *Vida
de Santa María Egipciaca.*" *Acta Poética* 20 (1999): 249–76.
Berger, Harry. *Fictions of the Pose: Rembrandt against the Italian Renaissance.* Stanford,
CA: Stanford University Press, 2000.
Bergström, Ingvar. "Masters of the *Vanitas* Still-Life." *Dutch Still-Life Painting in the Sev-
enteenth Century.* Translated by Christina Hedström and Gerald Taylor. New York:
T. Yoseloff, 1956.
Betancourt, Roland. *Byzantine Intersectionality: Sexuality, Gender, and Race in the Middle
Ages.* Princeton, NJ: Princeton University Press, 2020.

Bettella, Patrizia. *The Ugly Woman: Transgressive Aesthetic Models in Italian Poetry from the Middle Ages to the Baroque.* Toronto: University of Toronto Press, 2005.

Bloch, R. Howard. "Medieval Misogyny." *Representations* 20 (1987): 1–24.

Bloch, R. Howard. *Medieval Misogyny and the Invention of Western Romantic Love.* Chicago: Chicago University Press, 1991.

Bolter, Jay David, and Richard Grusin. *Remediation.* Cambridge, MA: MIT Press, 2000.

Brown, Catherine. *Contrary Things: Exegesis, Dialectic, and the Poetics of Didacticism.* Stanford, CA: Stanford University Press, 1998.

Brown, Peter. "Images as a Substitute for Writing." In *East and West: Modes of Communication: Proceedings of the First Plenary Conference at Merida*, 15–34. Boston: Brill, 1999.

Bruyne, Edgar de. *The Aesthetics of the Middle Ages.* Translated by Eileen B. Hennessy. New York: Frederick Ungar Publishing, 1969.

Burrus, Virginia. *The Sex Lives of Saints: An Erotics of Ancient Hagiography.* Philadelphia: University of Pennsylvania Press, 2004.

Bynum, Carolyn Walker. *Holy Feast, Holy Fast: The Religious Significance of Food to Medieval Women.* Berkeley: University of California Press, 1987.

Calvo Serraller, Francisco. *Teoría de la Pintura del Siglo de Oro.* Madrid: Cátedra, 1991.

Camille, Michael. *The Gothic Idol: Ideology and Image-Making in Medieval Art.* Cambridge: Cambridge University Press, 1999.

Camille, Michael. "Seeing and Reading: Some Visual Implications of Medieval Literacy and Illiteracy." *Art History* 8, no. 1 (1985): 26–49.

Campbell, Erin. *Old Women and Art in the Early Modern Domestic Interior.* Farnham: Ashgate, 2015.

Campbell, Erin. "Prophets, Saints, and Matriarchs: Portraits of Old Women in Early Modern Italy." *Renaissance Quarterly* 63, no. 3 (2010): 807–49.

Caro Baroja, Julio. "Religión, historia, y literatura." In *Ensayo sobre literatura de cordel. Fundamentos 109*, 395–408. Madrid: Ediciones Istmo, 1990.

Carruthers, Mary. *The Book of Memory: A Study of Memory in Medieval Culture.* Cambridge: Cambridge University Press, 1990.

Carruthers, Mary. *Experience of Beauty in the Middle Ages.* Oxford: Oxford University Press, 2014.

Carter, Julian. "Embracing Transition, or Dancing in the Folds of Time." In *The Transgender Studies Reader 2*, edited by Susan Stryker and Aren Z. Aizura, 130–43. New York and London: Routledge, 2013.

Cassidy, Laurie, and Maureen H. O'Connell. "Introduction." In *She Who Imagines: Feminist Theological Aesthetics*, edited by Cassidy and O'Connell, ix–xviii. Collegeville, MN: Liturgical Press, 2012.

Cazelles, Brigitte. *The Lady as Saint: A Collection of French Hagiographic Romances of the Thirteenth Century.* Philadelphia: University of Pennsylvania Press, 1991.

Cervone, Maria. *Poetics of Incarnation: Middle English Writing and the Leap of Love.* Philadelphia: University of Pennsylvania Press, 2012.

Chazelle, Celia. "Pictures, Books and the Illiterate: Pope Gregory I's Letters to Serenus of Marseilles." *Word and Image* 6 (1990): 138–53.

BIBLIOGRAPHY

Chrétien, Jean-Louis. *The Call and the Response.* Translated by Anne A. Davenport. New York: Fordham University Press, 2004.

Christian, William A. *Apparitions in Late Medieval and Renaissance Spain.* Princeton, NJ: Princeton University Press, 1981.

Cirnigliaro, Noelia Sol. "Versiones de la historia, versiones de la leyenda: Sobre la comedia hagiográfica de Lope de Vega." *Filología* 33, no. 1–2 (2000): 187–206.

Clément, Silvain, and A. Guitard. *Vitraux du XIIIème siècle de la cathédrale de Bourges.* Bourges: Tardy-Pigelet, 1900.

Colby, Alice. *The Portrait in Twelfth-Century French Literature.* Geneva: Droz, 1965.

Consavari, Elizabeth Carroll. "Tintoretto." In *Mary Magdalene, Iconographic Studies from the Middle Ages to the Baroque,* 135–60. Leiden: Brill. 2012.

Coon, Lynda L. *Sacred Fictions: Holy Women and Hagiography in Late Antiquity.* Philadelphia: University of Pennsylvania Press, 1997.

Copeland, Rita. "Rhetoric and Religious Community." In *Sacred and Secular in Medieval and Early Modern Cultures: New Essays,* edited by Lawrence Besserman, 135–48. New York: Palgrave Macmillan, 2006.

Corominas, Joan. *Diccionario crítico etimológico castellano e hispánico.* Vol. 3. Madrid: Editorial Gredos, 1980–91.

Cortina, Lynn Rice. "The Aesthetics of Morality: Two Portraits of Mary of Egypt in the *Vida de Santa María Egipciaca.*" *Hispanic Journal* (1980): 41–45.

Cotarelo y Mori, Emilio. *Bibliografía de las controversias sobre la licitud del teatro en España (Edición Facsímil).* Granada: Universidad de Granada, 1997.

Cruz-Sáenz, Michèle Schiavone, ed. *The Life of Saint Mary of Egypt: An Edition and Study of the Medieval French and Spanish Verse Redactions.* Barcelona: Puvill, 1979.

Cruz-Sáenz, Michèle Schiavone. "La *Vida de Santa María Egipciaca*: Texto juglaresco u obra de clerecía." In *La juglaresca: Actas del I congreso internacional sobre la juglaresca,* edited by Manuel Criado de Val, 275–81. Madrid: EDI, 1986.

Damisch, Hubert. "The Underneaths of Painting." *Word and Image* 1, no. 2 (1985): 197–209.

Danto, Arthur. *The Abuse of Beauty: Aesthetics and the Concept of Art.* Chicago: Open Court, 2003.

Dassbach, Elma. *La comedia hagiográfica del Siglo de Oro español: Lope de Vega, Tirso de Molina y Calderón de la Barca.* New York, Berne, and Berlin: Ibérica, 1997.

Delenda, Odile. "Livio Mehus. Cat. 63." In *María Magdalena: Éxtasis y arrepentimiento,* 204. Distrito Federal, Mexico: CONACULTA, Instituto Nacional de Bellas Artes, 2001.

Delgado, Ernesto E. "Penitencia y Eucaristía en la conformación de la vertiente occidental de la leyenda de Santa María Egipcíaca: Un paradigma de negociación cultural en la Baja Edad Media." *Revista de poética medieval* 10 (2003): 25–55.

Deyermond, Alan. "Thirteenth-Century Expansion: I.7 *Vida de Santa María Egipciaca.*" In *A Literary History of Spain: The Middle Ages,* 70–71. New York: Barnes & Noble, 1971.

Díaz, Emilio Orozco. "Sobre la teatralización del templo y la función religiosa en el barroco: El predicador y el comediante." *Cuadernos para investigación de la literatura hispánica* 2–3 (1980): 171–88.

Didi-Huberman, Georges. *La peinture incarnée*. Paris: Minuit, 1985.

Díez Borque, José María. "Algunas notas sobre géneros y espacios teatrales del Siglo de Oro." In *El redescubrimiento de los clásicos: Actas de las XV jornadas de teatro clásico, Almagro, julio 1992*, edited by Felipe B. Pedraza Jiménez, 123–39. Almagro, Ciudad Real, Spain: Universidad de Castilla-La Mancha, Festival de Almagro, 1993.

Duggan, Lawrence G. "Was Art Really the 'Book of the Illiterate'?" *Word and Image* 5, no. 3 (1989): 227–51.

Dulaure, Jacques-Antoine. *Nouvelle description des curiosités de Paris*. Paris: Lejay, 1785.

Dunkelman, Martha Levine. "Donatello's *Mary Magdalen*: A Model of Courage and Survival." *Women's Art Journal* 26, no. 2 (2005): 10–13.

Eden, Kathy. *Hermeneutics and the Rhetorical Tradition: Chapters in the Ancient Legacy*. New Haven, CT: Yale University Press, 1997.

Farago, Claire J. "On Leonardo da Vinci's Defense of Painting against Poetry and Music and the Grounding of Aesthetic Experience." *Italian Culture* 9, no. 1 (1991): 153–70.

Farmer, David Hugh. *Oxford Dictionary of Saints*. Oxford: Oxford University Press, 1992.

Felton, Craig. "The Paintings of Ribera." In *Jusepe de Ribera, lo Spagnoletto, 1591–1652*, edited by Craig Felton and William B. Jordan, 44–70. Fort Worth, TX: Kimbell Art Museum, 1982.

Felton, Craig, and William B. Jordan. "Saint Mary of Egypt." In *Jusepe de Ribera, lo Spagnoletto, 1591–1652*, edited by Craig Felton and William B. Jordan. Fort Worth, TX: Kimbell Art Museum, 1982.

Ferguson, Margaret. "St. Augustine's Region of Unlikeness: the Crossing of Exile and Language." *Georgia Review* 29, no. 4 (1975): 842–64.

Fernández Rodríguez, Natalia. "Veneno mortal para la juventud: Público y censura ante las pecadoras penitentes de la comedia nueva." *Bulletin of Hispanic Studies* 88, no. 8 (2011): 911–30.

Finaldi, Gabriele. "Ribera Paints the Magdalene." In *Jusepe de Ribera's Mary Magdalene in a New Context*, edited by Gabriele Finaldi, 17–34. Dallas: Meadows Museum, Southern Methodist University, 2011.

Flusin, Bernard. "Palestinian Hagiography (Fourth-Eighth Centuries)." In *The Ashgate Companion to Byzantine Hagiography*, edited by Stephanos Efthymiadis, 1:199–226. Burlington, VT: Ashgate, 2011.

Fraker, Charles F. *Celestina: Genre and Rhetoric*. London: Támesis Books, 1990.

Francomano, Emily. "'Lady, You Are Quite a Chatterbox': The Legend of St. Katherine of Alexandria, Wives' Words, and Women's Wisdom in MS Escorial h-I-13." In *St. Katherine of Alexandria: Texts and Contexts in Western Medieval Europe*, edited by Jacqueline Jenkins and Katherine J. Lewis, 131–52. Turnhout, Belgium: Brepols, 2003.

Garber, Marjorie. *Loaded Words*. New York: Fordham University Press, 2012.

García Sanz, Ana, and Juan Martínez Cuesta. "La serie iconográfica de ermitaños del monasterio de las Descalzas Reales." *Cuadernos de arte e iconografía* 47, no. 74 (1991): 291–304.

Gaunt, Simon. *Gender and Genre in Medieval French Literature*. Cambridge: Cambridge University Press, 1995.

BIBLIOGRAPHY

Giles, Ryan. *Laughter of the Saints: Parodies of Holiness in Late Medieval and Renaissance Spain*. Toronto: Toronto University Press, 2009.

Goldberg, Harriet. "Moslem and Spanish Christian Literary Portraiture." *Hispanic Review* 45, no. 3 (1977): 311–26.

Göttler, Christine. "The Temptation of the Senses at the Sacro Monte di Varallo." In *Religion and the Senses in Early Modern Europe*, edited by Wietse de Boer and Christine Göttler, 393–451. Leiden: Brill, 2012.

Graham, Heather Sexton. "Renaissance Flesh and Women's Devotion: Titian's *Penitent Magdalen*." *Comitatus: A Journal of Medieval and Renaissance Studies* 39 (2008): 137–54.

Grieve, Patricia. "Paradise Regained in *Vida de Santa María Egipciaca*: Harlots, the Fall of Nations and Hagiographic Currency." In *Translatio Studii: Essays by His Students in Honor of Karl D. Uitti for His Sixty-Fifth Birthday*, edited by Renate Blumenfeld-Kosinski et al., 133–54. Amsterdam: Rodopi, 2000.

Habert, Jean. "Italian Baroque Paintings: Marseilles." *Burlington Magazine* 131, no. 1030 (1989): 57–59.

Hamilton, John. *Philology of the Flesh*. Chicago: University of Chicago Press, 2018.

Haskins, Susan. *Mary Magdalen: Myth and Metaphor*. New York: Harcourt Brace, 1994.

Hénaff, Marcel. "Grâce, oeuvre d'art et espace publique." *La Beauté* 1, September 14, 2011. March 13, 2022. https://www.mouvement-transitions.fr/index.php/intensites/la -beaute/sommaire-des-articles-deja-publies/519-grace-uvre-dart-et-espace-public.

Herdt, Jennifer A. *Putting on Virtue: The Legacy of the Splendid Vices*. Chicago: University of Chicago Press, 2008.

Hernández Vargas, Jaime. "Dos viejas celestinas y hechiceras en la lírica quevediana: Fisonomía y retratos sociales como instrumentos punitivos." *La Perinola* 19 (2015): 161–80.

Higgins, Charlotte. "Master of Gore: The Violent, Shocking Genius of Jusepe de Ribera." *Guardian*, March 27, 2018. https://www.theguardian.com/artanddesign/2018/sep/19 /jusepe-de-ribera-art-of-violence-master-of-gore-dulwich.

Hirschkind, Charles. *The Ethical Soundscape: Cassette Sermons and Islamic Counterpublics*. Berkeley: University of California Press, 2006.

Hollywood, Amy. *Sensible Ecstasy: Mysticism, Sexual Difference, and the Demands of History*. Chicago: University of Chicago Press, 2002.

Howie, Cary. "As the Saint Turns: Hagiography at the Threshold of the Visible." *Exemplaria* 17, no. 2 (2005): 317–46.

Hughes, Krista. "Beauty Incarnate: A Claim for Postmodern Feminist Theology." *Revista Anglo Saxonica* 6 (2013): 103–26.

James, William. *Varieties of Religious Experience*. New York: New American Library, 1958.

Jansen, Katherine L. "Like a Virgin: The Meaning of the Magdalen for Female Penitents of Later Medieval Italy." *Memoirs of the American Academy in Rome* 45 (2000): 131–52.

Jantzen, Grace. "Beauty for Ashes: Notes on the Displacement of Beauty." *Literature & Theology* 16, no. 4 (2002): 433–38.

Jantzen, Grace. *Foundations of Violence*. Vol. 1, *Death and the Displacement of Beauty*. New York: Routledge, 2004.

Jay, Martin. *Downcast Eyes: The Denigration of Vision in Twentieth-Century French Thought*. Berkeley: University of California Press, 1993.

Jordan, William B., and Peter Cherry. *Spanish Still Life from Velázquez to Goya*. London: National Gallery Publications, distributed by Yale University Press, 1995.

Juárez-Almendros, Encarnación. *Disabled Bodies in Early Modern Spanish Literature: Prostitutes, Aging Women and Saints*. Liverpool: Liverpool University Press, 2017.

Karras, Ruth Mazo. "Holy Harlots: Prostitute Saints in Medieval Legend." *Journal of the History of Sexuality* 1, no. 1 (1990): 3–32.

Kassier, Theodore L. "Rhetorical Devices of the Spanish 'Vida de Santa María Egipciaca.'" *Anuario de estudios medievales* 8 (1972–1973): 467–80.

Kasten, Lloyd August, and Florian J. Cody. *Tentative Dictionary of Medieval Spanish*. New York: Hispanic Seminary of Medieval Studies, 2001.

Kelley, Mary Jane. "Ascendant Eloquence: Language and Sanctity in the Works of Gónzalo de Berceo." *Speculum* 79, no. 1 (2004): 66–87.

Kristeva, Julia. *Étrangers à nous-mêmes*. Paris: Fayard, 1998.

Laubriet, Pierre. *Un Catéchisme esthétique: Le chef-d'œuvre inconnu de Balzac*. Paris: Didier, 1961.

Leclercq, Jean. *The Love of Learning and the Desire for God: A Study of Monastic Culture*. Translated by Catharine Misrahi. New York: Fordham University Press, 1961.

Lévi-Strauss, Claude. *Le totémisme aujourd'hui*. Paris: Presses Universitaires de France, 1962.

Lo Re, Salvatore. "'Fresca e rugiadosa in quella penitenza': La Maddalena, Tiziano e Baccio Valori." *Intersezioni* 1 (1998): 33–46.

Lupton, Julia R. *Citizen-Saints: Shakespeare and Political Theology*. Chicago: Chicago University Press, 2014.

Mac Carthy, Ita. *The Grace of the Italian Renaissance*. Princeton, NJ: Princeton University Press, 2020.

Mackinlay, Shane. "Eyes Wide Shut: A Response to Jean-Luc Marion's Account of the Journey to Emmaus." *Modern Theology* 20, no. 3 (2004): 447–56.

Maier, John. "Sainthood, Heroism, and Sexuality in the *Estoria de Santa Maria Egipçiaca*." *Revista Canadiense de Estudios Hispanicos* 8, no. 3 (Spring 1984): 424–35.

Mâle, Émile. *L'art religieux de la fin du XVIe siècle, du XVIIe siècle et du XVIIIe siècle: Étude sur l'iconographie après le Concile de Trente, Italie-France-Espagne-Flandres*. 2nd ed. Paris: Librairie Armand Colin, 1951.

Mâle, Émile. *Religious Art from the Twelfth to the Eighteenth Century*. New York: Noonday Press, 1958.

Malvern, Marjorie M. *Venus in Sackcloth: The Magdalen's Origins and Metamorphoses*. Carbondale: Southern Illinois University Press, 1975.

María Magdalena: Éxtasis y arrepentimiento. Edited by Odile Delenda. Distrito Federal, Mexico: CONACULTA, Instituto Nacional de Bellas Artes, 2001.

Mariani, Daniela. "La chevelure de sainte Marie l'Égyptienne d'après Rutebeuf: Contraste des sources et de la tradition iconographique." *Perspectives médiévales* 38 (2017). Accessed March 27, 2022. https://journals.openedition.org/peme/12698#bodyftn36.

Marion, Jean-Luc. *Believing in Order to See: On the Rationality of Revelation and the Irrationality of Some Believers.* Translated by Christina M. Gschwandtner. New York: Fordham University Press, 2017.

Marno, David. *Death Be Not Proud: The Art of Holy Attention.* Chicago: University of Chicago Press, 2016.

Martínez-Burgos García, Palma. "El decoro: La invención de un concepto y su proyección artística." *Revista de la Facultad de Geografía e Historia* 2 (1988): 91–102.

Martínez-Burgos García, Palma. *Idolos e imágenes: La controversia del arte religioso en el siglo XVI español.* Valladolid: Secretariado de Publicaciones, Universidad de Valladolid, 1990.

Martínez-Burgos García, Palma. "La meditación de la muerte en los penitentes de la pintura española del Siglo de Oro: Ascetas, melancólicos y místicos." *Espacio, tiempo y forma* 12 (1999): 149–72.

Martínez-Burgos García, Palma. "Ut pictura natura: La imagen plástica del santo ermitaño en la literatura espiritual del siglo XVI." *Norba-Arte* 10 (1989): 15–29.

Mazzeo, Joseph Anthony. "St. Augustine's Rhetoric of Silence." *Journal of the History of Ideas* 23, no. 2 (1962): 175–96.

McDannell, Colleen. *Material Christianity: Religion and Popular Culture in America.* New Haven, CT: Yale University Press, 1995.

Menéndez Pidal, Ramón. *Poesía juglaresca y juglares: Aspectos de la historia literaria y cultural de España.* Madrid: Publicaciones de la Revista de Filología Española, 1924.

Meyer, Birgit. "Medium." In *Key Terms in Material Religion*, edited by S. Brent Plate, 140–44. New York: Bloomsbury, 2015.

Meyer, Birgit. *Religious Sensations: Why Media, Aesthetics and Power Matter in the Study of Contemporary Religion.* Professorial Inaugural Address. Amsterdam: Faculty of Social Sciences, Free University, 2006.

Meyer, Birgit, David Morgan, Crispin Paine, and S. Brent Plate. "The Origin and Mission of Material Religion." *Religion* 40, no. 3 (2010): 207–11.

Meyer, Birgit, and Jojada Verrips. "Aesthetics." In *Key Words in Religion, Media and Culture*, edited by David Morgan, 20–30. New York: Routledge, 2008.

Miles, Margaret. *Carnal Knowing: Female Nakedness and Religious Meaning in the Christian West.* Boston: Beacon Press, 1989.

Miles, Margaret. *A Complex Delight: The Secularization of the Breast, 1350–1750.* Berkeley: University of California Press, 2008.

Miles, Margaret. *Image as Insight: Visual Understanding in Western Christianity and Secular Culture.* Boston: Beacon Press, 1985.

Miller, Patricia Cox. "Is There a Harlot in This Text? Hagiography and the Grotesque." *Journal of Medieval and Early Modern Studies* 33, no. 3 (2003): 419–35.

Minnis, Alastair J., and Ian Johnson. "Introduction." In *The Cambridge History of Literary Criticism*, vol. 2, *The Middle Ages*, edited by Alastair J. Minnis and Ian Johnson, 1–12. Cambridge: Cambridge University Press, 2008.

Mitchell, W. J. T. *Picture Theory: Essays on Visual and Verbal Representation.* Chicago: Chicago University Press, 1994.

Moliner, María. *Diccionario de uso del español*. Madrid: Editorial Gredos, 1966–67.

Montoya Martínez, Jesús. "Juglar." In *Medieval Iberia: An Encyclopedia*, edited by E. Michael Gerli, 454–55. New York: Routledge, 2003.

Montoya Martínez, Jesús. "Retórica medieval ¿Continuidad o ruptura?" In *Retórica medieval ¿Continuidad o ruptura? Actas del simposio internacional, Granada, enero de 1995*, edited by Antonio Rubio Flores, 79–101. Granada: ADHARA, 1996.

Morgan, David. *The Embodied Eye: Religious Visual Culture and the Social Life of Feeling*. Berkeley: University of California Press, 2012.

Morgan, David, ed. *Religion and Material Culture: The Matter of Belief*. New York: Routledge, 2010.

Morgan, David. *The Thing about Religion: An Introduction to the Material Study of Religions*. Chapel Hill: University of North Carolina Press, 2021.

Morgan, David. *Visual Piety: A History and Theory of Popular Religious Images*. Berkeley: University of California Press, 1998.

Murphy, James J. "Saint Augustine and the Debate about a *Christian Rhetoric*." *Quarterly Journal of Speech* 46, no. 4 (1960): 400–10.

Musgrave, J. C. "Tarsania and Juglaría in the *Libro de Apolonio*." In *Medieval Studies Presented to Rita Hamilton*, edited by Alan D. Deyermond, 129–37. London: Támesis, 1976.

Nasrallah, Laura S. "The Rhetoric of Conversion and the Construction of Experience: The Case of Justin Martyr." *Studia Patristica* 40 (2006): 467–74.

Navarrete Prieto, Benito. "La Magdalena en la pintura española del Siglo de Oro." In *María Magdalena: Éxtasis y arrepentimiento*, edited by Odile Delenda, 48–63. Distrito Federal, Mexico: CONACULTA, Instituto Nacional de Bellas Artes, 2001.

Nehamas, Alexander. *Only a Promise of Happiness: The Place of Beauty in a World of Art*. Princeton, NJ: Princeton University Press, 2007.

Newman, Barbara. *Medieval Crossover: Reading the Secular against the Sacred*. Notre Dame, IN: University of Notre Dame Press, 2013.

Newman, John Henry. "The Glories of Mary for the Sake of Her Son." In *Discourses for Mixed Congregations*. London: Longmans, Green and Co., 1906.

Noble, Thomas F. X. *Images, Iconoclasm, and the Carolingians*. Philadelphia: University of Pennsylvania Press, 2009.

Nock, Arthur D. *Conversion: The Old and the New in Religion from Alexander the Great to Augustine of Hippo*. Oxford: Oxford University Press, 1961.

Pagano, Denise Maria. "Saint Mary of Egypt [Musée Favre, Montpellier]." In *Jusepe de Ribera, 1591–1652*, edited by Alfonso E. Pérez Sánchez and Nicola Spinosa, 158–59. New York: Metropolitan Museum of Art, 1992.

Panofsky, Erwin. "Erasmus and the Visual Arts." *Journal of the Warburg and Courtauld Institutes* 32 (1969): 200–27.

Parker, A. A. "Bandits and Saints in the Spanish Drama of the Golden Age." In *Critical Studies of Calderón's Comedias*, edited by J. E. Varey, 151–68. Farnborough: Gregg International, 1973.

Pedraza, Pilar. "El anciano y la vieja: Carne de Dios, carne del Diablo." In *El desnudo en el Museo del Prado*, edited by Rafael Argullol, 193–213. Madrid: Galaxia Gutenberg, 1998.

BIBLIOGRAPHY

Pereda, Felipe. *Imágenes de la Discordia: Política y poética de la imagen sagrada en la España del cuatrocientos*. Madrid: Marcial Pons Historia, 2013.

Pereda, Felipe. "True Painting and the Challenge of Hypocrisy." *After Conversion: Iberia and the Emergence of Modernity*. Edited by Mercedes García Arenal, 358–94. Leiden: Brill, 2016.

Pérez Sánchez, Alfonso E. "Ribera and Spain: His Spanish Patrons in Italy and Spain; The Influence of his Work on Spanish Artists." In *Jusepe de Ribera, 1591–1652*, edited by Alfonso E. Pérez Sánchez and Nicola Spinosa, 35–49. New York: Metropolitan Museum of Art, 1992.

Perry, Mary Elizabeth. *Gender and Disorder in Early Modern Seville*. Princeton, NJ: Princeton University Press, 1990.

Pfau, Thomas. "Rethinking the Image: With Some Reflections on G. M. Hopkins." *Yearbook of Comparative Literature* 57 (2011): 117–47.

Plate, S. Brent, ed. *Key Terms in Material Religion*. New York: Bloomsbury, 2015.

Plate, S. Brent. *Walter Benjamin, Religion, and Aesthetics: Rethinking Religion through the Arts*. New York: Routledge, 2005.

Podol, Peter L. "The Stylized Portrait of Women in Spanish Literature." *Hispanófila* 71 (1981): 1–21.

Portús, Pérez Javier. *Guía de la pintura barroca española*. Madrid: Museo Nacional del Prado, 2001.

Portús, Pérez Javier. "Indecencia, mortificación y modos de ver en la pintura del Siglo de Oro." *Espacio, Tiempo y Forma* 8 (1995): 55–88.

Portús, Pérez Javier. *Ribera*. Barcelona: Polígrafa, 2011.

Rambo, Louis R., and Charles Farhadian, eds. *The Oxford Handbook of Religious Conversion*. Oxford: Oxford University Press, 2014.

Réau, Louis. *L'iconographie de l'art chrétien*. Paris: Presses Universitaires de France, 1952–58.

Réau, Louis. *Les monuments détruits de l'art français: Histoire du vandalism*. Paris: Hachette, 1959.

Rennert, Hugo A. *The Spanish Stage in the Time of Lope de Vega*. New York: Hispanic Society of America, 1909.

Ricci, Teresa. "La grâce et la *sprezzatura* chez Baldassar Castiglione." *Bibliothèque d'Humanisme et Renaissance* 45 (2003): 233–48.

Rivera, Mayra. *Poetics of the Flesh*. Durham, NC: Duke University Press, 2015.

Robertson, Duncan. "Poem and Spirit: The Twelfth-Century Life of St. Mary the Egyptian." *Medioevo Romanzo* 7 (1980): 305–27.

Robertson, Duncan. "Twelfth-Century Literary Experience: The Life of St. Mary the Egyptian." *Pacific Coast Philology* 22, no. 1–2 (1987): 71–77.

Rodríguez G. de Ceballos, Alfonso. "Image and Counter-Reformation in Spain and Spanish America." In *Sacred Spain: Art and Belief in the Spanish World*, edited by Ronda Kasl, 15–36. New Haven, CT: Yale University Press for the Indianapolis Museum of Art, 2009.

Ross, Jill. *Figuring the Feminine: The Rhetoric of Female Embodiment in Medieval Hispanic Literature*. Toronto: University of Toronto Press, 2008.

Rubel, Helen F. "Chabham's *Penitential* and Its Influence in the Thirteenth Century." *PMLA* 40, no. 2 (1925): 225–39.

Ruffinatto, Aldo. "Hacia una teoría semiológica del relato hagiográfico." *Berceo* 94–95 (1978): 105–32.

Saint-Saëns, Alain. "Apology and Denigration of the Eremitical Body during the Spanish Golden Age." In *Religion, Body and Gender in Early Modern Spain*, edited by Alain Saint-Saëns. San Francisco: Mellen Research University Press, 1991.

Saint-Saëns, Alain. *Art and Faith in Tridentine Spain (1545–1690)*. New York: Peter Lang, 1995.

Saint-Saëns, Alain. "A Case of Gendered Rejection: The Hermitess in Golden Age Spain." In *Spanish Women in the Golden Age: Images and Realities*, edited by Magdalena S. Sánchez and Alain Saint-Saëns, 55–66. Westport, CT: Greenwood Press, 1996.

Saint-Saëns, Alain. "Saint ou coquin: Le personnage de l'ermite dans la littérature du Siècle d'Or." *Revista Canadiense de Estudios Hispánicos* 16, no. 1 (1991): 123–35.

Salih, Sarah. *Versions of Virginity in Late Medieval England*. Cambridge: Boydell & Brewer, 2001.

Sanchez, Melissa. *Queer Faith: Reading Promiscuity and Race in the Secular Love Tradition*. New York: New York University Press, 2019.

Sánchez-Castañer, Francisco. "Alusiones teatrales en *La Pícara Justina*." *Revista de Filología Española* 25 (1941): 225–44.

Sánchez Ortega, María Helena. *Pecadoras de verano, arrepentidas en invierno: El camino de la conversión femenina*. Madrid: Alianza, 1995.

Santayana, George. *The Sense of Beauty: The Works of George Santayana*. Vol. 2. Edited by William G. Holzberger and Herman J. Saatkamp Jr. Cambridge, MA: MIT Press, 1986.

Scarborough, Connie. "Seeing and Believing: The Gaze in the *Vida de Santa María Egipçiaca*." *La corónica* 42, no. 1 (2013): 299–320.

Sedgwick, Eve Kosofsky. *Tendencies*. Durham, NC: Duke University Press, 1993.

Sedgwick, Eve Kosofsky. *Touching Feeling: Affect, Pedagogy, Performativity*. Durham, NC: Duke University Press, 2003.

Severin, Dorothy Sherman. *Religious Parody and the Spanish Sentimental Romance*. Newark, DE: Juan de la Cuesta, 2005.

Simpson, James. *Under the Hammer: Iconoclasm in the Anglo-American Tradition*. Oxford: Oxford University Press, 2010.

Snow, Joseph T. "Some Literary Portraits of the Old Woman in Medieval and Early Modern Spain." In *"Entra mayo y sale abril": Medieval Spanish Literary and Folklore Studies in Memory of Harriet Goldberg*, edited by Manuel da Costa Fontes et al., 349–63. Newark, DE: Juan de la Cuesta, 2005.

Sohm, Philip L. *The Artist Grows Old: The Aging of Art and Artists in Italy, 1500–1800*. New Haven, CT: Yale University Press, 2007.

Solberg, Emma Maggie. *Virgin Whore*. Ithaca, NY: Cornell University Press, 2018.

Solomon, Michael. "Catarsis sexual: *La Vida de Santa María Egipcíaca* y el texto higiénico". In *Erotismo en las letras hispánicas: Aspectos, modos y fronteras*, edited by Luce López-Baralt y Francisco Márquez Villanueva, 425–37. Mexico City: Centro de Estudios Lingüísticos y Literarios; Colegio de México, 1995.

Spawls, Alice. "Portraits Put to Use—And Misuse." *New York Review of Books*, February 23, 2017.

Spinosa, Nicola. "José de Ribera, un español en Nápoles entre la realidad, la naturaleza y el color." In *Jusepe de Ribera, el Epañoleto*, edited by Nicola Spinosa and Alfonso E. Pérez Sánchez, 51–65. Barcelona: Lunwerg Editores, 2003.

Stoichita, Victor I. *The Self-Aware Image: An Insight into Early Modern Meta-Painting*. Harvey Miller Studies in Baroque Art no. 1. London: Harvey Miller, 2015.

Stoichita, Victor I. *Visionary Experience in the Golden Age of Spanish Art*. London: Reaktion Books, 1995.

Stowell, Steven. "Art and Compunction: Francesco Bocchi's Mystical Experience of Art." In *The Spiritual Language of Art: Medieval Christian Themes in Writings on Art of the Italian Renaissance*, 16–70. Leiden: Brill, 2004.

Swanberg, Ellen: "The Singing Bird: A Study of the Lyrical Devices of *La vida de Santa María Egipcíaca*." *Hispanic Review* 47, no. 3 (1979): 339–53.

Taylor, Barry. "La Fabliella de Don Juan Manuel." *Revista de poética medieval* 4 (2000): 187–200.

Taylor, Larissa J. "Apostle to the Apostles: The Complexity of Medieval Preaching about Mary Magdalene." In *Mary Magdalene in Medieval Culture: Conflicted Roles*, edited by Peter Loewen and Robin Waugh, 33–50. London: Routledge, 2014.

Taylor, Paul C. *Black Is Beautiful: A Philosophy of Black Aesthetics*. Hoboken, NJ: Wiley, 2016.

Tiffany, Tanya J. *Diego Velázquez's Early Paintings and the Culture of Seventeenth-Century Seville*. University Park: Pennsylvania State University Press, 2012.

Uría Macqua, Isabel. *Panorama crítico del mester de clerecía*. Madrid: Castalia, 2000.

Varona, María de Carlos. "Saints and Sinners in Madrid and Naples: Saint Mary Magdalene as a Model of Conversion and Penance." In *Jusepe de Ribera's Mary Magdalene in a New Context*, edited by Gabriele Finaldi, 79–90. Dallas: Meadows Museum, Southern Methodist University, 2011.

Vega, Carlos Alberto. *El transformismo religioso: La abnegacion sexual de la mujer en la España medieval*. Madrid: Pliegos, 2008.

Viladesau, Richard. *Theological Aesthetics: God in Imagination, Beauty, and Art*. New York: Oxford University Press, 1999.

Wack, Mary Frances. "The *Liber de heros morbo* of Johannes Afflacius and Its Implications for Medieval Love Conventions." *Speculum* 62, no. 2 (1987): 324–44.

Walsh, John K., and Billy Bussell Thompson. "The Myth of the Magdalen in Early Spanish Literature." In *The Myth of the Magdalen in Early Spanish Literature, with an Edition of the Vida de Santa María Magdalena in Ms. h-1-13 of the Escorial Library*, 1–27. Coll. Pliegos hispánicos 2. New York: L. Clemente, 1986.

Walsh, P. G. "The Rights and Wrongs of Curiosity (Plutarch to Augustine)." *Greece & Rome* 35, no. 1 (1988): 73–85.

Warner, Marina. *Alone of All Her Sex: The Myth and the Cult of the Virgin Mary*. New York: Knopf, 1976.

Waters, Claire M. *Angels and Earthly Creatures: Preaching, Performance, and Gender in the Later Middle Ages*. Philadelphia: University of Pennsylvania Press, 2004.

Waters, Claire M. "Dangerous Beauty, Beautiful Speech: Gendered Eloquence in Medieval Preaching." *Essays in Medieval Studies* 14 (1997): 51–63.

Weber, Alison. "Locating Holiness in Early Modern Spain: Convents, Caves, and Houses." In *Structures and Subjectivities: Attending to Early Modern Women*, edited by Joan Hartman and Adele Seeff, 50–74. Cranbury, NJ: Associated University Presses, 2007.

Weiss, Julian. *Mester De Clerecía: Intellectuals and Ideologies in Thirteenth-Century Castile*. Woodbridge: Támesis, 2006.

Williams, Rowan. "Language, Reality and Desire in Augustine's *De Doctrina*." *Journal of Literature and Theology* 3 (1989): 138–58.

Winiarski, Catherine E. "Adultery, Idolatry, and the Subject of Monotheism." *Religion and Literature* 38, no. 3 (2006): 41–63.

Winstead, Karen. *Virgin Martyrs: Legends of Sainthood on Late Medieval England*. Ithaca, NY: Cornell University Press, 1997.

Zeeman, Nicolette. "The Idol of the Text." In *Images, Idolatry, and Iconoclasm in Late Medieval England: Textuality and the Visual Image*, edited by Jeremy Dimmick, James Simpson, and Nicolette Zeeman. Oxford: Oxford University Press, 2002.

Zubillaga, Carina. "Introducción." *Poesía narrativa clerical en su contexto manuscrito: Estudio y edición del ms. Esc. K-III-4*. Buenos Aires: SECRIT, 2014.

INDEX

Aemilian of Cogolla, Saint, dream vision of, 68

Aertsen, Pieter, 38–39, 49

aesthetics, 6–7, 177n59, 193n2; catechism of, 13, 160; Christian, 172n12; and grace, 19; somatic, 175n43

Agnes, Saint, 101

Alfonso X: *Canticles of Holy Mary*, 84; *Siete partidas* statutory code, 67

allegoresis, 50, 80

Alvar, Manuel, 56, 90

Andrew, Saint, 48

Anna, Saint (widow and prophetess), 16

Anne, Saint (Virgin's mother), 16

apariencia, 157; spectacle of, 132–34; word and spectacle, as combination of, 132

Apelles, 98

Aquinas, Thomas, 137; and proper leisure, 135

Arellano, Ignacio, 153

Arguijo, Don Juan de, 33–34

Aristotle, 7, 122, 135

asceticism, 14–15, 51, 59, 85, 98–99, 102, 117–19, 123, 126–27; beauty in, 110; and concupiscence, 2; and penitence, 78, 88

Asterius, Saint, 32–33

Augustine, Saint, 51, 61, 84, 116–17, 119, 135, 138, 172n12; *Confessions*, 62; and "fleshly ears," 63; and incarnation, 64; *On Christian Doctrine*, 65–66; and "rhetorical heresy," 65–66; "rhetoric of silence" of, 64, 68; and speech and incarnation, analogy between, 64; and use, concept of, 65

Baldinucci, Filippo, *Vocabolario toscano dell'arte del disegno*, 114

Balzac, Honoré de, *Le chef-d'œuvre inconnu* (*The Unknown Masterpiece*), 13, 21, 160–65

Baroja, Julio Caro, 140

Barthes, Roland, 12; and invisibility of beauty, 175n43; *S/Z*, 11

Bartholomew, Saint, 101–2, 117–19, 124

beauty, 160–61, 173n29; and appearance, 131; and asceticism, 110; and body, 4; of Saint Catherine, 70–71; and eloquence, 70; and "freshness," extolling of, 114; and grotesque, 20, 94; as guide to divine, 172n12; and hagiography, 51; and holiness, 1–2, 8, 10–12, 15–16, 20, 26, 52, 198n67; immediacy of, 92; invisibility of, 175n43; of Mary Magdalene, 2–4, 14–15, 69, 109–11, 114; of Mary of Egypt, 2–4, 7, 9–10, 14–15, 16–17, 20, 45, 52–53, 57–62, 69, 75–76, 78–83, 85–86, 94, 109–11, 114–16, 120, 126, 128–29, 146–48, 152, 164; and noble birth, 59; of nude human body, 1; of old age, 127; as promise, 93; scar on discourses about, 93–94; and sin, 61; and temptation, 114; and ugliness, 93; in unexpected, 164; untimeliness of, 94; of Virgin Mary, 3–4

Berceo, Gonzalo de, 58, 68; *Miracles of Our Lady*, 84; *Poem of Saint Oria*, 69

Beresford, Andrew, 61

Berger, Harry, 45

Bergström, Ingvar, 38–39

226 INDEX

Betancourt, Roland, 176n55, 200n88
Bloch, Howard, 64
Bolter, Jay David, 27
Borromeo, Federico, 100
Botticelli, *Birth of Venus*, 98
Bril, Paul, 100
Brown, Catherine, 50, 185n24
Brueghel, Jan, 100
Burrus, Virginia, 15, 176n51
Bynum, Carolyn Walker, 7

Calderón de la Barca, Pedro, 136, 143; *El mayor encanto, amor*, 205n37
Camargo, Ignacio, 128, 130
Cameron, Averil, 81–82
Camille, Michael, 77, 82
Campbell, Erin J., 117, 126, 199n70
Caravaggio, 44–45; *Mary Magdalene and Martha*, 128
Cardona, Catalina de, 126, 196n35; as controversial figure, 106; cross-dressing of, 105, 117; as grotesque, 106–8; and penitence, acts of, 106; visibility of, 106
Carlos Varona, María Cruz de, 120
Caro Baroja, Julio, 140
Carruthers, Mary, 50, 66
Carter, Julian, 127
Cascales, Francisco de, 30
Catherine of Alexandria, Saint, 52, 60, 69, 71, 82–83, 185n27; beauty of, 70–71
Caxton, William, 60, 185n27, 189n74
Cazelles, Brigitte, 68
Ceballos, Alfonso Rodríguez G. de, 96–97
Cervantes, Miguel de, 138–39; *Don Quixote*, 144
Cherry, Peter, 49
chremamorphism, 42
Chrétien, Jean-Louis, 73
Christianity, 23, 63, 81–82, 105; fear of women in, 114; and fragility of life, meditation on, 123–24
Church of the Holy Sepulchre, 3, 10, 23–24, 44, 89, 141, 152–54
Cicero, 136

Cody, Florian J., 55, 91
Colby, Alice M., 82
comedia: *comedia de santos*, 141–42; *comedia nueva*, 134
Consavari, Elizabeth Carroll, 195n29
conversion, 113; as defined, 181n47; immediacy of, 33–34; of Mary of Egypt, 13–14, 23–25, 31–37, 42–44, 49, 52, 89, 91, 152–53, 155–57; temporality of, 24, 33; as transitional, 44; as unseen grace, 42
Coon, Lynda, 191n42
Copeland, Rita, 63
Cortina, Lynn Rice, 58, 80–81
Council of Trent, 14, 29, 45, 99, 100, 104–5, 129; Twenty-Fifth Session of, 31; and utility of images, 96
Counter-Reformation, 31, 99–100
Criado de Val, Manuel, 184n18

Damisch, Hubert, 163
Danto, Arthur, 92
Dassbach, Elma, 143
decorum, 95, 109, 120, 129, 184n14, 200n90; importance of, 96–97; and theater, 138
de la Torre, Don Jerónimo, 100; collection of portraits, 101–4
Delenda, Odile, 197n50
Delgado, E. Ernesto, 85, 89
desert saints, 100
Deyermond, Alan, 78
Díaz, Emilio Orozco, 132
didacticism, 129; ecclesiastic and profane traditions, relationship between, 185n24
Didi-Huberman, Georges, 159–60
Dominic of Silos, Saint, 69
Donatello, 197n50
Dunkelman, Martha Levine, 200n84
Dürer, Albrecht, 97–98

Eden, Kathy, 95
ekphrasis, 32, 83; and epideictic tradition, 80
eloquence, 83, 123, 156; in Christian hermeneutics, 66; of Cicero, 136; deceitful, 89; female, 69, 89; and hagiography, 51, 67–68;

INDEX

and idolatry, 62; of Mary Magdalene, 69–70; of Mary of Egypt, 62, 151; and masculine virtue, 63–64; in medieval texts, 66; as pandering, 66–67; of Saint Catherine, 70–71; and virtuous ethos, 63

England, 132, 136–37

Erasmus, 97–98; on acquired virtue, 135–36

eremitic saints, 100, 117–18; and landscape, close association with, 199n78

Euphemia, Saint, 32–33

eutrapelia, 135, 137

Farago, Claire, 28

Feiss, Hugh, 53, 55, 183n8

Felton, Craig, 115

females: and cosmetics, 128; and feminine holiness, 107; and femininity, types of, 116; hermits, 106–7; and lying, 128; mystics, 7, 104–5; and nudity, 110; religious, and disguising femininity, 105; signifying power of, 7; and spectacle, 157

Ferguson, Margaret, 62, 64

form, 9, 65, 70, 134–35, 138; and appearance, 51, 63; and content, 8; human, universality of, 28; importance of to hagiography, 20; importance of to religious experience, 19; materiality of, 174n32; and matter, 21, 66; mimetic, 161; poetic, 19, 58, 185n24

Fourth Lateran Council, 14, 67

Fraker, Charles, 67

France, 20–21, 136, 172n8

Frau Welt (Lady World) (sculpture), 79, 82–83

Garber, Marjorie, 10

García López, José Luis, 58

García Sanz, Ana, 100

Gaunt, Simon, 86

Gautier, Théophile, 50

Gentileschi, Orazio, 14–15

Giles, Ryan, 50

Goldberg, Harriet, 68

Golden Legend, The, 71, 96, 185n27, 189n74

grace, 135, 156; chameleon nature of, 177n59; and charisma, 20; and conversion, 42; and

images, 36; promiscuity of, 19, 164, 177n59; relational structure of, 19

Graham, Heather, 198n67

Gregory I, 4, 37, 74, 172n14; and "book of the illiterate," 25, 178n5

Gregory of Nyssa, 32; "On the Divinity of the Son and the Holy Spirit," 31

Grieve, Patricia, 81–82

grotesque, 106, 127; as aesthetic category, 107; decorative paintings, tied to, 107; inward possibility of, 108; untimeliness as feature of, 92–93, 108

Grusin, Richard, 27

gypsies, 145–46

hagiography, 9, 34, 50, 68, 109, 136–37, 139; beauty in, 51–59; and contemplative silence, 73; eloquence in, value and function of, 67; form of, 20; hagiographic drama, 130–31; hagiographic drama, objections to, 138; iconoclastic tendencies of, 71–72, 86, 89; iconophilic, 72; as imaginary, 2; and language, ekphrastic function of, 67

Hamilton, John, "philology of the flesh," 173n32, 174n33

Harpham, Geoffrey, 107–8

Haskins, Susan, 198n67

Herdt, Jennifer, 135

hermits, 118; female, 105; hermit saints, 100, 195n27

Hildebert of Lavardin, 87–88

Hirschkind, Charles, 6

holiness, 14–17, 24–25, 49–50, 54, 75, 109, 128–30, 160; conceptualizing of, 11; as difficult to see, 37–38; of female bodies, 51, 105; of humble objects, 48; as invisible, 38, 43, 92–93, 175n40; as surprising, 37, 40–41; as "undecidable," 43; in unexpected, 164; visibility of, 26

Hollywood, Amy, 7

holy harlots, 16, 24, 52, 59, 107–9, 143, 176n51

holy matrons, 16

holy women, 51, 86–87; bare calves of, 200n90

Howie, Cary, 15, 176n51, 181n41
Hughes, Krista, 8, 127
Hugh of Saint Victor, 27

iconoclasm, 13, 25, 34
idolatry, 52, 64–65, 70–71, 73; and eloquence, 62; and lust, sins of, 77
images, 37, 98, 129, 180n36; and grace, 36; holiness of, 35; immediacy of, 25–27, 31, 33–36, 49; mediation, as subject to, 36, 49; as pedagogical tool, 25; religious, attacks on, 96–97; and "seeing is believing," 11, 26, 36; "silent preaching," as form of, 34, 36; utility of, 96; worship of, 35–36
image theory, 34, 36–37, 49, 161
imitation, 135; proper use of, 139
immediacy: of beauty, 92; dream of, 35–36; of images, 25–27, 31, 33–36, 49; imagistic, 27, 29; Leonardian model of, 31; logic of, 27, 31, 49; model of, 27, 33; of painting, 30–31, 34; of perception, 46–47; temporal dimension of, 27, 33; of visual, 28, 30
incarnation, 8, 65, 75, 89–90, 113–14, 173n32, 180n36; and "fleshly ears," 51; mystery of, 36, 72–73; paradox of, 51, 74
interiority, 44, 46
"inverted still life," 38, 42, 181n44; "silent preaching," as going beyond, 39
Italy, 25, 44, 117

Jacobus de Voragine, 60, 71; *The Golden Legend*, 140
James, William, 181n47
Jansen, Katherine, 113
Jantzen, Grace, 4, 173n29
Jerome, Saint, 99, 119, 126
Jesuits, 137; and school theater, tradition of, 136
Jordan, William B., 49
Juvenal, 122–24

Kasten, Lloyd August, 55, 91
Kelley, Mary Jane, 68–69

La gitana de Menfis (Pérez de Montalbán), 9, 20, 140, 153, 207n56; *logos* in, 148, 156;

Mary of Egypt in, 130–31; plot of, 142–45; rogue theatrics of, 149–50; saintly miracles in, 129; *sermón* in, 130, 148–49, 152, 155–57; spectacle as wonder in, 158; surprises in, 141–42; title of, 145
Le chef-d'œuvre inconnu (*The Unknown Masterpiece*) (Balzac), 13, 21, 163–64; "Catherine Lescault" section of, 160, 165; "Gillette" section of, 160–61, 165; Saint Mary of Egypt, presence of in, 160–62
Leclercq, Jean, 65
Leonardo da Vinci, 27, 29, 95, 122; image theory, 37; immediacy, model of, 31
Lévi-Strauss, Claude, 10
logos, 130, 134, 148, 156
Lope de Vega. *See* Vega, Lope de
Lo Re, Salvatore, 197n50
Lupton, Julia R., 164
Luque, Francisco de, 132–34

Mackinlay, Shane, 181n43
Maier, John, 79
Mâle, Émile, 2, 111
Malvern, Marjorie, 114
Marion, Jean-Luc, 11, 20, 23, 38, 43–44, 175n40, 181n43; on "ontological invisibility of sainthood," 130
Marno, David, 19
Martínez-Burgos García, Palma, 97, 99, 199n78
Martínez Cuesta, Juan, 100
martyrdom, 15, 103, 115, 118, 200n90; and asceticism, 51; of Saint Catherine of Alexandria, 70; cruelty of, 32; of Saint Euphemia, 32–33; of virgins, 60
Mary, Virgin. *See* Virgin Mary
Mary Magdalene, 1, 24, 52, 101–2, 103, 116–17, 119, 140–41, 172n14, 197n50, 200n90; beauty of, 2–4, 14–15, 69, 109–11, 114; as Christianized Venus, 108, 111; daily ascent to heaven of, motif of, 111; female holiness, as Renaissance ideal of, 114; holiness of, 109; and horticulture, language of, 113; iconography of, 128, 176n50; luxury, attached to, 109; penitence of, 113–15; pictorial transformation of, 99–100, 111,

113; sacred eroticism, as icon of, 111; vanity, as foundational figure of, 4, 16; and Venus, 110, 114

Mary of Egypt, Saint, 8, 21, 27, 56, 74, 100–101, 136, 174n37, 197n50, 203n20, 204n31; aged body of, 75, 94–95, 108, 115; aged body of, beauty of, 15, 16–17, 52, 115–16, 120, 126, 128–29; aged but holy body of, 115; asceticism of, 85–86, 88, 117, 126–27; as "beautiful sinner," 61; and beauty, coexistence of with ugliness, 7; and beauty, relationship of to holiness, 9–10, 14, 20; beauty of, 9, 45, 52–53, 57–62, 75–76, 78–83, 85, 94, 109, 128–29, 146–48, 152, 164; beauty of as gift from God, 4; breast of, painting of, 115–20; clothing of, description of, 81–83; conversion of, 14, 23–25, 31–37, 42, 44, 52, 89, 91, 152–53, 155–57; conversion of, mystery of, 26; conversion of after encountering image of Virgin Mary, 13, 23–24, 33–35, 43; conversion of and mediation, 36, 49; conversion of as "discursive hyper-icon," 25; depicted in motion, 127, 162; in desert, 3, 34, 37, 43, 46, 157; and Diana, 110; Eastern branch of legend of, 34, 172n8; eloquence of, 62, 151; and female holiness, image of that shatters decorum, 120; as force of nature, 147; grotesque, in tradition of, 107–8, 127; as gypsy, 146; hair of, 15, 45–46, 85, 87, 109, 115, 118, 120, 126; and hermits, 118; and holiness, visibility of, 11, 43; holiness of, 3, 9, 13, 16–17, 85–86, 109, 124, 126, 128–30; holiness of and masculinization, 191n42; humility of, 88–89; and iconoclasm, 13; and idols, association with, 62, 77–78, 80–81, 90–91; and images, merits of, 13–14; image theory according to, 25–26, 49; image theory according to and dream of immediacy, 35–36; interiority of, 46; invisibility of, 44, 46; in Jussienne chapel, 1–2, 10, 13–14; in *La gitana de Menfis*, 130–31, 139–58; last gesture of, erotics of, 176n51; in *Le chef-d'œuvre inconnu* (*The Unknown Masterpiece*), 160–63; legend of, 2, 108–9, 124, 140–41, 159, 162, 172n8;

levitation of, 124; and mediation, awareness of, 20, 49; and memory, power of, 87; as metatheatrical figure, 142; modernity, as hinting at, 165; new theatrical practice, as figure for, 145; paradox of, 87, 90–91, 126–29, 164–65; penitent body of, 84–87, 94, 115, 141, 153, 163–64; prominence of as religious and symbolic, 2; as promiscuous, 11, 19, 163; and prostitution, association with, 81–82; queerness of, 16, 127; repentance of, 86; resilience, as image of, 120, 126; Ribera's portraits of, 46–47, 92, 94–97, 98, 108, 115–20, 122, 124, 126–29, 159–60, 182n51, 194n7, 200n90; as saint, 10–11, 13, 15, 19–20, 128–29; sensuality of, 75; sexual abandon of as "free gift," 19; shoes of, 82–83, 91, 164; as sinner, 10–11, 15, 19–20, 37, 53, 128–29; as "spiritual cross-dresser," 126; as strange and stranger to herself, 44; as strong woman, 126, 146; suffering of, 88; temporality of, 33, 161–62; theater, as figure of, 130; as transmasculine figure, 200n88; and ugliness, representation of as beauty, 86; and Virgin Mary, interaction with, 3, 90, 141, 157; vision, as object of, 89–90; Western branch of legend of, 75, 172n8; withered body of, 88; written sources for as hagiographic, 8–9; and Zozimas, confession to, 87–88

materiality, 8, 20, 24; of form, 174n32; of old person's body, 123; and religion, 2, 6–7, 19; of surface, 161; of words, 64

Matham, Jacob, *Kitchen Scene with Kitchen Maid Preparing Fish*, 39–41

Matsys, Quentin, *An Old Woman* (*The Ugly Duchess*), 118, 124

Maxentius, 60, 70

Mazzeo, Joseph Anthony, 64

McCarthy, Ita, 177n59

McDannell, Colleen, 6–7

mediation, 20, 27, 33, 47, 54; images as subject to, 49; importance of, 25, 36, 49; of material words, 62; and painting, 49; temporality of, 25; as visible, 36

Menéndez Pidal, Ramón, 56, 58, 183n12, 184n18

Meyer, Birgit, 7, 173n24

Miles, Margaret, 114, 116, 119

Miller, Patricia Cox, 107–8, 191n42; and harlot-saint, grotesquerie of, 86–87

Miseria, Juan de la, 105–6

Mitchell, W. J. T., and picturing theory, 25

Montalbán, Juan Pérez de. *See* Pérez de Montalbán, Juan

Morgan, David, 6–7, 26

Murphy, James J., 65–66

mysticism, 46, 99; and women, association with, 7, 104–5

Netherlands, 38

Newman, Barbara, 50

Newman, John Henry, 3

Noble, Thomas F. X., 180n36

Nock, Arthur D., 24, 181n47

Nolde, Emil, 162

nudity, 110–11

old age, 2, 16–17, 113, 118, 120, 126, 176n51; beauty of, 127; cruelty of, 117; depiction of, 122, 124; queerness of, 127; as repetition of past, 122; representations of, 116, 119, 122–23, 198n70; and sinfulness, 123

Oria, Saint, 68–69

Orozco Díaz, Emilio, 132

Otto, Rudolf, 173n24

Pacheco, Francisco, 31, 33–34, 42, 47, 111, 113; *Arte de la pintura*, 29–30, 32, 103

painting, 8; efficacy of, 32; immediacy of, 27, 30, 34; and likeness, achievement of, 29; and mediation, 49; and mimesis, insistence on, 26; and perception, 29; and space, 26; "there-ness" of, 28; and virtue, end goal of, 29–30

Paleotti, Cardinal Gabriele, 31–32, 198n70; *Discourse on Sacred and Profane Images*, 30, 107

Paul, Saint, 19, 97–98

Paul the Deacon, 203n20

Pedraza, Pilar, 118, 122

Pelagia, 24, 59, 81, 107–9, 126, 191n32

penance, 4, 45, 57–58, 99, 106, 113–14, 143

penitence, 14, 33–34, 36, 46, 85, 94, 99–100, 102, 106, 109, 113–15, 117, 119, 141, 163–64, 172n8, 174n38; and asceticism, 59, 78, 86, 88, 110; and holiness, 159; penitent figures, painting of, 110

Pérez de Montalbán, Juan, 136, 146, 154; *La gitana de Menfis*, 9, 20, 129–31, 140–45, 147–50, 152–53, 155–58, 204n31, 207n56

Pfau, Thomas, 36

Plate, S. Brent, 26

Plato, 51, 63, 66, 178n11; Plato's cave, 25

Pliny, 31; *Naturalis historia*, 47

Podol, Peter L., 78, 85

pornography, 92

portraiture: "fiction of the pose," 45; grand language of, 48

Portús, Javier, 100–102, 110–11

promiscuity, 9, 11, 105, 163, 174n34; of grace, 16–17, 19–20, 164, 177n59

prostitution, 33, 64, 81–82, 139, 149

queerness, 15, 16; of old age, 127

Quintilian, 51, 63

Réau, Louis, 13

Reformation, 25, 46

Rennert, Hugo A., 132

representation, 31, 46–47, 49, 62; of aged women, naked bodies of, 122; dangers of, 80–81; of female saints, 98; and "male gaze," 122; of penitent saints, 99–100, 104–5; and queering role of age, 122; and recognition, 40–41

rhetoric, 67, 131; and artifice of figuration, 63; and form, 51, 63; and language, 51; sensual appeal of, 131–32

rhopography, 48–49

Ribadeneira, Pedro de, 137, 139, 203n20

Ribera, Jusepe de, 9, 15, 16–17, 20, 44, 104; and asceticism, tropes of, 118–19; *The Assumption of Mary Magdalene*, 111, 112; oeuvre of, religious themes in, 100–101; as painter of dark and sinister subjects, 119–20; *Penitent Magdalene*, 101–3, 115; *Saint Bartholomew,*

101–2, 117–18; *Saint John the Baptist in the Desert*, 101–2, 115–17; *Saint Mary of Egypt* (Musée Fabre), 48, 94–95, 119–20, 126, 182n57; *Saint Mary of Egypt* (Museo Civico Gaetano Filangieri), 17, 45–46, 182n51; *Saint Mary of Egypt* (Museo Nacional del Prado), 101, 115–16, 118; *Saint Mary of Egypt in Ecstasy*, 18, 124–27, 159–60; *Saint Onophrius*, 101, 200n84

Rivera, Mayra, 174n33

Robertson, Duncan, 89, 91

Rodríguez G. de Ceballos, Alfonso, 96–97

Rojas, Fernando de, *Tragicomedia de Calisto y Melibea*, 66–67

Roman de la Rose, Pygmalion episode, 82

Rosa, Salvatore, 116, 122

Ross, Jill, 50–51, 63, 84, 183n6

Ruffinatto, Aldo, 58

Sadeler, Jan, 100, 195n27

Sadeler, Rafael, 100

Saint-Saëns, Alain, 99, 105–7

Salih, Sarah, 60

Sanchez, Melissa, 177n59

Sánchez Cotán, Juan, *Still Life with Quince, Cabbage, Melon and Cucumber*, 47–48

Sánchez de Villamayor, Andrés Antonio, *La mujer fuerte*, 126, 142

Sánchez Ortega, María Helena, 204n31

Santayana, George, 108

Sarmiento, Rafael, 132–33

Scarborough, Connie, 86

Second Council of Nicaea, 25, 31, 34–36, 96, 179n25, 180n36

Sedgwick, Eve Kosofsky, 16, 124

Severin, Dorothy, 50

signs, 65; ambiguity of, 68; linguistic, 27; sensuality of, 62; signifying, 83

silence, 12, 50, 65, 81–82; contemplative, 73; and female asceticism, 69; rhetoric of, 64, 68; and visions, 68–69

sinfulness, 3, 15, 34–35, 44, 59–60, 75, 119, 123, 129, 136, 143, 157, 172n8, 201n2; hermeneutic model of, 78; and holiness, 49, 74; narrative of, 99; and penitence, 100; as

representative, 61; as sexual impropriety, 172n14

Snow, Joseph, 198n70

Sohm, Philip, 122, 127

Solomon, Michael, 83–84

Sophronius, 2, 74–75, 80

Spain, 20–21, 25, 45–46, 98, 100–101, 126, 137, 185n24; and public theaters, social context for, 136; and "silent representations," 132; and spiritual treatises, popularity of, 199n78

Spinosa, Nicola, 119–20

Stendhal, 94–95, 119, 127, 193n5, 193n7; *De l'amour*, 93

Stoichita, Victor, 45–46, 48; and "split painting," 181n44

Surtz, Ronald E., 186n34

Synod of Salamanca, 97

Tamayo de Vargas, Tomás, 30

Taylor, Paul C., somatic aesthetics, 175n43

temporality, 33, 37, 163; of becoming, 161–62; of conversion, 24–25; and holiness, invisibility of, 92–93; linear, 14; as queer, 127

Teresa of Ávila, Saint, 8, 105; *El libro de las fundaciones*, 106

Tertullian, 64, 71, 77, 135; "On the Apparel of Women," 62–63; and public spectacles, critiques of, 134

Thaïs, 24, 59, 108–9

theater, 141, 148, 205n37; actors, degeneracy of, 134; and appearances, 131–32, 157–58; audience, misplaced empathy of, 134–35; Christian exemplarity, as medium for, 136; and Christian Republic, 131; concupiscence, as conduit of, 139; costumes, 149–50; critiques of, 134–35, 149–50; and decorum, adhering to rules of, 138; defense of, 130, 135, 139, 145; and false appearances, 139; and feminizing effects, fear of, 137; and hypocrisy, 134–35, 139; and imitation, proper use of, 139; and legitimacy, 130; and moralist's fear of feminine body, 139; negative effects of, 136–37; public theaters in Spain, 136; and putting on a face, practice

theater (*continued*)
of, 134; and religious content, 133; as *sermón*, 130; and sirens, comparison to, 137; and surprise as theatrical device, 132; and theatricalization of the temple, 132
Tiffany, Tanya, 42
Tintoretto, 100
Titian, 109–10, 122
transgender experiences, 127
Trethewey, Natasha, 41–42

ugliness, 11–12, 116; and beauty, 7, 86, 93–94; and time, 93
untimeliness, 126–27; of beauty, 94; and grotesque, 92–93, 108
Uría Maqua, Isabel, 185n24

vanitas, 48–49
vanity, 4, 15–16, 48–49, 71, 79, 85, 105, 117, 123, 191n32; female, 82–83; of poetry 55-56
Vasari, Giorgio, 110
Vega, Carlos Alberto, 117
Vega, Lope de, 9, 99, 136, 141, 143; *Arte nuevo de hacer comedias*, 134; *El divino africano*, 138
Velázquez, Diego, 46, 49; *Kitchen Maid with the Supper at Emmaus*, 41–42; *The Nun Jerónima de la Fuente*, 120, 121
Verrips, Jojada, 7
Vida de Santa María Egipciaca (*Life of Saint Mary the Egyptian*) (VSME), 9, 52–54, 56–58, 62, 66–67, 72–73, 75–76, 87, 90–91, 142, 162, 184n18; beauty in, troubling presence of, 79–80; and female body and eloquence, associations between, 89; and feminine body and corruption, 82; and footwear and female sexuality, association between, 82; as hygienic text, 83–84; pro-

logue of, 55; and representation, dangers of, 80–81; and *topos* of inexpressibility, 82; wonder in, 84
Villegas, Alonso de, 140, 203n20
Villegas, Bernardino de, 97–98
Virgin Mary, 1, 13, 15, 16, 25, 33, 35–37, 43, 52, 60, 62, 80, 89–90, 100, 108, 111, 113–14, 141, 148, 155, 157, 200n90; and blue, association with, 115; body and clothing of, 84; grace of, 19; as ideal beauty, 3–4; as incarnation of poetry, 91; and Marian devotion, 75; objectification of, 116; and Venus, analogy to, 97–98
virtue, 19, 57, 70, 90, 96, 126, 129, 131, 142; acquired, 135; ascetic, 3; as end goal of painting, 29–30; female, 198n70; masculine, 63–64; performance-centered vision of, 136; theatricality of, 135
Vives, Juan Luis, 117, 198n70
Voltaire, 2
Voragine, Jacobus de, 60, 71; *The Golden Legend*, 140
Vos, Maerten de, 100

Warner, Marina, 114
Waters, Claire M., 70–71
Weber, Alison, 196n35
Weiss, Julian, 69, 86, 89, 185n24
Williams, Rowan, 64–65
Winstead, Karen, 70

Zeeman, Nicolette, 67–68
Zozimas, 3, 15, 16, 34, 37–38, 43, 46, 57, 75, 86–91, 109, 124, 126–27, 129, 142, 147–48, 150–52, 154, 156–57, 159, 172n8, 181n41, 207n56; as Mary's suitor, depiction of, 141, 143–45, 149
Zubillaga, Carina, 184n18, 185n24